THE *Strange Death* OF PRESIDENT HARDING

FROM THE DIARIES OF

GASTON B. MEANS

A Department of Justice Investigator

AS TOLD TO

MAY DIXON THACKER

New York

GUILD PUBLISHING CORPORATION

19 WEST 44th STREET

1930

The Strange Death of President Harding

by Gaston B. Means

As told to May Dixon Thacker

Foreword by Sam Sloan

First printed in 1930 by Guild Publishing Corporation,
19 West 44th Street, New York NY

Current Printing September, 2008 by
Ishi Press in New York and Tokyo

ISBN 0-923891-39-0
978-0-923891-39-8

Ishi Press International
1664 Davidson Avenue, Suite 1B
Bronx NY 10453
USA
917-507-7226

Printed in the United States of America

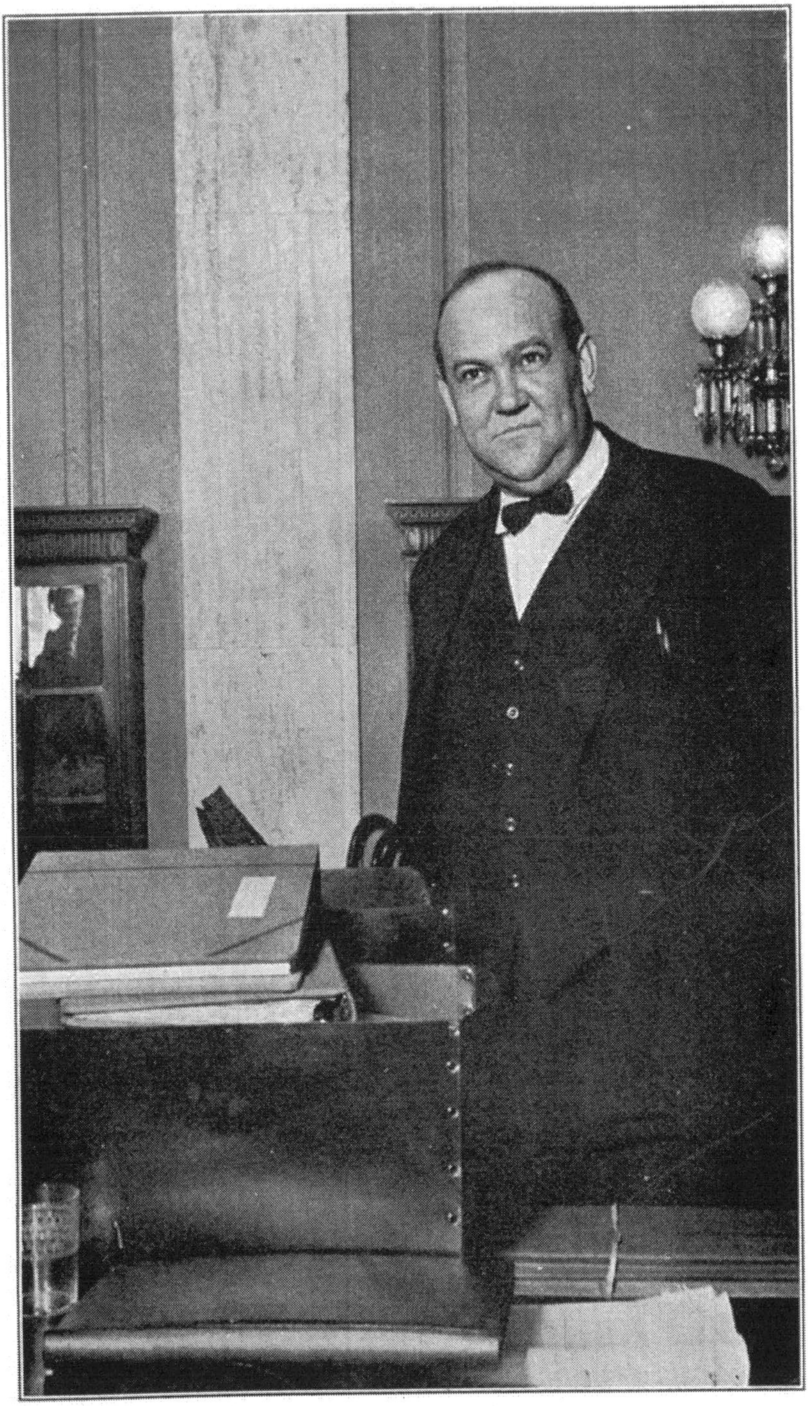

Gaston B. Means

Ex-Department of Justice Investigator. Star witness for the United States Government in the Harry M. Daugherty, Teapot Dome, and other sensational investigations, as he appeared in the Committee Room, in the United States Senate Chambers, with some of his diaries.

THE STRANGE DEATH
of
PRESIDENT HARDING

The Strange Death of President Harding by Gaston B. Means

Foreword

The cover photo to this book is one of the last ever taken of President Harding and his wife, Florence, before their untimely deaths. It was taken in July, 1923 on board the U.S.S. Henderson during their trip by ship to Alaska. Behind them is a lifeboat on the deck of the ship. Harding appears to be healthy, yet he died only a few days later.

This plus a variety of other circumstances created suspicion that Harding had been murdered, especially since his wife, Florence, refused to agree to an autopsy. Then, Florence herself died only one year later.

There is renewed interest in Harding during the current presidential election campaign, for several reasons. One is that Harding was a United States Senator when elected president and only he and John F. Kennedy were elected president while they were senators. This year, both of the candidates, McCain and Obama, are US Senators, so one of them will be elected.

Another reason is the long standing rumor that President Harding was part Black. This rumor is based primarily on the book entitled "*WARREN GAMALIEL HARDING: PRESIDENT OF THE UNITED STATES*" by William Estabrook Chancellor, published by The Sentinal Press in 1922. However, shortly after publication, the plates and the bulk of books stored by the Sentinal Press were taken away by agents and destroyed. It is rumored that the plates were dumped into the Ohio river. The book thus became one of the rarest bibliographical items in twentieth-century American history. Only five copies are known to exist, one of which is on sale

on the Internet for $2550.00 !!

The destruction of that book did not stop the rumor that Harding was part-Black from spreading and indeed may have enhanced it. Thus, if Barak Obama is elected President, it will be said that he was the SECOND Black president.

A more important reason for renewed interest in President Harding is that it is becoming increasingly apparent that Harding got a "bum rap" when he was called the worst president that America ever had. When I was in high school, my American History teacher taught me that the two worst presidents America ever had were Grant and Harding. Grant has still not been rehabilitated. (My next project?) However, there is a strong case to be made that Harding was one of the best if not the very best president America ever had.

Largely on the strength of this book, "*The Strange Death of President Harding*" and on the so-called "*Teapot Dome Scandal*", Harding became known as the worst president the United States ever had.

Of late, there has been a re-examination of President Harding, who was president from 1921 to 1923. A recent book entitled *Warren G. Harding*, by John W. Dean, who, as the cover blurb notes in a massive understatement, is "*no stranger to presidential controversy*" makes a strong case that not only was President Harding not the worst, but he was perhaps the best president the US ever had.

The Fall Guy in the *Teapot Dome Scandal* had been Albert Fall. However, Fall had served as Justice of the New Mexico Supreme Court and had been for many years a United States Senator before joining the Harding Administration, so it seems difficult to understand why Harding had to take the fall for Fall.

Harding had many accomplishments as president, far more than most presidents. For example, President Harding was the first to require all departments of the government to have a budget. Harding cut government expenditures by one billion dollars. Harding brought about the economic reforms that started "*The Roaring Twenties*", a period of unequaled economic prosperity in America.

Strangely, Woodrow Wilson is regarded by the general public as being one of the best presidents America ever had, but in reality he was one of the worst. When Wilson left office, the government was in a state of chaotic disarray. Harding managed to clean up most of it during his only two years as president.

There seem to be only three reasons why Warren G. Harding is regarded as the worst president, or at least one of the worst:

1. The Teapot Dome Scandal

2. The book "*The President's Daughter*" by Nan Britton

3. This book, "*The Strange Death of President Harding*"

I have now published or reprinted four different books by people who knew President Harding personally. All but this last one have expressed favorable views about President Harding. The other three books are:

1. *My Thirty Years Backstairs at the White House* by Lillian Rogers Parks ISBN 092389196X

2. *The President's Daughter* by Nan Britton ISBN 0923891234

3. *Dolly Gann's Book* by Dolly Gann ISBN 0923891080

The first book above was by two domestic servants who worked in the White House for a total of 50 years, including the years when Harding was president. They personally liked both President Harding and his wife, Florence, saying that Florence was plagued by "bad luck". It was this book that caused me to re-think my views about President Harding.

The second book was by President Harding's mistress, Nan Britton. She definitely liked, loved and admired President Harding. There is absolutely no doubt that she really was the President's Mistress. However, the book did a lot of harm to the president's reputation, especially the part about how she used to have sex with the President in the White House while the wife was away. In view of what we now know about other presidents who did the same thing, including Presidents Roosevelt, Kennedy and, to some extent, Clinton, this hardly seems shocking any more.

The third book, by the sister of Charles Curtis, the Vice-President under Herbert Hoover, was also by someone who knew and liked Harding.

A book I am in the process of reprinting right now and will be out soon is "*A Dead President Makes Answer to The President's Daughter*" ISBN 0923891013

This is a rare book. Very few copies were sold, but I have been able to obtain one in mint condition.

Finally, I will reprint the book "*WARREN GAMALIEL HARDING: PRESIDENT OF THE UNITED STATES*" by William Estabrook Chancellor, if I can ever find one, but, no, I am not willing to pay the $2550.00 demanded for the only copy available for sale.

Returning to this book, "*The Strange Death of President Harding*" by Gaston B. Means, I have a special reason for interest in it which has to do with the game of chess. This will seem surprising, but

most of the main characters in "*The Strange Death of President Harding*" had an impact on the world of chess.

This was because of an International Chess Master named Norman T. Whitaker who was, at one time, one of the top two or three chess players in America. Whitaker lived in Washington DC on M Street, near the White House, and was a close associate of Gaston B. Means. Whitaker also knew Evalyn Walsh McLean, who was a close personal friend of Florence Harding and whose name is frequently mentioned in this book. Evalyn Walsh McLean later wrote a book entitled "*Father Struck it Rich*", which is still popular.

I do not know whether Whitaker knew Harding personally, but I believe that Whitaker probably did know him, as he lived nearby and both Whitaker and Harding tended to know people like each other and to frequent similar places.

Norman T. Whitaker and Gaston B. Means later became involved in a side con related to the Lindbergh Kidnapping. The Lindbergh Kidnapping was "the crime of the century". On March 1, 1932, the 20 month old baby of famous aviator Charles Lindbergh was kidnapped and held for ransom. Evalyn Walsh McLean knew that Gaston B. Means was a former FBI agent who also often associated with criminals (like Whitaker) and she asked Means if he was in contact with the kidnappers and knew how to get the baby back.

Means, realizing that Evalyn Walsh McLean was a "mark", replied that yes, indeed, he was in contact with the kidnappers and could arrange the return of the baby if the ransom was paid.

Evalyn Walsh McLean agreed to pay. In fact, she agreed to pay, and did pay $104,000, even more than the real kidnappers were demanding.

However, Gaston B. Means was not really in contact with the kidnappers and had no idea who they were. He just wanted the ransom money.

Therefore, he called in his friend, chess master Norman T. Whitaker, to impersonate one of the kidnappers and to collect the ransom money.

Here, there are at least two different versions of what happened. According to the 1955 book "*The FBI Story*" by Don Whitehead, pages 94-96, Whitaker was the bag man. Means gave Whitaker the code name "The Fox" and, as "The Fox", Whitaker went to the home of Mrs. McLean and collected the ransom money.

However, Means then got greedy. He told Mrs. McLean that the kidnappers were demanding even more money. Mrs. McLean had no cash left independent of her husband, but she owned a lot of jewels and had even once been the owner of *The Hope Diamond.* When she went to pawn the jewels to raise the ransom money to give to Means, her husband found out and called in the FBI who arrested Means and Whitaker. Means and Whitaker were both convicted. Means died in prison. Whitaker got out after only serving a few months. The Lindbergh baby was found dead, having been killed only a few hours after being kidnapped. The body was immediately cremated, which contributes to many current conspiracy theories. The money was never recovered.

However, a relatively recent book, *Shady Side: The Life and Crimes of Norman Tweed Whitaker, Chess Master*, by John Samuel Hilbert, published in 2000, pages 114-128, tells an entirely different story:

Hilbert had access to the complete papers of Norman Tweed Whitaker, who died in 1975. According to his account, Whitaker may not have been guilty. The first ransom money of $104,000 that had been paid had been paid in marked money. The kidnappers

had realized it (and indeed this part was true, as the first money that had been paid to the real kidnappers had been marked, which is how they were caught). Also, unlike the account in "*The FBI Story*", Whitaker had not been the one who had picked up the money. In fact, Whitaker had a perfect alibi, because at the time of the Lindbergh Kidnapping and the payment of the $104,000 a few days later, Whitaker had been on trial in Florida for Grand Theft Auto and thus could not have been involved. Whitaker thereafter for the rest of his life made his living by suing and winning judgments against newspapers, every time they reported that he had collected the Lindbergh Kidnapping ransom money.

According to Hilbert's book and other sources, Evalyn Walsh McLean had a summer home in Aiken, South Carolina. Whitaker went there to see her. He told her that the Lindbergh baby was in Juarez, Mexico, across the border from El Paso, Texas. He then proceeded to drive Mrs. McLean in his (possibly stolen) car from Aiken South Carolina to El Paso, Texas, a distance of 1586 miles. There, he told her that the kidnappers, who were safely across the border in Mexico, had offered that if Mrs. McLean provided $35,000 in new ransom money, they would exchange it for $49,500 of the old ransom money plus the baby. The kidnappers did not want the money they had previously received because they knew it was marked.

According to *Shady Side: The Life and Crimes of Norman Tweed Whitaker, Chess Master*, by John Samuel Hilbert, page 121, what Whitaker was really convicted of was "attempted" extortion. He or Means had claimed that the Lindbergh kidnappers had refused $49,500 of the ransom money paid by Mrs. McLean because the serial numbers on the money had been published. Therefore, they demanded replacement money in the amount of $35,000, in exchange for which they promised to return the original $49,500 plus the baby. This exchange was supposed to take place in Juarez, Mexico.

However, Mrs. McLean did not have any more money, so she returned to Washington DC to pawn her jewels. That was when her husband, who was the owner and publisher of *The Washington Post*, found out and called in the FBI.

Also, according to another source, "The Fox" was not a code name for Whitaker. Rather, Mrs. McLean mistakenly believed that Whitaker's name was Fox. Albert Fox was a well-known chess master and a friend of Whitaker, and he or a person with the same name had also been a reporter for the *Washington Post.* Perhaps due to a mistake or confusion, Mrs. McLean thought that Whitaker was Fox. Albert Fox was also the name of her attorney who was representing her in her divorce case against her husband, who was the owner of the *Washington Post.* Later, the newspapers, including *The New York Times*, picked up the story and mistakenly reported "The Fox" as a code name for Whitaker.

The book by Hilbert also found a noteworthy coincidence. Albert Fox, the attorney, later sued Mrs. McLean for $35,000 in attorney's fees. However, $35,000 was the same amount of money that Mrs. McLean was trying to raise as ransom money to pay the Lindbergh kidnappers. Was this just a coincidence?

Now, here is the killing point: Once, when I was researching chess history, I spent many days in the San Francisco Public Library looking for tournament newspaper reports of the 1923 Western States Chess Championship in San Francisco, which had been won by Whitaker. Looking at an aging issue of the *San Francisco Call*, I saw the headline "HARDING DEAD". I discovered that at the very moment that Warren G. Harding had died in San Francisco, Norman T. Whitaker, chess master and notorious international criminal, had been virtually at the scene of the crime. Harding had died in a private hotel room in the Palace Hotel on Market Street in San Francisco, which is now the Sheraton Palace Hotel. Whitaker had been, at that very moment, right across the street on the 4th floor of the Mechanics Institute at 57 Post Street playing his game for what was regarded as the US Open Chess Championship, a tournament that Whitaker had won.

Therefore, having discovered this coincidence, I wrote a spoof or joke newspaper story that Whitaker, who was in fact a notorious womanizer in addition to being a criminal, had been the lover of Florence Harding and, while playing his chess game against Samuel D. Factor, in between moves, while his opponent's clock was ticking, he had walked across the street to the Palace Hotel, where, by prior arrangement, Florence Harding had let him into the private hotel room where Florence and President Harding were staying. They had planned to make love but, when President Harding discovered this, Whitaker had killed Harding, and then had gotten back to the chess game before his opponent, Samuel Factor, had yet moved, and therefore Whitaker had been able to kill Harding with such a perfect alibi that nobody had even suspected this, until I, the super-sleuth Sam Sloan, had discovered this 70 years later.

Of course, this was a joke, or at least was intended as such, but all of the basic facts were true. Harding really did die on August 2, 1923 in a private hotel room in the San Francisco Palace Hotel while Whitaker was across the street in the Mechanics Institute at 57 Post Street playing his game for the US Chess Championship against Samuel D. Factor.

All of these facts were completely true.

Now, all I had to do was make up a few invented facts, which were that Whitaker knew both Florence Harding and President Harding, which I believe was probably true based on what we know about Whitaker and Harding, since Harding was known to frequent gambling dens and illegal drinking parlors on K Street, only two blocks from where Whitaker lived on M Street. So, the only really invented fact was that Whitaker had been the lover of Florence Harding, and even that was not impossible as Florence had been a woman whose virtue was suspect.

So, now I had it all. I even added that Whitaker had actually lost the chess game to Samuel D. Factor. This was explained by the fact that he had been distracted from the chess game by the break he had taken to go across the street to kill the President of the United States, and he had become flustered, which had caused to him to lose to Factor, but he had won the rest of his games and so had won the championship anyway.

Now, of course, you will want to see the chess game that proves all of this. So, here it is:

[Event "Western Association Championship"]
[Site "San Francisco, Cal."]
[Date "1923.08.02"]
[White "Factor,Samuel D"]
[Black "Whitaker,Norman Tweed"]
[Result "1-0"]
[ECO "D64"]

1.d4 e6 2.Nf3 d5 3.c4 Nf6 4.Bg5 Nbd7 5.Nc3 Be7 6.e3 O-O 7.Rc1 Re8 8.a3 c6 9.Qc2 a6 10.Bd3 dxc4 11.Bxc4 b5 12.Bd3 c5 13.Bxf6 Nxf6 14.dxc5 Bxc5 15.Ne4 Be7 16.Nxf6+ Bxf6 17.Bxh7+ Kh8 18.Be4 Rb8 19.O-O b4 20.Bc6 bxa3 21.Bxe8 axb2 22.Bxf7 bxc1=Q 23.Rxc1 Qd7 24.Qg6 Rb5 25.Be8 Rc5 26.Re1 Qd8 27.Ba4 Bb7 28.Bc2 Kg8 29.Qh7+ Kf8 30.Rd1 Rd5 31.Nd4 Bxd4 32.exd4 Qg5 33.f4 Qg4 34.h3 Qg3 35.Rd3 Qe1+ 36.Kh2 Qf2 37.Rg3 Qxd4 38.Qh8+ Ke7 39.Rxg7+ Kd6 40.Qb8+ Kc5 41.Rxb7 1-0

It can clearly be seen from this chess game that Whitaker was playing below his normal strength and thus proves that Whitaker killed Harding while the game was being played.

Needless to say, I knew Whitaker. The last time I met Whitaker (before he died) was in 1962 and he had given me a ride in his VW bug from a chess tournament in Raleigh North Carolina to Virginia where I lived. I finally got up the nerve to ask Whitaker about Gaston B. Means and about the Lindbergh Kidnapping. I had never had the courage to do this before. One does not just say, "By the way, Norman, how did the old Lindbergh Kidnapping go?"

Whitaker answered my question by talking about all the dirty tricks Means had done to Whitaker. I am so sorry that I did not write down his exact words. All of us chess players knew Whitaker and knew about his side involvement in the Lindbergh Kidnapping, but I know of no other chess player who ever asked him about this. I did not write it down and do not remember what he said, except he started talking about all the dirty tricks Means had done. Whitaker was driving his VW at the time and I really wish I had taken notes on what he said, but alas I did not. I now believe that Whitaker may not have been in on the scam and possibly really believed that the Lindbergh Baby was being held in Juarez, and thus was not guilty. Why would he drive 1586 miles, a trip of three or four days, with a fabulously wealthy woman, if he knew that it was all just a scam?

One person who obviously must have asked Whitaker about this was Al Horowitz, owner of *Chess Review* magazine. The often told joke is that whenever Whitaker came to see Horowitz in his office, Horowitz would say, "Hello Norman. Pull up an electric chair!"

Now as you read this book, *The Strange Death of President Harding*, you will see how this all comes together. Means apparently wrote this book while serving time in prison for perjury. He passed the sheets to an accomplice, May Dixon Thacker. I believe that few of the facts in this book are true. However, I believe that Means constructed this story in much the same way that I created the story proving that Whitaker killed Harding. Means knew all the people in this book. Means certainly knew Florence Harding and her husband, President Warren G.

Harding. Almost without doubt, he knew everybody or almost everybody whose name is mentioned in this book. Conveniently, by the time this book was published in 1930, almost everybody whose name is mentioned in this book was dead and no longer available to refute Means' accounts.

Now, you will ask: Since I obviously do not believe what is written in this book, why do I publish it?

The answer is that although this book is not about history, it *is* history. At the time of this book, two years before the Lindbergh Kidnapping scam, Gaston B. Means, a former FBI agent, had every appearance of being a respectable, honest and credible person. Thus, this book was widely believed and is one of the prime reasons why Warren G. Harding is widely considered to be the worst president America ever had.

Secondly, as Means really did know all the people mentioned in this book, and since this book describes events that could possibly have happened, it tells us something about those people, even though the events it describes were often not true.

To me, the tip-off that reveals that the book is not true is that it contains long dialogs of conversations that supposedly took place. Few men would be able to remember conversations in such detail years later, especially since Means was in prison in 1930 when this book was written.

Therefore, with these caveats, I present this book to you:

Sam Sloan
Bronx New York
September 20, 2008

"Without, or with offence to friends or foes,
I sketch your world exactly as it goes."

—Byron

Contents

List of Illustrations

Preface

I FIRST met Gaston B. Means in the Atlanta Penitentiary, —was introduced to him by the Chaplain. I heard snatches of his story and was deeply interested. I felt at that time that he would be doing a real service to his country if he would, without dissimulation, tell his story to the world.

This he has now done.

The story is in no way a reflection on the American political system. On the contrary, it is a vindication of this system. It clearly reveals how a Great Party was tricked and how it has extricated itself with a dignity and poise and surety of purpose unexcelled in history.

It was the *human interest* story, however,—not the political—point of view that impressed me most. That this human interest happened to focus on the White House and with the President and his wife made it all the more appealing and important.

My treatment is a sympathetic one.

The facts of the narrative belong to Gaston B. Means. I simply assembled these facts and put them in proper form.

MAY DIXON THACKER.

Foreword

"If Gaston Means should talk!"

I almost spoke the words aloud as I stepped my six foot, two hundred avoirdupois through the iron-grilled outer door of the Atlanta Penitentiary on the forenoon of the 19th day of July 1928, and breathed once again for the first time in three years the sweet clean pure air of God's outside world.

Although I am that much maligned individual—Gaston Means, himself—I was at that moment conscious of viewing myself objectively, as a personality separate and apart. I was acutely conscious that this public malignment that had branded me before the world was the direct result of super-developed powers of dissimulation instilled and ingrained into me from early boyhood through a rigid life training as investigator and detective. For I had now to realize anew as I had been doing for many months in the close confines of prison walls,—that I, Gaston Means, was the only living human being who held accurate knowledge of dangerous truths concerning many social, political, financial and international secrets.

As I stood outside the door, I nodded a last farewell to the big guard stationed there, who manipulated so skillfully the soft click of the outer door lock and I threw back my head drinking in the first glories of a new free life. Then, suddenly, vividly, there passed before my mind in rapid tragic sequence—one by one—the ghostly procession of other persons who had known some of these secrets. There were in this procession: C. F. Cramer, Jess Smith, Lawyer Thurston, John T. King, C. F. Hateley, Warren G. Harding,

Mrs. Florence Kling Harding, General Sawyer, and last—Thomas B. Felder,—all representing supposed suicides or sudden deaths.

I alone remained—who knew!

*. * * * * * *

What was going to happen to me?

I knew that I was a good investigator.[1] My bitterest enemies had all conceded this. I knew that I knew how to keep my mouth closed, because I had! Because of my ability at dissimulation I knew that the shrewdest cross-examiners on numerous occasions, had been unable to bring to light any facts that I did not want to tell. Should I—and must I—and would I—tell it now? In defense of myself? Would I tell the true inside story of the Harding Administration?

Why should I tell it?

It flashed through my mind whether Col. T. B. Felder's sudden death—suicide or murder—was fortunate or unfortunate for me. Had he lived, I knew and many others knew, that he was prepared and was just about to reveal to the world the multiplied scandals during the era referred to by John W. Davis,[2] the Democratic candidate for the presidency, in his speech of acceptance, as "those melancholy years." Col. Felder's intention to do this was in defense of himself. Should I resort to his intended method? Or—should I remain silent?

How did I know that this was Col. Felder's intention?

Col. Felder was capable of telling the whole story of the Harding Administration from start to finish. He had been my attorney all through my troubles and he was also a close intimate friend of Mr. Harry M. Daugherty, former Attorney General of the United States and a close intimate

[1] (See Appendix "A" for notes referred to in the text.)

friend of Jess Smith and others involved in the Harding intrigues.

During my incarceration, many visits had been paid to me by those close to Col. Felder, including an ex-Governor of a state and a United States Senator. In addition I had been taken to New York City from the penitentiary on several occasions for the purpose of using me, if I would so consent, in connection with the prosecution of Harry M. Daugherty, ex-Attorney-General of the United States and Thomas W. Miller, Alien Property Custodian during the Harding Administration.

On these visits naturally the opportunity was offered me to discuss situations and conditions with Col. Felder who had been my defense attorney and who himself had been convicted with me in the Glass Casket Case. Col. Felder had said to me that if the United States Supreme Court refused a review of his case and would not blot out the stigma of a conviction and the fine that had been imposed on him,—which automatically disbarred him from his law profession,—it was his purpose to give to the world the whole story in every hideous detail.

The Supreme Court did deny him a review of his case. When this happened Col. Felder began at once to make arrangements for his exposure. He left New York City for the South.

But prior to his leaving New York City for the South he had communicated to me his intentions. He told me to expect him at the penitentiary in Atlanta in order that I could make available to him the documents and records that I had that would enable him to bring about the exposure that he had in mind. He had the sure belief that it would vindicate him.

Col. Felder had first gone to his old home town, Dublin, Ga., to get documents and records that were stored there.

From there, he went to Florida to make personal contact with certain parties. From Florida he came to Savannah, Ga. He had outlined to me that, whether I worked along with him in the exposure or not, whether I corroborated his statements with documents that I had or not—that his mind was made up to tell the entire story to the American people and appeal to their sense of justice and fair play. Then, I received a wire from Col. Felder saying that he was on his way to Atlanta to see me.

From the day he left New York City until he arrived in Savannah he was under constant surveillance and his intentions were fully known to those who would be most adversely affected by his exposure.

Col. Felder stopped in Savannah as was his plan. Before the story had gotten into the newspapers I was informed that he had died there suddenly.

Soon thereafter the papers carried the story of Col. Felder's death: the New York and Washington papers copied.[8]

No autopsy was performed. He was alleged to have died from "alcoholic poisoning." Just when he was about to leave Savannah, Ga. for Atlanta to visit me at the penitentiary he was found dead.

This had happened two years ago.

The fact that pressed itself upon my consciousness as I first breathed the air of freedom was simply this: what is going to happen to me now? I alone remained—who knew!

I am out! My wife is standing beside me on the top step: a tiny little woman with brave heart and big courage. My ten year old son was standing at my other side.

Yes—I was out! And—I had paid! My slate was clean! God! I had paid! Nobody could do anything to me—

now. And yet—I remembered with a start, a word of caution from the warden, Mr. Snook, within the walls, spoken just as I was saying goodbye:

"Watch your step, Gaston! Don't forget—it is legally and technically possible for Mrs. Willebrandt, or some other influence, to revive those *nol prossed* indictments. It has never been done—but it can be. It is possible. Don't forget that."

"If Gaston Means should talk?"

I knew that this same question has been in the mind of the world for years. Again and again I have been approached by editors and publishers and newspaper men. I knew—that many possessors of vast new fortunes had squirmed through restless nights wondering—if Gaston Means would talk? I knew that official Washington during the Harding Administration stiffened and blanched at the possibility—and then—later—relaxed with a comforting knowledge that Gaston Means was in a Federal prison. Gaston Means could not talk. The gray dank walls of Atlanta's bastille held his sure silence.

I recalled—how sensational trials of high officials had been staged and played and passed on. How they had furnished sardonic entertainment and cynical amusement for the peoples of two or three great nations. And—Gaston Means was in prison—silent.

Well—time has a way of going on and TRUTH has a way of coming out. You may dig a grave and bury it under the sod but the inexorable laws of life and God will not let it stay buried.

Between my wife and boy I walked down the long granite steps. I helped them into a waiting car that a friend had sent. I got into another car with a Deputy Marshal and he took me to a Commissioner's office where I signed final papers that released me. Then I hurried to the hotel where my wife and boy were stopping.

They met me at the door of their rooms. My wife! My boy! Loyal souls that had never faltered or questioned. How could I ever atone to these two! I had no other thought or object to live for! Just that! After all—how much simpler life is when it is reduced to but one equation and all complications have been eliminated. Those years in prison had certainly done this for me.

I was out—at last! Not a day's parole had been granted me. Although I had a model record and had been recommended for parole by the Parole Board in Atlanta,—the Department of Justice in Washington refused to confirm it. They had exacted the full pound of flesh. I had "served" to the last second of my "time."

Well—what would I do now?

I had no money. Although many millions of dollars had passed through my hands I had gone to prison—penniless. My wife had been teaching public school in Concord, North Carolina, all these three years, earning a meager living for herself and my boy.

I had the check given me by the Warden—$15.00—this liberal compensation from the government for three years of life—$15.00.

* * * * * * *

Constantly—there has been the question in my mind:—should I tell my story in its entirety to the world? Many people, including my wife, had been urging me to do this,—not as a bid for public sympathy—indeed far from it—not so much as a personal vindication, for, so far as that goes,

I knew that I had broken the law and had been punished,—but as an absolute and positive obligation.

I am not a writer. I know nothing about publishers. I am and have always been a cold-blooded Investigator. But I knew a woman in New York who was a writer. I went to New York and called to see her at her home on Riverside Drive.

We discussed the writing of my memoirs. She put me in touch with a Publisher and at their insistence before another twenty-four hours had passed, arrangements had been made for the publication of my book of Memoirs. It was decided that this story should be of what I know concerning many of the political and social intrigues leading up to the mysterious death of President Harding.

During the Harding Administration, I was Investigator, associated with William J. Burns, Chief of the Bureau of Investigations of the Department of Justice. I was also employed by Mrs. Harding for personal investigations and assigned to her, officially. I know—as no other living person—the entire confidential story of the White House during those years.

Much has been written about the Harding Administration. The *truth* has never been told—or the half of it. The more conspicuously great the individual, the greater the incentive to slander him—for the interest is commensurate with the eminence of the person slandered. Such, indeed, might have been the case with President Harding. It is my purpose to put all the FACTS before the public and ask the American people to be both Judge and Jury.

The veil that public sentiment drew over the tragedy and sorrow of a nation at the time of his death will be pierced, not by the hot eye of prurient imagination,—but by cold *facts* of *truth.*

Being also entirely aware of the fact that I am regarded as a consummate liar,—it is difficult for the lay mind to distinguish between trained dissimulation and lying—a master-intriguer,—a master-juggler of truth, I explained to the Publishers with great emphasis, that I did not expect to be believed on my word alone, but that I could back up with indisputable documentary evidence, every incident and fact in my story. I told them that all of my documents and papers were in a warehouse vault in Washington—perfectly safe and secure. I had there sixteen trunks and nine packing cases filled with documents. Remember—I had been in control of the German Secret Service work prior to our entry into the World War, and very closely associated with Captain Boy-Ed.[4] I had also worked for the British Government, the Mexican Government and the United States Government—and for such individuals as J. P. Morgan, H. C. Frick, and other leaders in commercial and political life, through my association with William J. Burns. Because of the very character of my work, I had come in contact with the greatest political and commercial leaders in our land.

And so it was brought about that Gaston Means is going to talk!

I also said to the Publishers:

"I do not fight women or children. I would never do anything that would hurt a woman or a child. I would never degrade a woman or besmirch an innocent. Had Nan Britton not already told her story, I would remain forever silent. But what I have to say now—cannot in any way reflect on Nan Britton or her daughter."

* * * * * * *

Gaston Means is going to talk!

As the story unfolds, one must brush aside century

TELEPHONE CHICKERING 4100

HERALD SQUARE HOTEL
114-120 WEST 34TH STREET
IN THE HEART OF THE SHOPPING AND THEATRICAL DISTRICTS
NEW YORK

Aug. 15th, 1928.

My dear Mrs. Thacker:

I think you will agree that it has been constantly my purpose and intention to show to you undisputable documentary evidence verifying any and all statements that I have made to you.

It is not my intention for you as an author at any time, to publish any statement of mine that I am unable to verify myself with undisputable, self-evident documentary evidence -- or to place you in a position where you can verify my statements by personal interviews and convince yourself that my statements are always the facts as to what transpired in matters I refer to.

Therefore -- if you will look at the documents that I present to you and make the necessary investigation to confirm any of my statements,-- which I insist upon your doing -- I will assume always full responsibility for all such statements.

And also -- I insist that you show to the publishers the documentary evidence verifying any and all statements I may make to you, from time to time,

Sincerely,

Gaston B. Means

steeped veneers of civilization and go back to the late sixteenth and early seventeenth centuries and medieval days of the reign of the Borgias.

The very kernel—the vital tragic web-mystery of the entire Harding Administration has never been told or hinted. It has been garbled and distorted and buried beneath an avalanche of untruths and misrepresentations. It is in reality a scarlet thread—a crimson cord that cements and binds the whole fabric together, producing a fantastic and dramatic tapestry effect through which this thread interlaces and entangles—politicians, bankers, capitalists, industrialists, worth-while world and underworld characters,—high officials, cabinet-members and even an ex-President in the White House. A crimson cord—dipped in the life blood of a broken hearted woman—once, our First Lady of the Land.

I will take up this crimson cord and unravel the knots and tangles for all the world to see.

This story will not be a chronicle of piety. It will be a record in American life of certain very important and very human men and women in a very human age—hypocritical, greedy, grasping, debauching, lustful. A period that has been red with the blood of nations and pale with passion at white heat. A period of vivid color, of soft allurements and coldest steel—of swift movements, speed-mad—of high ambitions, of dazzling lights and impenetrable blackness—of trusts dishonored and basest treacheries,—of amazing contrasts and blatant conspiracies and hidden murders.

It will be a record of *truth* and *facts.*

The little tragic "House of Mystery" on H Street next

to the old Shoreham Hotel, made famous and infamous through the Harding Administration and the "Little Green House" on K Street—will become mere insignificant incidents,—compared to 903—16th St., N. W. where my "home" was made for me.

THE STRANGE DEATH

of

PRESIDENT HARDING

Chapter I

Mrs. Harding Employs Means as Private Detective

"Mrs. Harding wants me to come to the White House."

This idea held a tenacious minor key in my consciousness all the time I was dispensing with the routine business at my desk in the Department of Justice, after the lunch hour at one o'clock on a late October day in 1921.

Buttoned securely in an inside coat pocket reposed a note that had been handed to me at eleven o'clock that morning. Shortly after ten o'clock, my phone had rung and I was told that the private secretary of a prominent man in Washington, Mr. Edward B. McLean, whose wife was a very special friend of Mrs. Harding—had a letter for me. And would I come to the lobby of the Shoreham Hotel right away? I had never met this secretary but he said that he would know me.

I closed and locked my desk and went to the Shoreham Hotel. As I entered the lobby, I was met by a young man of perhaps thirty, with clear-cut features and faultlessly dressed. He said simply:

"Mr. Means."

It was not a question but a statement, for he knew me. Then he took an addressed envelope from a pocket and handed it to me and said: "I am instructed to deliver this to you."

I replied: "Thank you."

No other word was spoken between us. I glanced at the envelope and saw that it was of the usual social stationery of the White House. In an upper left hand corner was engraved: "The White House." In the lower left hand corner was written: "Very personal and confidential." I recognized the handwriting of Mrs. Harding.

I put the letter in a pocket and returned to my desk at the Department of Justice I finished the work that was clamoring for attention before noon. I did not open the letter until I had found a secluded place free from interruption where I was entirely alone, during the lunch hour. The note thanked me for what I had done for her, and asked me to come to the White House at once—that she wanted to talk to me.

The note practically summoned me to the White House to see Mrs. Harding. It had been several weeks since I had been assigned to a very special piece of investigating for Mrs. Harding. To refresh my memory as to exactly how many days it had been,—I drew my diary from a pocket.

I have always kept a diary. It is an accurate record of every hour of my days and nights. This was part of a self-imposed rigid discipline as an Investigator. This diary has always been a valuable asset. If I want to know, for example, where I was and what I was doing on the 15th day of July, 1917,—all I have to do is to refer to my diary and I will find a detailed account of every hour of that day.

Glancing through the pages now—I saw that it had been three weeks and two days, since I had been working for Mrs. Harding. It had come about in this way.

William J. Burns who was at the head of the Investigation Bureau of the Department of Justice, sent for me to come to his office.[5] My desk was on the first floor while his offices were on the seventh. Mr. Burns met me in an outer office, when I appeared in answer to his summons. He explained:

"Gaston—I have an important visitor in the office." He told me that it was General Sawyer—with a special mission from Mrs. Harding. It seems—that Mrs. Harding was a great believer in fortune tellers and soothsayers and star-gazers and crystal gazers. I had heard rumors of this, just as everybody else in Washington. When President Harding was Senator, Mrs. Harding had gone with four other Senators' wives to consult a certain rather famous soothsayer—a Madam X. They were told by this prophetess at that time, that one of their husbands would one day be President. There was a public record of this occurrence in the newspapers.

After Mr. Harding was President, Mrs. Harding had gone on two occasions to the home of Madam X. She went ostensibly to have her fortune told. Mrs. Harding believed implicitly—so it was said—in this woman's supernatural powers of clairvoyance and divination. When the President learned of these visits—he was tipped off by a reporter as it was getting into the newspapers, he put a stop to them immediately.

A Sunday article appeared in one of the Washington papers about that time, telling the history of these magic arts,—laying the foundation for the story that Mrs. Harding was an ardent disciple. It was hinted that Mrs. Harding sincerely felt that the nation could not be properly run by the President without the aid of this soothsayer.

I had heard these things so I was not altogether unprepared for what Mr. Burns told me. It seems that when it became impossible for Mrs. Harding to either call at Madam X's home or have her come to the White House, she conceived the idea of writing questions that she wanted answered and sending them to Madam X by a special friend whom she had brought with her to Washington, a Mrs. Whiteley.* She put these questions in the form of a serial questionnaire. Mrs. Whiteley would carry the papers out to Madam X and she would keep them for several days,—dream over them, and then Mrs. Whiteley would call for

* In this, as in a few other instances involving minor characters, fictitious names have been substituted for the true names.

them and take them back to Mrs. Harding, who would write new questions.

I had never seen Mrs. Whiteley but knew her by reputation as a rather small brunette, always well and becomingly dressed: a vivacious and alluring personality. Mr. Burns told me that Mrs. Harding would sometimes speak of her as nurse, and then again as companion and I have heard her referred to as servant.

The serial questionnaire had been going back and forth carried by Mrs. Whiteley for some time. Many of these questions would be concerning matters of state,—of various appointments, of what Congress would do—or what the Senate should do in connection with certain important bills, and concerning judicial and diplomatic appointments and other executive and diplomatic appointments,—but also there were many questions of a most intimate character—about the President.

Mr. Burns told me—that this soothsayer in her zeal, had made a recent attempt to come to the White House and that this had been reported to the President. And he had such strong feelings in the matter and had expressed them to Mrs. Harding—that she had become alarmed about the serial questionnaire that contained her questions in her own handwriting and the answers in the handwriting of the soothsayer,—knowing that this paper was in the possession of Mrs. Whiteley. When she asked Mrs. Whiteley for it, she was told that it had been destroyed. But Mrs. Harding was not satisfied and had sent Gen. Sawyer to consult Mr. Burns. Mr. Burns briefly outlined the case to me, standing in the outer office. He told me that the matter was not to be known to anybody in the world but himself, myself, Gen. Sawyer and Mrs. Harding. "I'll introduce you to Gen. Sawyer," he said as we went into the inner office.

Sitting in this office, I saw a little, high-strung nervous

man: highly polished and shining—shining face, shining shoes, shining glasses, shining buttons on his dapper uniform, shining false teeth—shining everything. At a glance, I had him catalogued according to my profession: a self-centered egotist.

Mr. Burns spoke:

"Gen. Sawyer—this is Gaston Means. I can assure you that any matter that you take up with him in behalf of Mrs. Harding will be treated in the right way. In order—that you may know if there is a break anywhere down the line,—I'll not listen further to the story and I want you to tell it only to Gaston. He will let you know if what you want to accomplish can be done. I'll assign him personally—to handle it. It will not go further."

Mr. Burns left us alone. Gen. Sawyer began:

"I am an emissary from Mrs. Harding." Then he repeated the story that Mr. Burns had already told me and emphasized the very urgent need—that these most important papers in Mrs. Harding's handwriting and the answers in the handwriting of Madam X be recovered. All the questions had been answered—except the last serial of the questionnaire—that was pending. He concluded: "Do you think it's possible to get these papers?"

"Do you know the address of Mrs. Whiteley?" I asked.

"I can get it for you. I don't know it," was his reply.

"Can you also get the address of this soothsayer—Madam X?"

This address he gave me.

The next remark of Gen. Sawyer gave me my first important clew. He said:

"Mrs. Whiteley says—the papers have been destroyed, you understand. . . . And whatever you do, do not annoy Madam X. She is a dangerous woman. She has unbelievable powers. I myself have consulted her many times. Why—she can cast a spell over you! Whatever you do, don't antagonize her! These papers are not in her hands. If they have not been destroyed, Mrs. Whiteley has them."

He then entered into a long and technical and scientific dissertation about soothsayers and this amazing Madam X who could cast a spell. He spoke of her remarkable powers in delving into the subconscious mind—her clairvoyant gifts.

I asked him—if he believed in witches and fortune-tellers. He replied with great earnestness.

"Yes. There is much to it. It is as yet an unexplored field. As science advances—we will know that these extraordinary powers are—a connecting link between man and God. They are gifts, directly from God."

He was patronizingly patient with my ignorance and I tried to look intelligent. After he had further eulogized the soothsayer and reiterated many times his own absolute faith in her, I returned to the one important question: Mrs. Whiteley's address. He said he would send it to me privately—just on a card with no name. I gave him my home address. He gathered up his military cap, gloves and stick and papers, with little pecking movements and with the wiry strut of a bantam rooster, he went out. I remarked to Mr. Burns:

"Is that man a nut—or what?"

He replied with a smile: "We are forced to deal with all sorts of people."

With the official assignment from Mr. Burns to Mrs. Harding, I began my investigation. I dictated a short note to Gen. Sawyer telling him to tell Mrs. Harding to arrange it diplomatically—that she would not need the services of Mrs. Whiteley until further notice. Mrs. Whiteley lived with her husband in an apartment in the city. I did not want my men to trail her to the White House. I could not have my agents hanging around there.

I took eight men in this surveillance:—"shadow" men.

These "shadow" men are of distinct type: small and of neutral personality, non-de-script—men who would not attract notice anywhere. These men were not great investigators, but they were the pick of the Department of Justice "shadow" men. They had been instrumental, through their shadow work, in bringing about the successful prosecution of a great number of cases in which the United States Government was interested.

I called to my office the one of these eight men whom I knew was most experienced. I gave my instructions to him. First—I wanted to see Mrs. Whiteley myself, but I described the lady to him with careful accurate detail as she had been described to me by Gen. Sawyer. I gave him her home address, and told him that when a woman of this description entered this apartment, he would know that she was Mrs. Whiteley.

I wanted two men working on shifts of eight hours each, day and night, to keep her and her home under constant surveillance and, to use the technical term, "tail" her whatever she does and wherever she goes. I wanted the two extra men to be used for emergencies:—that is, to follow anyone else who from Mrs. Whiteley's actions might be a special intimate friend of hers. I made available to these men sufficient funds to hire taxis or any other mode of transportation that Mrs. Whiteley might resort to, with full instructions to keep me posted over the telephone—besides their daily official reports that were always written.

Within a day or so, I found that she was making frequent calls at the Veterans' Bureau of which Col. Forbes was then in charge, but it developed that she went there—to visit Gen. Sawyer's offices that were in the building. This seemed peculiar.

My men kept me posted almost hourly. They would 'phone for instance that "we've put her to bed, the lights are out," or "we've taken her to Childs to lunch—alone" or "we took her to Huyler's to lunch with a woman friend" or "we've gone to market and bought the groceries" or "we're having a coca-cola at the corner drugstore" and so on.

Knowing that she was going to the Veterans' Bureau, I selected an extra man to talk to her in the entrance on one occasion, so that I could see and observe her. I waited with him at the time she was expected to arrive. I was standing over by a window reading a newspaper intently—when my man gave me the signal that she was coming. I continued to read, of course. He made pretext and engaged her in conversation. I saw at once, that she was a woman peculiarly attractive to men. She had a small trim erect little figure, was well and becomingly dressed—I judged about 38 years old. But her greatest attraction lay in her eyes,—alluring, inviting,—eager for adventure. She had all the marks of a woman gambler who plays a game,—not at cards over the poker table, but by subtly controlling men.

That night I gave orders to tap her telephone wires.

Two days later, one of the men reported that he had rung the bell of her apartment disguised as an agent,—that the lady had opened the door herself and had smilingly declined to be interested in anything he might have for sale—but he reported that she lived in the usual five room apartment, decidedly better furnished than her husband's salary or position would seem to justify. And—most important of all, through an open door leading into another room, he had caught a glimpse of a young *colored* girl with a broom and dustpan. This one fact was more important to the case than all the elaborate system of espionage with which I had surrounded her: the mere fact that she had a young *colored* girl as her maid.

Immediately, I withdrew all my "shadow" men. I sent to New York for a young negro man investigator. I reported to Gen. Sawyer, of course, from time to time, and he seemed delighted that I had Mrs. Whiteley under surveillance. And then constantly, every day—he would 'phone me to know where she was and what she was doing. I could not understand this—at the time.

My negro investigator from New York arrived promptly. He came to the office. He was a neat appearing mulatto. His name was Harry Peoples. I said to him:

"I've a nice little job for you. You'll like it. All I want you to do—is to make the acquaintance of a certain young colored girl—make love to her——"

He laughed: "The usual thing?"

"The usual thing. But listen—this is an important affair and must be done speedily and right."

He was an intelligent young fellow and went to work. I handed him $100.

Within forty-eight hours, he was back in the office with his report.

"I met her," he grinned.

"How?"

"I followed her, Sunday, to Sunday school—and got in the same class."

"Good . . . Now listen. You cultivate the acquaintance as rapidly as you dare. Get into the apartment. . . . Find out if Mrs. Whiteley has a special bureau or desk or drawer or anything that she keeps carefully locked. Understand?"

"Sure. Want me to get a key to the apartment?"

"As soon as possible."

Another two days, and he returned with a key. He had slipped it from the girl while they were at a dance,—long enough to have a duplicate made. And he also reported that she had a carefully locked desk.

Luckily for us,—just about at that time, only a few days intervening, Mrs. Whiteley and her maid went to Baltimore for a little visit. I knew that Mr. Whiteley's business kept him away from home all day long.

Harry Peoples and I entered the apartment. He showed me the locked desk—which was an old secretary that stood in a corner.

"You a-gonna break the lock?" Harry asked.

"Never break a lock, Harry—if it can possibly be avoided," I replied.

We made a paraffin impression of the keyhole,—slipped out and had a key made and returned within two hours.

We opened the desk. We found many loose papers but not the papers we were searching for. However, pushed back in a corner I saw a box. I reached my hand under and pulled it out. It was a black metal bank-box—locked. It was about twelve inches long and eight wide. Because I had no key to this, I carried it to the Department of Justice,—sent Harry out to have a key made from another paraffin impression.

He returned with the key and we opened the box. The box was placed on the center of my desk in my office. I bent over it eagerly. It was filled with loose papers,—it seemed. I lifted a thickly folded mass and flipped them open carelessly. But in an instant, I knew that I had found exactly what I was searching for. It was a long serial questionnaire,—the questions written in one handwriting and the answers in another.

I said: "Here we are—Harry—this is what I'm after. You can go now—report tomorrow."

I was alone. I sat down at my desk and glanced through those questions. "My God!" I muttered under my breath. And I knew why Mrs. Harding was so eager to get these questions back. What questions! What answers! What would happen—if they should ever become public? I dared not try to think! Well—she should have them back.

Then I lifted a bundle of letters from the box. Letters

to Mrs. Whiteley? What could these precious things be? I opened one and gave a sort of gasp when I read its amorous salutation—then I turned over the pages to find the signature.

"My Lord—they're from Gen. Sawyer!"[6]

I spoke aloud in surprise and consternation. I read a few of the letters, and as I read, the paramount issue of this particular investigation veered.

In all of my wild career of spectacular adventure,—I had always had an instinctive reverence for the sanctity of the home. And—whatever might be my own personal beliefs and prejudices in the matter, I knew darn well—that Mrs. Whiteley's conduct with Gen. Sawyer at the White House as told in those letters, ought to be stopped. I knew—what the American public would think about it. And—so far as I had been able to know, Mr. Whiteley was an honest, honorable man.

It was not Mrs. Harding's questionnaire, important as it assuredly was to her, and that Mrs. Whiteley had stolen and kept hidden for her own purposes,—it was not to protect President Harding from publicity concerning the soothsayer,—that was the paramount issue with me at the moment, *but* to stop Mrs. Whiteley and her conduct with Gen. Sawyer. I understood why Gen. Sawyer had lied to me, when he told me that he did not know Mrs. Whiteley's address. It was a silly useless lie.

My mind was quickly made up.

I took the entire contents of the box and bundled them together and sent them by registered mail to Mrs. Harding—marked "Personal and Confidential, from Gaston Means." Also I enclosed a letter to Mrs. Harding in which I told her

—that while I was glad to return her papers to her,—that I was not greatly interested in the soothsayer-matter—that I considered it inconsequential in comparison with another matter revealed by the investigation: Gen. Sawyer's letters to Mrs. Whiteley. That I was sure it would be a matter of vast importance to her and to the American people—that the White House, the "home" as it were of the nation, should not be desecrated as evidenced by those letters.

And it was her reply to this communication,—that now summoned me to the White House to talk with her. I had been in consultation with her several times, during the course of the investigation, but I had a very different feeling that afternoon and one that I could not explain. Could I only have foreseen into what vast complications that interview was to lead—perhaps I would have understood. And perhaps I would not have gone at all. For—the serious effect that that interview was to have on my own future destiny, finally culminated—in cutting out of my life—thirty-eight months, spent in the Federal Penitentiary in Atlanta . . . But suddenly, I sat erect,—closed my desk and started for the White House.

II

Mrs. Harding seemed vastly pleased with my conduct of the Whiteley affair and each time I saw her to make my personal report, she had hinted that she would soon assign me to some very important investigations.

In the meantime, with her deep insight into intrigues of all kinds and her inborn suspicious nature—she had evidently tested me out to her satisfaction.

There was a reporter on the *Washington Post* whom she knew extremely well, and she tipped off this reporter that he could probably get some interesting social items from me, if he were clever enough to make me talk. She assumed that perhaps I might be flattered to be interviewed by a society reporter.

The man came to see me in the office. He was affable, suave, smiling.

"Well—what do you want?" I inquired.

"Just to ask a few questions—social questions. I'm from the *Post*—" he began. I was very busy that morning and interrupted.

"From the *Post?* Write out your questions and bring them to me."

He sat down and covered a sheet of legal paper with questions. I glanced at them, folded the paper and put it in my pocket saying,

"Come back tomorrow and I'll see."

The questions pertained largely to social matters at the White House and at the home of Mrs. Boyd—one of Mrs. Harding's best friends.

I took the sheet of questions to Mrs. Harding and asked her what to do with them. She told me afterwards that the reporter had said to her that 'nobody could get that guy to open his mouth,' and when she said that I saw through her little strategy.

III

It was a murky cold day in October. I glanced at my watch—3:15. It had been raining through the night and early morning. Drops of water still glistened on the soaked foliage of the trees and hedges and shrubbery. The rain had pelted down a vast harvest of dead leaves. They were blowing on the pavements as if trying to scurry to shelter.

It is but a short walk from the Department of Justice to the White House. I did not enter the front gate, but circled the corner and walked up the curved driveway that leads to the east entrance of the Executive rooms.

In the dripping wetness, I saw that the yard men had already begun raking off the dead leaves from the White House lawn, and were tossing them into waiting carts.

There was death in the air that day, but it was death that presaged new life. It always does. Everything must die—before it can live again. What an endless cycle—*life*, I mused. An endless cycle, indeed: sure, inexorable.

I stopped and picked up a leaf of silver maple. It was stiff with age and curled and cracked at the edges. Its surface was wrinkled and hard, glowing dully in crimson and gold and amber,—like the face of a painted old woman! I tossed it aside with disgust.

A little squirrel darted from an undergrowth and scurried across the pavement in front of me, carrying in its uplifted paws,—a small portion of its winter storage of food. A flurry of birds emerged from the top of a crepe myrtle tree that bordered the path,—their wings poised, perhaps for a long flight southward to warmth and sunshine.

The rows of shrubbery bordering the building itself, already blighted by frost even in a sheltered nook, drooped and hung limp and impotent, leaning downward toward the earth, as though impatient for a final surrender.

I shivered in the raw, damp atmosphere, as I entered the east door of the White House. I was promptly escorted through the net-work of narrow corridors and up to the second floor, to the door of Mrs. Harding's private suite.

As I was silently following my guide, I had been thinking to myself: "And this is the home of the President of the United States." Well—it is no more sacred to him than my little home is to me, and I knew that I was but one of millions who feel the same way. Man has always preserved the sanctity of his home. Haven't we seen pictures of even the primitive Caveman standing at the door of his cave, with a great big long knotted stick,—ready to defend the sanctity of his home? Civilization has not moved from this fundamental principle of life—and it never will.

I had scarcely rapped on the door when it was opened by Mrs. Harding herself.

IV

"You are prompt, Mr. Means," was her greeting as I entered.

"That is part of my profession," I replied.

Mrs. Harding was standing very straight and stiff,—with head and chin held high. She was dressed in soft, flowered silk of lavender and gray. Her hair was arranged with studied care: each hair exactly in its place. Over her shoulders was a scarf of transparent silk. Her neck was encircled by a black velvet band.

"It is a disagreeable conversation that we must have this afternoon, isn't it?" she asked, brightly, seating herself comfortably at the end of a couch and arranging a pillow behind her.

"I trust—more profitable than disagreeable," I replied sitting down opposite in a straight stiff chair.

"First—let me thank you for your miraculous work. I do consider it little short of a miracle that you got my papers for me. I depend on Madam X more than on anything or anybody on earth, for you see—it is through her—that I can help my husband."

"It is difficult for me to understand that," was my laughing rejoinder.

"President Harding—Warren—is always blind to the faults of his friends. Everybody knows that. It is I who must be ever alert to guard and protect him—and I could never do it without Madam X. You may not understand but it is the truth."

"You really do—believe in Madam X?" I asked quizzically.

"Absolutely! And—she tells me that I am a 'Child of Destiny'."

Mrs. Harding kept her face in repose always. Any nervousness was indicated by her hands. She constantly clasped and unclasped the four fingers of each hand.

"But now—Mrs. Whiteley? I need not tell you what a shock these letters from Gen. Sawyer to her—were to me! Why, I could scarcely believe my eyes! And as you say—it is a matter of vast importance."

She paused a moment and then suddenly changed the subject by asking: "Do you always have to make your reports to Mr. Burns?"

"Unless otherwise instructed. He is my superior officer."

"But if I should give you at any time—some very personal work to do for me,—investigations, you know,—would you have to tell Mr. Burns about it? I would pay you."

"Not necessarily, if I could get his permission."

"But—I would not want Mr. Burns to know a thing about it. . . . My husband has burdens that the world knows nothing about—and must know nothing. There are forces—devilish forces, working against him. And they will destroy him, if I do not protect him."

She had become excited and emphatic.

"I feel sure—that could be arranged," I assured.

I was beginning to be curious to know what new investigation she could be hinting. "Forces"—working to destroy the President? As abruptly, she returned to the former subject.

"You know—Mr. Means—it is hard for me to understand people who do things like Mrs. Whiteley and Gen. Sawyer,—for my own married life has been so perfect—well, I just can't understand."

"Yes?"

"I've been married thirty years! Could you believe it?"

As I looked at her, I could indeed believe it. She was an old woman,—a little withered old woman,—with a face like an autumn leaf,—and no expert masseur or hairdresser, or paint or cosmetics could ever make her anything else. I wondered—how much older than the President she really was? I had heard—nine years. It seemed entirely possible.

"I feel in a reminiscent mood this afternoon," she was saying. "And so,—shall I tell you a bit of history? Besides, I shall want you to always understand—that nothing has ever intervened or come between, my husband—President Harding—and myself. You may think it strange that I say these things to you. I have reasons—vital reasons! Listen. From our very first meeting, Warren Harding and I knew—that we were kindred spirits. It was love at first sight. . . . And the path of our love-romance was not made easy. . . . My father bitterly opposed. And—I had worshiped my father. He was a banker, a rich man, and he and I had always been pals. I was his pet. Warren was a struggling publisher of a little daily newspaper that had known nothing but difficulties."

This was not new to me but I was interested in the telling of it, by her. She went on:

"But love laughs at obstacles. On July 8th, 1891,—with a smile of joy on my face and a deep sweet confidence in my heart, I walked out of my father's home, knowing that its doors would be closed against me,—perhaps forever. I cast my life's fate on the man I loved and I have never had cause to regret it. My father did not speak to me—for seven years. But—I was happy. Warren completely filled my life."

Yes—that was perfectly possible, I concluded to myself.

"I have always been at his side, encouraging, agreeing heartily with his every purpose and ambition. . . . Not long after we were married, Warren was sick and I went down to the little newspaper office to take his place. I went,—expecting to stay a few days. . . . I stayed for fourteen years. . . Although I had direct charge of the circulation department, I kept in close touch with every detail of every department."

I wondered—if she could ever be placed in any position where she would not want to dominate every detail? I did not think so. I listened attentively.

"Every evening during all the years, we walked home from the office,—arm in arm. We used to sit at either side of our library table on long winter evenings—"two souls with but a single thought", and work over our "exchanges" to find good stuff to reprint. . . I never lost courage or ambition. It was all for my husband. I was keenly interested in public affairs and public men. I devoured all current news of the day. And yet—I was always a successful home-maker, for my husband's friends were my friends. I lived—only for him."

I recalled that this had been frequently quoted in the newspapers. She went on:

"Then—came his meeting with Harry Daugherty. It was at Richwood—way back in 1898. Did you ever hear the story?"

Without waiting for my reply, she continued:

"Warren was at the school house pump, washing the mud from his shoes. Mr. Daugherty came up to the pump—and the acquaintance began. There was a political meeting in Richwood. Warren was not billed to speak that day, but

Mr. Daugherty insisted that he should. Mr. Daugherty has often said that he knew from that first chance meeting—that Warren Harding was destined to go far politically. . . . Of course, I had always known it! During the two terms in the Ohio Senate, the friendship deepened. It was Harry Daugherty who really made him run for Lieutenant-Governor of Ohio. . . . Always in everything, Harry Daugherty has been behind Warren—with his amazing political insight. He always said—that Warren looks like a President. To me—of course, he has the regal look of a King! I believe Mr. Daugherty put much store by Warren's handsome appearance. Once seen,—he could never be forgotten."

In this, I heartily agreed. Warren Harding was an amazingly handsome man.

"And so—he climbed steadily upward," she continued,—a far-away look creeping into her intellectual eyes. She smiled. "Our life together has been ideal. My mentality could keep pace with his—often would stride ahead of his. We had the same ambitions. And, while of course, we might differ in little unessential things—our home life has been perfect. I asked nothing for myself. I lived—through him. And—I had made him what he was. I knew it. He knew it."

This explained in a measure what I had heard: that Mrs. Harding felt that she was the divinely appointed arbiter of the President's destiny! Had she not brought him up, step by step, and placed him in the highest office in the gift of the greatest nation on earth?

"Were you here at the inauguration?" Again, a sudden change of subject.

"No. I was not. Unfortunately," was my lament.

"Ah—it was a marvellous day! I wore a blue hat—most becoming,—and chinchilla furs and carried a great bunch of

American Beauty roses. I felt just like a bride—and I was told that I looked like one. And Warren wore the same smile as my young bride-groom of thirty years before."

I shifted my eyes and looked out of the window.

She continued: "In the brilliant sunshine of that Washington March day, amid the plaudits of assembled thousands—with banners and flowers, music and oratory—the flash of steel, the blaze of decorations, the booming of cannon,—*I*, the *wife* of Warren Harding saw the goal and summit and crowning glory of my life-ambition: the inauguration of my husband. He was President of the United States. I was First Lady of the Land."

She had every reason to feel elated, I very soberly concluded. Every reason. But I could somehow say nothing. Evidently, I was not expected to make comment, for she continued:

"And after it was all over,—and the day was done, and we were alone in our room that night,—he put his arms around me and with eyes swimming in tears, he said: 'Duchess—I owe it all to you. You did it. The future—is—golden—'. . . . Had there ever been the slightest doubt of my husband in my mind,—it was gone then,—forever. He loved me. He had always loved me. He would always love me. Warren Harding never betrayed a friend in his life. What had his wife to fear—ever? He is the soul of honor. My trust in him is perfect—perfect."

Again—I could not look in her face—for sheer pity. Or if not pity—something else that kept my eyes averted.

"So—you see—I have my Prince Charming still with me. The beautiful dreams of my girlhood have come true again and again through long happy years. Thirty years! I ought to be a perfectly happy woman. Don't you think so?"

Again, she was clasping and unclasping the four fingers

"To me, of course, he has the regal look of a king!"

of her hands. There was an alert, vivacious, forced note in her voice. I truthfully replied:

"It surely does seem so."

"Oh—I am! I am! I am!" She replied with an emphasis not to be mistaken. And yet,—it was her very emphasis and repetition and reiteration that lodged a stubborn questioning in my mind and made me remember a flood of recent rumors that had been floating around Washington. And—I happened to know a few embarrassing things about these rumors. But I gave her close attention as she continued:

"It is true—that Warren was most reluctant to allow his name to enter the Presidential race. You knew that? He shrank from it. Later—I was to understand why. I did not —then."

She paused a moment and then continued hurriedly as though to cover up a possible slip—of having said too much.

"But Harry Daugherty was determined.[7] He camped on Warren's trail—at our home, in the office, even at meals—he talked of nothing else. Then Harry set himself rigidly to the task of convincing me,—for he said, if he could do that—that victory was won. And it was!"

She laughed, clasping and unclasping the four fingers of her hands. Suddenly, the hands became quiet, she leaned forward and spoke with great earnestness:

"I've told you all this—Mr. Means—so you could the better realize how I feel—about preserving the sanctity of the home. The White House typifies the *'home' of the nation.* It must be protected from any slander or any shadow of scandal. It must be, like Cæsar's wife, above suspicion. The foundation of the government rests on the purity of the home. That is largely *my* responsibility. I shall always prove myself watchful and diligent. . . . The White House as the *'home'* of the nation, is a sacred place and nothing shall come into it that 'defileth or maketh an abomination'. I don't often quote Scripture but that expresses exactly what I mean."

"Which would exclude Mrs. Whiteley and Gen. Sawyer?" I ventured the question.

"Mrs. Whiteley—yes. I shall reprimand her severely. But—I must be cautious. . . No country can rise higher than the home of its people. The very progress of civilization depends on the thoughts we think and the deeds we do—back in our homes. A nation becomes decadent—as its homes become decadent, and never before."

The words sounded familiar. Had I read them somewhere? Anyhow—it was not an original thought.

"Mrs. Whiteley knows how strongly I feel about these things. And—I thank you from the bottom of my heart, for not covering up this matter."

That she was not disposed to include Gen. Sawyer in her displeasure—was a little queer. Then came another sudden change of subject:

"Have you ever seen—the President's inauguration present to me! I am so proud of it. See?"

She raised her head and touched a beautiful diamond studded ornament on the front of the black velvet band that encircled the wreck of her throat. "Isn't it a lovely thing? Really beautiful! No woman in the world could be happier than I. It is what has kept me so *young*—always."

She moved suddenly and stood up. Evidently, the interview was over.

"And—we understand each other, don't we? You are to find out from Mr. Burns if you can be allowed to do some very *personal* work for me—and report directly to me and to no one else. You understand?"

I, too, had stood up. "Yes, I understand."

"And—you are to continue to keep Mrs. Whiteley under

surveillance—until—until we can—get rid of her—you understand."

"I understand."

Once again—a sudden change of subject.

"Oh—I want to tell you. President Harding had a very wonderful 'creed' under which his newspaper—the *Marion Daily Star*—was editorially conducted. It is a fine creed on which you should model your own work and life and career."

"What is it?" I asked.

"I will quote only the most important excerpts:

" 'Remember there are two sides to every question. Get them both.'

" 'Be truthful. Get the *facts.*'

" 'I would rather have one story exactly right than a hundred half wrong.' "

She spoke the words with a triumphant intonation as though she were quoting from the mouth of an oracle, and waited for my comment, which was:

"Excellent!"

"Can you remember—or shall I write it down for you?"

"I can remember. I shall never forget."

And—I never have!

"Get the FACTS."—The life slogan of President Harding!

Abruptly, she extended her hand.

"Good afternoon."

I bowed low over her hand, not failing to notice the pale white thinness of it, the interlacing of tiny blue veins, the nervous trembling—every mark of pitiless age.

It had been a puzzling interview. I had a feeling that she had carefully rehearsed it. And it was not long before I knew its far-reaching significance.

As I walked back to my desk at the Department of Justice,

one little incident in that interview held in my mind, President Harding's inauguration gift to Mrs. Harding. . . A diamond ornament for the front of the black velvet band that she always wore around her neck. Was not this—perhaps, unconsciously on his part—a supreme gesture of pity—and futility? A black band of velvet encircling an aged throat: that tragic badge of lost illusions, of dead hopes:—that final surrender! And he had tried to dress it up—remove its somber stigma—with a glittering diamond ornament.

And I also decided that there was a certain man whom I must see and ask a lot of questions. And that man was—Jess Smith.

Chapter II

Jess Smith Summons Means to the "House on H Street"

Mrs. Harding was reputed to be familiar with everything pertaining to governmental affairs to the last detail. After the interview with her, described in the preceding chapter, I felt that she not only was familiar with every phase of state and diplomatic strategy,[8] but that she intended to continue to be the central moving factor: the determining factor.

She had placed Warren Harding in the highest position in the gift of the greatest nation in the world,—and assuredly, she had no intention of abandoning him now to the intricate mechanisms of that position and its dangers.

Mrs. Harding was a woman of brains: cold, logical, calculating. And even as little familiar as I was, at that time, with the personnel of the group immediately surrounding the President, I knew and had heard enough to foresee endless complications and intrigues.

Certainly—it was a strangely assorted bunch of diplomats and statesmen that President Harding had ensconced in his Cabinet and in the Department of Justice.

Mrs. Harding's description of their "perfect and ideal" home lacked conviction. Indeed—I knew differently. I wondered if she herself believed in the pretty fable? I did not think so. And to visualize a love scene between the President and his wife was entirely beyond the imagination of man.

She was an old woman: withered, nervous, highstrung—tenaciously holding on to the illusion of youth and fooling nobody but herself.[9] Had she been another woman, I would have felt pity for her, but pity is something that no one could feel toward Mrs. Harding. Her personality was resentfully adamant—toward pity.

I had already seen enough of the President to know that he could no more resist a pretty girl or woman than he could resist food, when hungry. And I had already come in contact with two cases. He loved life. The sheer joy of living raced in his veins!

There was that woman from Marion, Ohio. She had been a milliner in Marion. We will call her Mrs. Milliner. She had been a campaign worker before the election. She had a very fine voice and sang frequently in campaign work.

There was a rumor that she had also had occasion to be in Paris at the same time that President Harding happened to be there on one of his European trips while he was Senator.

At any rate, Jess Smith had told me that she was one of the President's ex-flames, and as he termed it a "lullapalooza", a favorite expression of Jess Smith.

Mrs. Harding had forbidden her to come to the White House. But Mrs. Milliner was clever and resourceful and whenever there was a delegation from Ohio at the White House receptions,—it didn't matter who or what: high school girls, camp fire scouts—anything, she would always be in the line and walk along with them. And she would grab the President's hand and he would have hard work getting rid of her. She would hold up the line in spite of all that the Secret Service men could do.

Jess Smith actually consulted me professionally—for me to tell him how on earth Mrs. Milliner always managed to know the exact day and hour these various delegations would appear. I asked him to get me his Columbus and Cincinnati newspapers and in the very papers he handed me, were two notices of expected delegations. It was too simple.

Upon one occasion, Mrs. Milliner had become so insistent and held up the receiving line so long that the President had called his secretary—to show her into his office until the reception was over and he could talk with her.

No one knows what happened in that scene, of course. But Jess Smith told me that she had a bunch of letters from the President and, unless she was treated with more consideration, there would be trouble.

They had to get those letters, he said. Then Mr. Douglas Boyd, always a loyal and aggressive friend of the President, conceived a clumsy idea of inviting Mrs. Milliner to visit Atlantic City and there pull a sort of badger stunt. They invited her and she came to Atlantic City, but she arrived—substantially chaperoned and the stunt was off. A complete failure.

So Mr. Boyd, confident in his rough horse-play manner of adjusting difficulties, 'phoned Mrs. Milliner at Atlantic City and told her plainly that he wanted the letters and if she would come to his office in Washington and bring the letters—he would pay her the price for them.

She came to his private office with her chaperone who proved to be a middle aged lady. He asked Mrs. Milliner if she had brought the letters and she told him that she had them—he understood her to say—in her shirt waist. So as quick as a flash, to the woman's incredible amazement, he snatched the front of her shirt waist and tore it off—but did not get the letters.

Mrs. Milliner began to cry while he raved at her and told her that she had lied to him. Between sobs, she protested that she had not lied—that the letters were in the shirt waist of the chaperone. Nothing daunted, the valiant Douglas snatched the shirt waist off the middle aged lady—and got the letters. Which eventually cost the gentleman some $15,000—in a compromise settlement to keep the matter out of court.

But the President's letters were secured and Mrs. Milliner came no more to the White House. Her husband was quickly given an assignment as keeper of a lighthouse on one of the great lakes near Detroit—at a safe distance from Washington.

When he told me of this incident, Jess Smith had also mentioned another girl from Marion, whose name I did not catch,—who was extremely jealous of Mrs. Milliner and hated her and it seems that Mrs. Milliner was also jealous of this girl.

Jess Smith was known by everybody as Harry Daugherty's "man Friday". Just what his relation to Mr. Daugherty was, no one ever knew, except as a faithful and confidential friend. He was the best dressed man in Washington. He loved expensive clothes and many of them. He had a desk at the Department of Justice but was on no pay roll there. Much of his time was spent in the Attorney General's office, studying the stock market quotations. He lived with Mr. Daugherty at the Wardman Park Hotel.

I did not care to make a point of going to see Jess Smith to ask the questions that I wanted to know but was alert for the first opportunity that might present itself.

I did not have long to wait. One night about 3 A.M. my home phone rang,—the private extension at the head of my bed. I was sound asleep but at its first tingle, was wide awake. It was Jess Smith.

"Means? Is that Gaston Means?"

"Yes."

"This is Jess Smith. Say—come around to H Street quick as you can get here—will you? There's a—little trouble—" his voice trailed indistinctly.

"Who's giving me this order?"

"What the hell difference does that make? Come on—quick!"

The receiver was hung up. I slipped into my clothes, ordered the car that was always at my disposal and hustled around to H Street. Everyone knew of the many gay midnight suppers there. And I knew that the hilarity sometimes threatened to get beyond bounds.

So I was not altogether unprepared for the scene that I walked into when the door was opened for me. The rooms were in wildest disorder. The dinner table had been cleared —evidently for the dancing of chorus girls—dishes were scattered over the floor—bottles lay on chairs and tables. Everybody had drunk to excess. Half drunken women and girls sprawled on couches and chairs—all of them now with terror on their painted faces.

I was approached by Mr. Boyd who told me—that somehow, accidentally, when they were clearing the table for the girls to dance (girls from the musical comedy then playing in town) and everybody was throwing bottles or glasses—that a water bottle had hit one of the girls on the head and she—seemed—badly—done—up——.

I saw President Harding leaning against a mantel with his guards standing near. He looked bewildered and I whispered to the man next to me that they better get the President out and away first,—and under my breath I added to myself—back to his "perfect and ideal home". I had been told that no one enjoyed these late suppers more than he.

I found the unconscious girl stretched out on a sofa in a rear hall, with two of her companions frantically rubbing her hands and sprinkling water over her face.

I immediately saw the seriousness of the situation. I dared not 'phone for a doctor or an ambulance so I picked the seemingly lifeless figure in my arms and carried her out to my car and took her to a hospital behind the Hamilton Hotel. She was unconscious for days and was finally operated on. I grew alarmed and so made out my own official reports for self-protection.

The next day Jess Smith came into my office. He was plainly perturbed.

"It was a bad business—that girl!"

"I'll say so."

"How did you leave her?"

"Still unconscious."

"Well—keep it under cover. You understand?"

"Of course."

"Suppose that girl dies?" Jess asked.

"It's quite possible," was my calm reply.

"You do! My God—man, what will happen?"

"Nothing. They will operate,—she will die. It will cost big money."

Jess Smith shrugged his shoulders,—but his face was white and he was trembling. Jess had little real nerve.

"Well, it takes big money to cover 'overhead expenses', at H Street. They will charge this item to 'overhead expense'.

"Do you happen to know—who it was that hit her?" I asked.

"What difference does that make?"

Jess threw himself into a chair and lit a cigarette.

"It keeps us all busy—protecting the President's philandering gayeties—but that's part of the little game—so who's crying? That girl from Marion's giving all sorts of trouble again, too."

"Thought she had gone to a far lighthouse—" I ventured.

"Oh—I mean—the *other* one—another of his little 'Janes' that he brought out from Marion. She is determined to come to the midnight supper parties—and it won't do. Nobody wants her—not even the President."

"What is her name?" I asked.

"Her name's—Nan Britton. She wants to climb the social ladder along with the rest of us, I reckon."

"Does the President like her?"

"Does a cat like cream? She's a young—very young and pretty girl," he answered, "and her father was one of the President's oldest friends."

"What's she doing in Washington?"

"Self-culturing herself, I reckon. The President first gave her a job as one of his very personal confidential Secret Service agents. You know—there's a fund of $100,000 put aside for this purpose,—which does not have to be accounted for——"

"You know all about funds—eh?" I inquired quizzically, for Jess Smith's reputation was well known.

"Trust me for that," he laughed. "She ran away with herself on that job however and he had to let her out."

"How?"

He leaned back in his chair, recrossed his legs and twirled his cigarette between his fingers, his eyes fixed on its glowing end.

"The President was going on a week-end trip on the *Mayflower*. Mrs. Harding wasn't going. Nan Britton was hell bent—to be on that trip so she hurries to the dock—and like a little fool—tells the guards and Secret Service men that she holds precedence over them and they must let her pass, which was perfectly true. She operated under credentials of the State Department. She wore a badge as Confidential Messenger. But—they didn't let her pass. They knew better."

"That automatically fired her?"

"Sure. She's a pest."

"Why not get rid of her?" I asked.

Jess Smith stood up, threw his cigarette into a tray and spread out his hands in a final gesture.

"Oh—well—" and he went out.

I wondered. They were getting rid of all the rest of them. Why not Nan Britton?

What did Jess Smith mean about the "little game"? It was all part of their little game, he had said,—to protect the "President's philandering gayeties." What was their little game? Who was in on it? And was that what Mrs. Harding had meant about "devilish forces" threatening to destroy the President?

Chapter III

The Undercover Headquarters of "The Clique"

I AM relating the events in this story as they actually occurred, and as I lived them.

Before President Harding was elected I knew that Mr. Harry M. Daugherty was to be Attorney-General of the United States, and I believed that Mr. William J. Burns was to be Chief of the Bureau of Investigation of the Department of Justice. I also knew that the plan was to consolidate all of the Secret Service work under one head, including the Prohibition, War, and Treasury departments. All were to be under one head,—but this consolidation never materialized.

May I indulge here in just a little personal reminiscence that may help my readers to get the proper slant on some of the activities in this narrative?

My father was a lawyer: one of the leading lawyers in the county. When I was ten years old, he gave me a pony. This pony was equipment for my first detective experiences. My father was a shrewd man. When an important case was about to come to trial, he would send me on my pony around to the different country stores. He instructed me to buy some candy, and to sit down by the stove and eat the candy. But primarily—I was to listen attentively to everything that was said in the store, by everybody,—especially anything that had a bearing on the important case he had,—soon to be tried. That night, I would write out for him all that the men had said.

When the case was begun, some of these men would invariably be called as possible jurors or witnesses. They would be cross-questioned by my father. Once a man professed to have formed no opinion on the case on trial. My father said:

"Weren't you at the Boss Mill store on Friday, about four weeks ago?"

"Yes."

"Didn't you buy an iron preserve kettle at that store on that day?"

"Yes. I did."

"Well, didn't you remark,—that you believed this man was guilty."

"I remember. Yes, sir."

"Stand aside."

Oh, how I thrilled at a scene like this! Who would ever suspect that a ten year old boy, sucking a stick of candy,—was a detective and on the job?

I had an uncle, Geo. W. Means. He was a great detective and investigator in his day and saw years of service in the U. S. Treasury Department. Geo. W. Means was Chief of Police of the town while my father was Mayor.

As I grew in years, I would go around with this Uncle George. I saw many lynchings. I saw my father and uncle do many brave deeds that nobody else would do. All of this early training had its full weight and influence on my life career.

Mr. J. W. Cannon, the multi-millionaire cotton manufacturer of Concord, North Carolina, knew my father well and he knew me. Mrs. Cannon said that she always felt that her children were safe if Gaston Means were with them.

After school, I used to go down to the cotton mills and hang around and make ten or fifteen cents to spend. During these years, I gathered much information about cotton mills and the help employed, and I picked up many little technicalities on how to evade the law.

When I finished college, I studied law. For two years,

when I was nineteen and twenty, I was Superintendent of the grade schools of Albermarle, North Carolina. There were thirty-two teachers working under me.

While in New York, employed by the German government,—I first met Mr. William J. Burns. He told me that he saw in me a brain of exceptional analytical power. He employed me in 1910,—as undercover man. I was already an investigator with life training when I took my first assignment with him.

After Mr. Harding's election there was serious opposition to the appointment of Mr. Daugherty and the same wing of the Republican party that opposed Mr. Daugherty, was also bitterly opposed to Mr. Burns.

Something had to be done about this. Consequently I was sent on an extended trip all over the country and especially through the South. I had numerous letters from prominent men written to Mr. Harding, urging that Mr. William J. Burns be named. These letters came apparently unsolicited. I also conducted everywhere a regular propaganda with the newspapers in Mr. Burns' interest. This placed Mr. Harding in a position to say to the opposition:—"Look at all these letters and newspapers commending Mr. Burns."

Mr. Burns was appointed, but the consolidation fell through.

Mr. Burns received his appointment some months before I received mine,—that is, formally, for, the moment he stepped in, I stepped in also.

I was officially sworn in,—in September. I had been working with Mr. Burns since the inauguration—and before.

I had been living at the Bellevue Hotel. It was convenient to the Department of Justice. In September I moved my family to Washington and we lived at the Bellevue. From the Bellevue, we went to live with a private family. After an interval of several months, we came back to the Bellevue,—

I had retained a room there all the time. From the Bellevue, we moved to the Gordon Hotel. I was always living within five minutes walk to the Department of Justice. I was a night and day man,—subject to call at any moment. From the Gordon Hotel we moved to 903—16th Street, N. W.

My salary at the Department of Justice was $89.33 1/3 a week. That was the sum total of my official pay; but considerably more came to me *from outside sources.* Thus, my house rent was $1,000 a month. I was provided with five excellent servants, including my boy's nurse. A five or six thousand dollar Cadillac car with chauffeur was always at my disposal—day and night,—none of this, of course, was paid for by the Government.

Jess Smith made the arrangements in renting this house and in fitting it up for our purposes. The lease was signed by my father-in-law, W. R. Patterson, who lived with us. It was a peculiarly well located house with a front and a rear entrance. A lane ran along back of the yard,—wide enough to accommodate the parking of a car. My car stood there always,—opposite the back gate. This lane or alley twisted a circuitous route that led within a short block to the Department of Justice. That was my usual way of going.

The house faced on 16th Street and was three stories high with a full English basement.

It was this English basement that formed the chief attraction. It was a substantially built house and each floor was a separate and distinct housekeeping unit.

Most of my time was spent in the English basement. It afforded most comfortable office facilities. There were six rooms and a bath room.

The front room—very large—was my office. There were two telephones: one confidential, unlisted. There was my mahogany rolltop desk and swivel chair. I had an individual, confidential filing cabinet on rollers. Nobody carried the keys but myself. Mr. Patterson's desk, similar to mine, with his chair. Two typewriters on two typewriter desks—three regular filing cabinets—two excellent couches, convertible into comfortable beds—chairs. On the walls, hung many very fine maps,—chiefly waterfronts of the entire country. There was a large beautiful white marble mantel. Open fireplace,—convenient for burning papers. The windows were iron-barred. The entrance was doubly iron-barred. A narrow hall ran all the way through this basement, with rooms at one side.

Just inside the front doubly iron-barred door,—was a small dark reception hall with a settee and chairs, used as a waiting room to the office. That reception room was not a pleasant place:—spooky.

Directly back of the office was the bath room and back of it was a large file room. Behind the file room was the dining room: a large comfortable well-furnished room,—easily accommodating twenty guests at the table. Back of the dining room was a laundry, enormous, which made a most excellent "bar" and service room. The white enamel concrete wash tubs were ideal for ice-packed champagne bottles and liquors and wines.

The handsomest room we had down there was our kitchen: large wood and coal stove, a gas stove and an electric stove. Every modern convenience and luxury.

My monthly grocery bills amounted to hundreds of dollars, more hundreds of dollars than my entire salary.

The house was magnificently furnished from basement to attic: everything included: dishes, silver, linens,—everything.

As I have said, Jess Smith made all the arrangements and he made them well.

The back yard was the strategic point of interest. We had a back gate that was as strong as the door of a bank vault. Entering this gate (with special key), one was then inside a steel cage,—confronted by another gate, equally as strong and opened only by another special key. All around the yard, extending several feet inside the fence—and above the fence some thirty feet, was placed double iron net work, of fine mesh, but thick and strong as the grating protecting a bank. Part of this is still around that yard in Washington. In summer this high iron grating was camouflaged with vines.

The basement and yard of 903—16th Street, N. W. was an arsenal, and there never was an hour, day or night, that a watchman was not on guard. In the front office someone sat always,—day and night. At any moment,—instantly—I could throw on every corner and crevice of this entire back yard, by a system of switches, great electric lights,—properly placed.

Of course, I had to spend a certain amount of time each day at my desk at the Department of Justice. I had to earn my salary of $89.33-1/3 per week.

I understood my position and my office,—clearly. My duties,—intricate, and complicated, as they were,—amounted in the ultimate to a perfectly simple equation:—*I was to do as I was told and ask no questions.*

Although Mr. William J. Burns was my official superior officer in the Department of Justice, I used to receive instructions from time to time from Jess Smith,[10] Harry Daugherty, and others.

For me to tabulate the monies received by me and cared for by me, and turned over to Jess Smith, would fill a volume. And this brings me to a more detailed description of the iron-barricaded back yard of 903—16th St., N. W.

I spent much time in that back yard—for the benefit of the neighbors,—working and arranging flowerbeds around the fence—and in building a swing for my boy.

While doing these things, I dug a square hole about three and a half feet in the center of the yard. After getting down a couple of feet or so, I had a wooden platform built that fitted into this place,—with an open space in the center. Then, I dug down and through that center for twenty feet, —and lowered into this twenty-foot-deep hole a terra-cotta pipe about eight inches in diameter.

That was our bank—our safe deposit vault—in case of fire. That is where we buried our 'talents' that drew no interest, according to Biblical lore. I had a small steel box,—which I kept lowered into this pipe by a strong rope.

Always, in this buried pipe in my back yard at 903—16th St., N. W. in the steel metal box, let down by a rope,—reposed thousands of dollars. I have had there as much as $500,000 at one time and never less than $50,000. Sums less than $50,000 I usually kept on my person or entrusted to my wife for safe keeping.

I remember at one time, my wife carried for three weeks, pinned to her clothing,—$60,000. Often she would carry $40,000 and lesser amounts. I was the safe deposit bank for all graft for the 'gang', operating through Jess Smith, until some one would be making a trip to Washington Court House, Ohio, where it would be deposited in a bank there.[11]

My home, 903—16th St., N. W. was an arsenal, and the secret undercover executive chambers for the "gang".

I was kept well supplied with stenographers, but my confidential work was done on dictaphones and nobody was permitted to transcribe it but Mrs. Patterson.

We had many visitors there,—many high officials in "on the know". Col. Miller spent much time there, as also did Col. Felder, and others well known during the Harding Administration.

Almost daily, we had banquets of the finest food and the finest wines.

When the cares of State pressed heavily and the tension grew great at the Department of Justice, there was always this place that all of us knew where we could go and be quiet and discuss conditions and make plans, and reach conclusions as to future acts, without annoyance from any outside source.

Jess Smith, when under the slightest mental strain, and he was frequently under one, would find refuge here and roost on one of the big couches in the dining room.

The front door,—the formal entrance to the house above the English basement, was never opened. An iron bar was across the inside of that front door.

Jess Smith was paymaster for all "overhead" expenses.

The "Little Green House" on K Street was a social side issue. Also, the "House of Mystery" on H Street.

903—16th Street, N. W. was the real executive undercover chambers of the Harding administration. We had no social banquets or midnight suppers or dances there. The stern undercover work of the *government* alone occupied our attention: Jess Smith, Mr. Daugherty, Col. Miller, Col. Felder, and myself.

Bear in mind that always,—separate and distinct, were my family affairs and my official affairs. None of my Department of Justice friends ever went upstairs. My assumption always was that they came on business. Col. Miller was the only one who ever ate with the family in our private dining room, upstairs.

All mail came through the basement office. I rigged up an ingenious mail box, that extended all the way across the central front window of the bay window in the office. It was made of wood,—the width of the window and perhaps nine inches deep and six inches broad. That box is still on the house.

I could pull the lid up from the inside to receive mail,

903-16 St. N.W., Washington, D.C.
"The undercover executive headquarters for the 'gang'."

and if I pulled down the shade of that window, it was impossible for the mailman or anybody else to see or know who was receiving the mail. Registered letters, telegrams, special deliveries,—everything—came through this mail box,—and was signed for in this way.

When President Harding took his oath of office, his big task was to bring a war-stricken nation "back to normalcy". "Back to Normalcy with Harding" had been the campaign slogan.

I realized very soon that he had gone about this task in a very funny way, and I was mixed up in it—up to my neck. Well—I reasoned,—I might as well sit on the band wagon, where I have been put! I could use a million or so myself for my wife and boy. But I am here to say that had I dreamed of the hectic days and nights to follow, I'd rather have put my wife and boy on a one-mule farm, back in the sticks of North Carolina.

Chapter IV

Why Daugherty Made Harding President

Of course, I had no trouble at all in getting permission from my superior officers to make my reports directly to Mrs. Harding and to no one else, as she so expressly desired. As I had been going to Mrs. Harding's so frequently at the White House, she became nervous that someone might make comment, knowing that I was connected with the Department of Justice, so she conceived the plan of meeting me at different times at the home of some of her friends. There we could talk at length and with no fear of interruption.

It was in early December that I made my first trip to Mrs. Boyd's home to meet Mrs. Harding, at her special request by phone. It is a beautiful, magnificent mansion of a very rich man and his wife. Mrs. Boyd was a most charming little hostess and mother. From my first meeting with her, which was some months before the beginning of this story, she impressed me as an ideal of noble womanhood.

I arrived before Mrs. Harding,—always prompt by habit and instinct. I was met at the door by a colored butler. I stood in a small square entrance hall. On one side was the dining room. It was this door that he opened and escorted me into,—the dining room. Through the opposite door, I caught a glimpse of a large shadowy, book-lined library where a great fire of logs was burning,—casting flickering lights over polished mahoganies and deep-piled Oriental rugs.

The dining room was immense and, I saw at a glance very exclusive. A conference here would be free from interruption, as the butler rather ostentatiously demonstrated when he carefully closed the entrance hall door behind him.

I sat down in one of the hand carved dining room chairs. I did not have long to wait, for in a very few minutes I heard the doorbell and a fluttering noise of someone coming through the front door and into the hall. A loud whispered conversation—and the door noiselessly opened and Mrs. Harding appeared in the aperture. She was bundled in a long dark fur coat,—with a gray hat and gray flowing veils, draped over the hat and across her face and coiled around her neck.

I arose. She stood still a moment, very straight and stiff. Then she slipped inside the door, turned and closed the door herself as she said:

"Have you waited long?"

"No. Only a few minutes. No matter."

She drew off her gloves with jerky nervous movements and put them with a large gray and black beaded bag on the dining room table. Then she unwound the scarfs and veils from around her neck, using the same nervous jerky movements, this time with her head also. I helped her remove her fur coat and placed it over the back of a chair. Her nervous fingers busied themselves with the laces on the front of her black flowered dress.

"Mr. Means—did you get authorization to work for me and report to me, alone?" she asked sharply.

"Yes, I did."

"Then,—Mr. Means, I need not tell or ask you that you will not repeat one word that I say to you. I am going to take you into my confidence."

I placed for her the big end-chair that I had been sitting in and she sat down. I drew up another one and placed myself in it, near her. I felt at that time, that Mrs. Harding would never really take any human being into her confidence, but in this,—future events proved that I was mistaken.

She began abruptly to discuss the business at hand.

"You may not know that President Harding—Warren—has suffered heavy losses recently in the stock market."

This was an entirely new topic of conversation with her, and I could not help but wonder to what she might be leading.

"I have heard rumors—" I hesitated.

She looked sharply at me. She said:

"There is something very strange about it. I firmly believe that he has been taking his tips from Harry Daugherty. Do you know if Mr. Daugherty has sustained losses—also?"

"I do not know."

"It is not so rumored?"

"Well—no. I haven't heard. But of course——"

She interrupted: "Is it possible for you to find out—confidential matters that are discussed down at the Department of Justice? Can you find out—what Harry Daugherty and Jess Smith are doing—on the market? Do you know Jess Smith?"

She was sitting straight and unrelaxed in the chair,—hands tightly clasped in her lap.

"Very well," I replied.

She raised her careful eyebrows: "I shouldn't think he would be a very difficult person to cultivate. A little flattery about his clothes—his vanity——"

"I understand. I know him."

"Cultivate Jess Smith!". It was a command.

"Get his confidence and find out for me if Mr. Daugherty is buying the same stocks that he is recommending to Warren. I do not believe it. Can you find this out?"

"Oh—I think so."

"Warren Harding is a child in business matters," she continued. "When we came to the White House we had accumulated a comfortable little fortune with our newspaper and wise investments,—but it would never have been done, had it not been for me! I have always had to be the financial head of the house."

I believed it. I noticed that the multitude of parchment-like wrinkles on her cheeks were flushed and her eyes almost glistened. She was plainly laboring under excitement.

"Why Warren's friends should want him to lose his money—I cannot understand, for they certainly have Warren completely and at all times under their power and control."

Her voice had gradually risen and as she finished there was almost a note of hysteria.

"You didn't know this?" she went on. "Well—it's the truth! Warren could not get rid of Harry Daugherty, his Attorney General, if he wanted to."

"He appointed him?" I queried.

She laughed. It was not a pleasant laugh.

"Yes. He appointed him—Attorney General of the United States at the Department of Justice. There was bitter opposition. All the world knew that many prominent Republicans opposed—but under no circumstances could Warren Harding afford not to appoint Harry Daugherty to whatever he wanted to be. Attorney General at the Department of Justice was his choice—Harry Daugherty's choice. There were—reasons—*reasons*." [7]

As her voice trailed off indistinctly, I thought to myself that certainly these reasons must be powerful ones.

She continued. "But—surely it is not necessary for Warren to be guided by tips on the market from Harry Daugherty and Jess Smith. If he wants to play the market, the proper thing to do would be to seek the advice of Mr. Weeks or other cabinet members more capable of giving sound, financial advice."

I was relieved to be again on safer ground. I said:

"Let me be sure to understand. You want me to find out,

—if Mr. Daugherty buys the same stocks he recommends to President Harding?"

"Exactly. And do you know that a crowd of brokers have come down to Washington from Ohio and have opened a brokerage office at the Willard Hotel? It is absurd. There are a number of other brokerage firms here in Washington. Why I myself have made some money in a proper way through these offices when Warren was Senator."

"You like to play the market, too?" I ventured.

"Yes. Why not?" she snapped. "Now—I want you to find out what is going on down in that office at the Willard: —Ungerleider is the name."

"You want me to make a contact there?" I asked.

"Is that what you call it? Contact? Of course. Yes. Do these two things for me: find out if Harry Daugherty is speculating in the same stocks he is advising Warren to buy," she repeated emphatically. "Why—Warren is losing everything he's got!"

"I understand. And——"

"Investigate the Ungerleiders. Find out what is going on down there."

"I understand—perfectly," I assured.

"Then—do you know, after Warren had lost so disastrously—that Mr. Daugherty comes to Warren with a *sure* proposition by which he can redeem all these losses, which I firmly believe were sustained through treacherous tips."

"Yes?"

"It was all so simple. . . . The President was to issue an order for an investigation of violators of the Sherman Anti-Trust Act—and thereby reap a fortune for himself,—fluctuate and break the market, you understand. Mr. Daugherty could always explain to his friends who are violators of this Sherman Anti-Trust Act that it was not his fault because the President had ordered the investigation. He is trying to convince Warren that only by this policy can he redeem the unfortunate and very heavy losses—that it will take such heroic measures."

She paused. . . . I was beginning to see a great light!

"Can't you see what enemies this would make—for Warren? I do not want—I will not have Warren do anything that will create antagonism in any quarter. He has never made enemies. He shall not begin now!"

She was becoming nervous again,—clasping and unclasping the four fingers of her hands.

"Warren must not antagonize. I have always thought that more flies can be caught by sugar—than with vinegar."

Again she paused. But I knew that she yet had something to say. She went on in a moment:

"Of course, Warren must redeem his losses,—but there are other ways. One must have money. One can do nothing—be nothing, without money, not even in the White House. Money is power."

Again she paused and I thought to myself that there are times when Mrs. Harding could almost equal but never quite excel the banalities of her distinguished husband. She continued:

"And yet, I can confide in you, that even above the question of the power of money,—we must think of—the second term. He—shall—have—it!"

I felt at that moment that the question of a second term was decided once and for all. Suddenly she smiled, disturbing the rigidity of her countenance in an astonishingly unique way. Her eyes shone with a fanatic's prophetic light, as though the luminous future was already casting its rosy light upon her. She said:

"And then—a grand triumphant tour of all the capitals

of Europe! A-and, I have plans! I felt on the day that I witnessed my husband's inauguration, that I had reached the summit of my ambitions. It was wonderful—marvelous! Why—now, I am beginning to feel that that glorious day—was but the beginning!"

Suddenly she stood up.

"Our earnest little suffragettes who strived so long and hard for the mere right to vote,—to have a single voice in the government of our nation, might do well to recall that in the latter half of the 16th Century all Europe was governed by women. Did you know that? England was ruled by Elizabeth; Scotland by Mary Stuart; Portugal by the Infanta, daughter of Eleanor; Navarre by Queen Anne; the low countries by the natural daughter of Charles V; Spain by Isabella of Aragon; and France by Catherine de Medici. In instances it is true they ruled through men—but none the less, they ruled.

"Also the fact exists that during the three most glorious epochs of English history,—the Crown was worn by a woman.

"America needs to be taught a lesson. 'First Lady of the Land' shall take upon its silly misnomer, a regal dignity. I am a 'Child of Destiny'."

She paused, her eyes gleaming. Again the interview was closing. I rose also. We stood facing each other. She said:

"Now any suspicions that would affect the possibility of a second term must be avoided at all costs! It *shall* be avoided. I'm already taking a more marked interest in Warren's foreign diplomatic appointments than in any other business of the government,—looking to the future—to the grand triumphant tour of the world—all the kings and rulers of Europe—and of the world. This is the age of woman. . . For the first time in American history, a woman shall be recorded as a real factor—a power—and not have to go by that insipid and uninteresting and moth-eaten title: First Lady of the Land! Silly!"

The low chuckle with which she pronounced the last word had nothing of mirth in it. It was more like the purring of a female tiger, intent, threatening.

Chapter V

Jess Smith Tells His Story to Means

As MY car glided from the picturesque doorway of the Boyd home, the uppermost impression in my mind was Mrs. Harding's dramatic declaration of her great plans: first her determination that the President should have a second term and that nothing should be allowed to interfere, and then—for her and the President to make a grand and triumphant tour of all the capitals of Europe and of the world. I saw the new dazzling heights to which Mrs. Harding had pinned her star of destiny. I could picture the two of them: the President indeed looking every inch a King among men,—and she—well, she felt young and she thought that she looked like a bride and she felt like one—so I let it go at that!

But before I had reached home, I was already mentally turning over my new assignment. As is my usual custom, I tried to throw my mind back to remember someone I knew who also knew the Ungerleider Company. I did not want to ask Jess Smith in this connection. I was getting just a bit wary of Jess Smith anyhow. I had been told to "cultivate Jess Smith" by Mrs. Harding—but I had had cause to believe that Jess Smith was likewise cultivating me and I did not know for what purpose. He was always hanging around my office these days. And, of course, everything Jess Smith did—had Mr. Daugherty behind it. No—I wouldn't ask Jess Smith about the Ungerleider Company. I'd undoubtedly need him for more complicated things.

During the next day, I inquired of two or three people and they knew little or nothing, but the fourth man I asked said he knew the Ungerleider Company well.

"Are you interested in making speculations?" he asked.

"Oh—possibly."

He was affable. "All right. I'll take you down and introduce you to the floor manager or possibly to Mr. Ungerleider."

The next day we met at the Willard and he took me to their offices which were on the mezzanine floor just off the lobby. Very imposing offices. He introduced me to Mr. Ungerleider himself.

"Are you interested in any particular stocks? You want to invest?" Mr. Ungerleider inquired.

I smiled. "I want—to do many things. But yes, I may."

He was polite. "Make yourself at home. You can always find interest in the board and ticker. Let me know when I can serve you."

I hung around a while watching the board and ticker, but made no investment. However, I got busy outside and in a day or so, sent them several customers, being very sure that the Ungerleiders would understand positively that I was sending these customers,—swinging them around from the older firms, as it were. This gave me a friendly entree to the private offices; which soon enabled me to get hold of a list of their customers, ostensibly to be able to send them further customers.

Heading this list were the names of Warren Harding,—Harry Daugherty and Jess Smith and many Assistant Attorneys General and other government officials of prominence.

However, I soon found out that Harry Daugherty and Warren Harding had invested in the same stocks and both had lost. This refuted what Mrs. Harding had suspected.

I duly carried this information to Mrs. Harding but she

was unconvinced. Mrs. Harding was an able business woman.

"This is not conclusive evidence at all," she informed me somewhat impatiently.

"It is what you asked me to get," I reminded.

"Yes. But—I know Mr. Daugherty. Now you find out if he is not dealing with other brokerage firms in the city,—hedging, speculating, to cover his own losses with the Ungerleiders. That would be exactly what he would do. Find out."

And this condition proved to be true. I quickly learned from Jess Smith that he was dealing with one of the largest brokerage firms in Washington. But—whether he had hedged on sales and purchases of stocks on margin, as against his transactions with Ungerleider Company, I never quite figured out, for just at that time, the situation in Washington on more important matters became so fast and furious, that the documentary evidence I had discovered from these two brokerage firms was forgotten for the time.

II

Jess Smith was in my office every day. Poor Jess. He was a typical city department store floor walker, transplanted into alien aisles. Before coming to Washington he had been in the dry goods business, I was told, all his life. He was not a weak character in his own environment. He could discuss intelligently and with interest with any woman—materials, laces, ribbons, all dry goods,—but transplanted into big finance and diplomatic circles,—he was at a total loss. In trying to handle men of iron and steel,—strong sinewed diplomats, he was entirely out of his element, a complete failure.

And how he loved clothes! He always had about thirty suits and all accessories to match. I had heard that he did not hesitate when out of the city to wire government officials to send him certain suits from his wardrobe and he would describe the suits as a woman does a dress. He had several handsome diamond rings, but I had noticed that his favorite was one set with diamonds and two large rubies.

Jess Smith was about 55 years old, florid complexion, smooth broad face, dark hair tinged with gray,—deep-set, rather shifty hazel eyes. He knew and felt that he was out of his element in Washington but he was heroically trying to adjust himself and live up to his present exalted state. He firmly believed that clothes were his greatest asset in this exalted state: that men judge each other by the clothes they wear. I never saw him enter an office, without first rearranging his tie, pulling down his vest, fixing his cuffs just so,—taking off his hat and patting and smoothing his hair like a woman. He must be exactly, sartorially correct before meeting anybody. I was told that he was a wonder—selling ribbons to the ladies over the counter and matching colors and quality and materials.

Jess Smith worshiped Harry Daugherty with a dog-like devotion. He wanted to do and be exactly what Mr. Daugherty expected of him—and I have always thought that he succeeded perfectly. And yet, he was personally determined to get out of the whole Washington business everything that was coming to him.

Of his personal life, all I knew was that he had married a woman in Ohio and that they were divorced.

One day, Jess was sitting in my office very much in the dumps. He was dressed that day in gray: gray hat, gray tie flecked with lavender, gray tweed suit, gray gloves, handkerchief with gray and lavender threads hand-woven around the edges in an upper pocket and gray silk socks. Jess always carried out his color scheme to the last detail.

He had come into the office and flopped into a chair, with a groan. This was not like Jess Smith. He never flopped.

"Say old man—what's up?" I asked.

He favored me with a frown.

"Nothin'."

I looked him over and laughed.

"Go home and change your clothes. Gray is cold. You need to wear yellow and red today—to 'brighten the corner where you are'."

"Shut up."

"Any death in the family?"

No reply.

"Lose in the market—or in the little game last night?"

No reply. I was becoming amused. He looked like such a big helpless baby.

"In love? Want me to investigate her and see if she loves you?" I further persisted.

"To hell—with your impudence."

"All—right," I drawled good naturedly, turning back to the work at my desk that his coming had interrupted. "I just thought I'd be helpful,—cheer you up a bit."

Suddenly he asked: "You knew—I'd been married?"

I chucked. "Many do."

My hands paused among the papers. I really didn't get back to work for I believed that he wanted to talk and might say something I ought to hear.

"Mr. Daugherty never could stand her," he continued. "Well she—he—she wasn't his type at all, you understand. You know—he wants only the most cultured, lady-like, pedigreed, refined—all that. Society bred. You know."

I very naturally interposed:

"Good Lord! She wasn't his wife!"

He gave no heed to my irrelevance.

"Well—we—she and I—we got along all right. Life with her was—oh hell—there are some things even men don't tell to each other."

I was conscious of lifting my eyebrows.

"I'm not asking," I reminded.

"We quit. She's out in Ohio."

"Divorced you said?" I asked.

"She got it. And—it wasn't infidelity and it wasn't—oh well—what difference does it make. She got it."

I didn't exactly see what he was driving at so said nothing and waited for further enlightenment.

"But now—that I'm here, she wants to come back. Harry Daugherty will never stand for it. And I'm going to have her come on for a visit anyhow. No harm in that, is there? She's been here for a few days once or twice already."

What queer little kettle of fish was this, I wondered.

"She can come back and forth from Ohio. I'm in a position now to help her out a lot in every way."

"Is she in love with you?"

"No."

"Just what were the grounds for divorce?" I persisted.

"She got the divorce," he repeated doggedly.

"Sure it was not infidelity?"

"It was not."

He had me guessing. But I felt sorry for him. He was a good enough sort and couldn't get much out of life at best. Mr. Harry Daugherty had him chained to his chariot wheels. A willing slave to be sure, but a slave, nevertheless.

"Does Mr. Daugherty require you to like the kind of women he likes? Was that in your contract? It takes all sorts of women to make this little world."

"It does. Even the President tried a new type."

"Really?"

"Who is she?"

"Oh, he likes her all right,—but it didn't amount to much. His friends told him he must stop going to her house. It was beginning to attract attention. It was easily managed. He stopped."

"Stopped what?"

"I dunno—do you? Stopped going there, of course. He'd been getting by with the flimsiest excuses."

"Getting by whom? What?"

"Mrs. Harding, of course. He has to get by her with everything. She watches him like a hawk and nags and nags—eternally. She never lets up! Not Mrs. Harding. You see—she's gotten an inkling about—Nan Britton."

A-ah, this was something I would like to hear. But I appeared indifferent and again looking over some papers on my desk, I carelessly asked:

"What about Nan Britton?"

Quick as a flash, Jess stiffened. Evidently, he thought that I already knew whatever there was to know about Nan Britton.

"I dunno—do you?" Again he parried, using that favorite hedge expression of his. On second thought, he decided that I was bluffing.

"Say—you couldn't have been around the Department of Justice and not know something about Nan Britton!" he affirmed. "Quit trying to kid me. I got trouble enough. You're bound to know that there's reason—reason a-plenty why the President signs anything and everything that the 'gang' asks him to—unless Mrs. Harding happens to catch on, which does happen sometimes. Not often. Right now—oh boy—there's a delicious brew stewing! Mark my word—he'll do it! He'll appoint just who the 'gang' tells him to, too. Child—we've got him sewed up in a bag. He has got to do what they say and don't you forget it."

"And—Nan Britton?" I again ventured.

"Aw—think it over! Don't be so dumb and innocent. Were you born that way—or did mother train you?"

He stood up. He was plainly troubled and I believed that I rightly inferred that it was about his ex-wife who wanted to come to Washington to live.

Just then my phone rang. He was standing directly over the phone so I said:

"Answer that, Jess. But—wait. Better pull down your vest and smooth your hair and fix your tie. No telling who that might be——"

He was already speaking.

"Hello. Means? Yes. Just a moment."

He handed me the phone but stood still where he was.

It was Mrs. Boyd's voice that greeted me. She had a message from Mrs. Harding. Would I come to the White House right away?. I hung up.

"What the devil are you talking to her for?" he asked sharply.

"Mrs. Boyd?" I saw that he knew her voice. "I work for many people, Jess."

"And you think you're damned smart, don't you? Telling me to smooth my hair before I pick up a phone. Let me tell you this and you can profit by it. The first quality of a gentleman is neatness."

He was ludicrously serious. I tried to shock him.

"Aw—say—I think a man can be plowing in a corn field and still be a gentleman—see? That's just one little difference between you and me, Jess Smith. No harm."

I was arranging my desk to close it.

"Come again. So long," I hinted.

He called goodbye as he sauntered out.

"Nan Britton? Think it over!"

I sat at my desk and tried to do just that. There was much food for thought here. I had heard various muffled rumors around the Department of Justice that made me positive that there was something peculiar—very peculiar, going on. Something—menacing, that could not be strangled or coped with in the usual ways. What was it?

And the figure that had stood out in my consciousness as the one sinister power behind this maze—was the figure of that girl Jess Smith was always talking about. I had never seen her. There was something different here—something unusual about the girl Nan Britton, otherwise she would have been sent out of Washington long ago and kept out.

Was the President really seriously infatuated with Nan Britton, I wondered? The idea was absurd to me. No man in love with any one woman could behave as I had seen President Harding behave in the presence of young girls and attractive women. That deduction was final in my mind. Nan Britton was but one of many—and yet, there was something connected with this Nan Britton that apparently made the President fear her.

Could she by any possibility—be his own daughter—by some former entanglement, I wondered, floundering around in my mind to find a key to the situation. Why—President Harding was almost old enough to be her grandfather.

Ah—perhaps it was this very thing, her extreme youth that made her different from all these other girls and women. He had known her—all her life. Her father was one of his best and oldest friends. Could something have happened in Marion—perhaps—something that would sound very sordid and ugly in print? She was the young daughter of an old friend—she had been extremely young. There are certain laws: to betray the very young daughter of an old friend—. Could this something have happened in her own home, perhaps—or in his—when there was no Department of Justice detective to phone for—to come quickly and cover up?

And did this girl hold the key to the power of Mr. Daugherty and the other members of the Cabinet—over the President? I had never been able to reconcile the power these men seemed to hold over President Harding—with his indifference to money. It was not money power they were manipulating—neither was it political power.

Mrs. Harding had never mentioned Nan Britton's name to me. But all the time she had been leading up to something. Did she know anything about Nan Britton? Possibly not. Possibly so! And—yet—I had a strong feeling that she would never speak of Nan Britton to me. Again I put on my hat and started for the White House.

Chapter VI

Mrs. Harding Tells Means About Nan Britton

I ENTERED the White House as usual through what I now called the 'viaduct entrance'. The guards within the White House knew me by this time and passed me quietly on to Mrs. Harding's private apartment upstairs.

I found her door slightly ajar when I rapped. Through the aperture, I could see her standing across the room looking out of a window. I noticed that in her right hand she had gripped some folds of the lace curtains at the window and that this hand was nervously crushing the folds.

She turned in a flash at my first rap and almost ran across the room.

Her face as usual was in repose, only her eyes glistened with a repressed excitement.

"Mr. Means. Come in."

She darted behind me and closed the door herself. Then she sat down as usual on the end of a couch and arranged a pillow at her back. She made a firm effort to appear at ease and unhurried.

"I'm feeling fine this morning," she announced. "My masseur has just finished her treatment. She tells me that I have the firm flesh of a young girl. See?"

She held up her arm. The loose violet-colored chiffon sleeves fell away in soft folds.

"My arms are smooth and firm and white,—aren't they? I am very proud of my arms. And—you have noticed I am sure, that my walk has the same elastic spring that I had as a girl. I am really proud of my walk. I have kept myself young—and I always intend to."

"No one is ever any older than they feel," was my not very original rejoinder.

"Exactly. Now, Mr. Means—I have much to say to you this morning. I have decided—to take you into my confidence. But tell me first—do you at any time have to make any statements or explanations to Mr. Burns—about what you are doing for me?"

Invariably she asked this question every time she consulted with me.

"Never," I reassured, as I had done many times before. "I bring copies of all my reports—to you only. No one else sees them or knows anything about them. Mr. Burns does not want to know. It is positively a relief to him not to have to know. I am carrying out your own ideas in this matter to the minutest detail."

"And you have been officially assigned to me for my own particular personal work?"

"Exactly that. I make reports only to you," I repeated.

She seemed satisfied and more at ease. She began to talk in a steady flow of words as though excited.

"Well—there is a secret that lies buried deep in my heart—that I have never discussed with anyone except Madam X. And by the way, you must go to see Madam X. You must know her. She can help you in your work for me. She is a marvel. She can give you information that you could get nowhere else. She knows this secret I am about to tell you. It is a sacred matter,—and not of a business nature at all,—but very personal and intimate. To a certain point I have taken my friend Mrs. Boyd into my confidence also,—for this matter is a social problem as well."

She had me guessing, of course, and yet I felt that I knew to what she must be leading. I was amazed, however, when she classified this very personal, intimate secret as a "social" problem. Mrs. Harding was always a cold and logical reasoner.

She held a handkerchief with a narrow lace border which she crushed in her hands. She reclasped her fingers.

"Now—Mr. Means,—I know men and I know their weaknesses. And about all a good woman can do is to—forgive and hope, and hope and forgive,—always expecting happier things in the future."

There surely seemed nothing for me to say to this.

"Many public men—many great men have had their careers utterly ruined—and the lives of all their loved ones totally wrecked—by—indiscretions. They have had to forfeit everything that was dear to them—by an act of weakness. . . ."

She paused,—clasping and unclasping her hands but the expression of her face did not change. She continued:

"I must now tell you of just such an instance. And I would not speak of it—only—only—the consequences are growing into a nightmare day and night—like a sword of Damocles hanging over my head—all the time. And it is also hanging over President Harding. I am thinking of him—more than of myself. I want to save him—from his folly. I *must* save him! And what I am doing now—is to save him far more than myself."

After this long ethical preamble,—very quickly and out of a clear sky, as if impelled almost against her will she said:

"Warren Harding has had a very ugly affair with a girl named Nan Britton from Marion. It goes back to the actual childhood of this girl."

Ah—I was to be told the story of Nan Britton after all and by Mrs. Harding herself.

"I became suspicious of this girl Nan Britton when she was but a child in Marion. She was a greatly over-developed child and wore extremely short dresses above the knees. It was not considered quite decent. And she was always doing everything on earth that she could—to attract Warren's attention. This over-development tended to attract men—on the streets and together with her unusually short dresses, why she attracted attention of course and not in a very nice way. Why, I have watched men—watch her—even before she was in her early teens. And I could see from Warren's eyes and manner that this young girl affected him—by her very presence."

I had no doubt of the truth of this and many others could also bear witness. She continued:

"I felt that Warren encouraged her too much in the silly stuff that she would write for the paper—our *Marion Daily Star*. She would bring her work in—I knew it was merely an excuse—but would never leave any of the material, unless she could give it to him in person. And even right there in the office, she would edge up to the side of his desk and even try to sit on his lap and I could see that Warren liked to put his hands on her. And—when we would go driving, I also noticed that Warren always liked to drive around by the Britton home. Frequently, when she would come to our house or to the office, I have had to tell her that it was time for her to leave. Actually, I would have to do this. And this was—even before Warren was in the Senate—years ago. . . . On one occasion I spoke to her mother about it, in a diplomatic way, of course."

Mrs. Harding was well versed in diplomatic ways, I knew and just then I had a wee feeling of pity for the mother of this girl to whom Mrs. Harding had to speak diplomatically about her young daughter. I said nothing.

"I told her mother that Nan's craziness over Mr. Harding was all a joke of course and laughed at by people in town,—but that sometimes these silly jokes lead to serious consequences. An adolescent girl's consuming adoration for a man—a man almost old enough to be her grandfather—was not a nice joke—even so. And that I felt that she should talk to

Nan and tell her that she should have more sense and not encourage such jokes—silly as they are—and also that she should stop her from walking back and forth by the office as frequently as she did and looking in—to see Warren. But—I was told by others, that her mother could do nothing with her."

What a hectic, varied life Mrs. Harding must have had, I mused. And then—there also flashed across my mind something of the vision—of what a life Mr. Harding must have led—all these years! She had said—their home life was ideal. People have different "ideals", unquestionably.

As she paused, I saw that her face was white as chalk, under the carefully and daintily rouged and wrinkled surface and that she was laboring with an inner excitement that was acute. Her immobile countenance seemed to have frozen. Her eyes narrowed and glistened through half-closed lids—like slits covering a raging fire.

I really felt alarmed and started to suggest a change of subject, when she again made one of her quick unexpected speeches:

"This girl Nan Britton has a child and she claims that Warren Harding is the father of it!"

A-ah! So—that was it. Jess Smith had been right: I was dumb. But I was now beginning to see—many things. At that moment, I was too surprised and astonished to speak.

"I don't believe it!" she snapped. "I don't believe a word of it."

There was no room for question or doubt in her words or accent. She did not believe it.

Now that she had the thing actually spoken, she seemed to command herself once more.

"No use for me to tell you how I found this out," she said. "A hundred little things put together—day by day.

Some time I may tell you. I shall not take the time now. And it is not important."

What was it Jess Smith had told me about "nagging"? Had she actually nagged this thing out—day by day, hour by hour,—year by year. She was now alert to give instructions.

"Mr. Means—you can see that I have work for you to do. Much work. And it is all vital and important. But first and above all else,—I want you to find out—just exactly *when* their improper relations began. Can you do this?"

This took me a little by surprise. If she "don't believe one word of it"—I said:

"There are usually ways of finding out—most anything. Have they been corresponding—writing to each other?"

"How do I know?" she quickly snapped.

How—indeed, I thought. This was evidently a tender point that she had not yet found out.

"How old is this child?" I asked.

"Around two years."

"Where is it?"

"In Chicago, her sister—a Mrs. Scott Willets is supposed to have adopted it."

"Where is Nan Britton?"

She shrugged her shoulders and her lips tightened.

"That girl! Oh—everywhere! She stays with this sister in Chicago sometimes—God alone knows where she calls home. But listen! You can find out. I want you to find out and put her under surveillance immediately, day and night. Will you do this?"

I was calculating.

"It will cost much money," I ventured.

She brushed aside this angle with a wave of her hand.

"I don't care what it costs. I will be responsible. I will pay whatever it costs. Find out where she is at once. Get your best "shadow" men.[12] Begin at once and report to me every day. Will you do this?"

There seemed nothing left but for me to say:

"If you assign me to it."

"And—you must find out for me when their improper relations began. If there are letters,—I must get them. You got the Whiteley papers and the Sawyer letters. I know that you have the ability, for I have tested you out and I know that you can be trusted. I suppose—I might find other investigators with like ability,—but I feel sure I can never find one in whom I could place such confidence, and with whom I can share most secret intentions and plans. You have demonstrated to me—that nothing can make you break a confidence. You must take this assignment and carry it through successfully. I shall depend on you. Will you?"

I spoke: "Do I understand correctly? I am to find out for you through whatever channels I can—just when the improper relations began—with your husband and Nan Britton."

She was quick to correct emphatically.

"Or—if there have *been* improper relations at all. I am not convinced of that—yet."

"I—see. I misunderstood. I thought that had been established."

"No!"

Just at that moment there was a rap on the door. Mrs. Harding stood up quickly and said:

"Come in."

President Harding entered. I also rose to my feet, of course. He had on a light overcoat and held his hat and gloves in his hand. Every time I saw Mr. Harding, I was impressed anew with the real beauty of the man and the charm of his person. I used the word "beauty" advisedly. He was as handsome as an Apollo,—yet his head and shoulders held a classic grandeur that the mere word "handsome" was inadequate to express.

Bowing to Mrs. Harding but before speaking to her, he said to me:

"Mr. Means? I think I've met you before."

He came forward and shook my hand. He had indeed met me several times before—in other places, however. He smiled. There was a rare kindly twinkle in his eyes. I saw that he too remembered those other places.

"Mrs. Harding tells me that you are a very wonderful investigator," he informed.

Here Mrs. Harding hastily explained:

"The President understands all about your investigation for me."

I was relieved to get the cue.

"I am always glad to be of any service that I can—to Mrs. Harding," I replied inanely.

He laughed.

"Keep her informed. She likes to know all about everything that's going on."

"I've found that out," I replied.

He turned toward her and spoke:

"I will be detained all day. Will not be home for lunch. But, of course, at dinner as usual."

She took several quick steps toward him. She spoke eagerly, almost angrily:

"Are you going to play golf—with Jess Smith?"

He smiled again—that rare, winning smile.

"I believe that is the plan," he quietly replied.

Mrs. Harding shook her head impatiently:

"Now, Warren,—Jess Smith is working this golf *racket* with you for a purpose."

The President raised inquiring eyebrows.

His comment was:

"He plays a fair game."

"You know what I mean. He is a scout—for the gang. Warren,—be careful what you say and what you promise."

I happened to know that for once her suspicions and surmises were entirely correct. Jess Smith was Mr. Daugherty's scout—to feel out the President—and golf was their best point of contact. Mrs. Harding did not play golf.

She was persistent:

"You won't make any promises?"

Again the President smiled, as he took several steps backward toward the door. I was included in the smile.

"Not today, my dear."

He opened the door and bowed again as he said "Goodbye" and went out.

For a full minute after the door was closed, Mrs. Harding stood still gazing at it, clasping and unclasping the four fingers of her hands.

"Sit down," she commanded, again taking her seat on the couch and motioning me to the chair. I sat down.

"I am not through yet. There is another matter that has been crowded out of my mind. They—are now after the President to sign certain papers. I upset their plan completely about the investigations into violators of the Sherman Anti-Trust Law, for I put my foot down and simply told them that Warren Harding would not sign the orders for those investigations—to fluctuate and break the market. They had expected to clean up millions—right there. I balked that! Why—just think of the enemies such a thing would have made for the President. That and that alone—would actually have endangered his second term. Don't you see that it would?"

I did indeed see.

"Yes. I think it would," I conceded.

"Now they say—that these papers they are urging him to

sign and he won't tell me what they are—that these papers will make not enemies but powerful friends. Mr. Means—I do not trust these men. They hate me. I know it. Warren has promised me that he will not sign any papers until he tells me about it, and until I have had time to go into the matter thoroughly. I always try to be present when any of them come to the White House. Warren is just as eager for a second term as I am. It is my belief—that he would never consent to—oh, many other things—unless terrific pressure was brought to bear upon him. And—that pressure will be brought."

I wondered if Mrs. Harding knew of the President's Executive Order on May 31st, 1921—transferring the Oil lands from the Navy to the Department of the Interior? I wondered—if she realized the significance of that order, and its possibilities. Had they succeeded in keeping this Oil matter from her? I rather thought myself that she had guessed rightly—that pressure would be brought.

She went on:

"Mr. Means—I believe it is Harry Daugherty that brings this pressure and I believe it has something to do with this girl Nan Britton. You know—Harry Daugherty was scheming for Warren Harding to be President for—many—many—years. And he was doubtless also at the same time, during those years, scheming and calculating how he could get that President completely in his power. I believe he has encouraged Warren Harding with Nan Britton—it may be from the very first. It may have been all part and parcel of his plans."

She paused but I made no comment.

"There is some excuse—perhaps—if there is ever excuse, for other men to be unfaithful to their wives. But—there is no excuse for Warren Harding. Now—is there, Mr. Means?"

To save my soul I couldn't have spoken had she expected me to and waited for the answer, but she didn't. She went on:

"I am never ill! I have never been ill—in my life except when it was brought on by mental worry. That's God's truth! And I have kept myself young and attractive. We are on the same mental plane—the President and I. Our union has been ideal—for more than thirty years. There has never been the slightest excuse for Warren Harding to ever look at another woman! Never! Never!"

I said nothing. What could a man say?

Again she stiffened and sat erect.

"Now—Mr. Means—listen carefully. I have other important work for you and you might as well begin at once. I want you to make a life investigation of Mr. Daugherty, and Mr. Fall and Mr. Weeks."

"Phew! That's a sizeable order! Do you happen to know what it costs to make a life investigation of an individual?"

"I don't care what it costs! I want to know everything about these men. Everything there is to know. And I know you are the one man in the world who will get all this information for me. I'll pay. It may come to the point that only by counter-strokes can I stop all this—this—why it's a form of blackmail, isn't it? I want to be prepared. I must —like Napoleon's Josephine, be ever watchful,—discover every danger and remove it from his path. I will be his protecting rampart and a barrier to the flood of any treachery. Investigate these men for me at once."

"It will cost thousands of dollars," again I reminded.

"I tell you—I don't care what it costs! I want it done. Get your men started and bring the reports to me as fast as they are brought to you. Be thorough—and swift. I may need this information at any minute. You understand?"

I did.

Chapter VII

Means "Takes" Nan's Diaries and Letters

My new assignments were very definite. They were herculean. I was to find out exactly when and where improper relations had begun between President Harding and Nan Britton, taking for granted, as I was positive that Mrs. Harding herself had done—that there had been relations. Also I was to put Nan Britton under surveillance. I was to make a complete life investigation of Mr. Daugherty and Mr. Fall and Mr. Weeks.[12]

I engaged the proper men and set them to work. The assignment to find out where and when improper relations had begun between the President and Nan Britton, of course, I allowed no one to handle but myself.

Experience had given me some foundation facts in my profession. If a woman is in love with a man and they are meeting clandestinely,—or if a woman is having improper relations with a man, she always has in her possession some kind of tangible or documentary evidence. I have never known this to fail. She keeps some sort of "souvenirs" or "keepsakes"—or she has letters, regardless of any and all promises to destroy. I was confident that somewhere, in her possession, Nan Britton had letters from President Harding.

Acting on this fundamental belief, I set myself the task to find whatever evidence there might be in existence.

I had promised Mrs. Harding that I would go to see Madam X. This was such utter foolishness to me, I was tempted not to go at all. But I remembered how implicitly Mrs. Harding believed in this soothsayer and how she apparently depended on her. Besides, I had told her that I would go, so I set out for the visit. In fact, this visit was included in my orders.

Not receiving any help from Madam X, which I duly reported, I went ahead with my own program.

First I made a trip to Chicago to get the lay of the land as it were. I stopped at the LaSalle Hotel.

I had little difficulty in finding the apartment house on the south side of Chicago where the Willets family, Miss Britton's sister and her husband lived. My agents who were by this time keeping Nan Britton under surveillance had given me the needed data. I found out that Mr. Scott Willets was a musician and played in an orchestra down town. Mrs. Willets had a position down town likewise. I knew that the child was not then with them. They were supposed to have adopted her. But at this time she was away with Nan Britton,—on a farm.

I carefully looked over the territory. I found out the names and addresses of the owners of the apartment building—in case of any future entanglements—and I put Mr. and Mrs. Willets under surveillance. I only had two regular men and one extra for this task. It was not a rush surveillance. My purpose was to find out the daily habits of the family—where they mailed their letters, if they had a servant, who their friends were and so forth. I merely wanted to know their daily habits and routine.

I did not tarry long in Chicago. As soon as I returned to Washington, I sent what we call a "roper" out there to Chicago, with his wife. I instructed them to rent an apartment in the same building where the Willets lived. I selected a "roper" who was also a musician to form a better contact and friendship. There did not happen to be a vacant apartment at the time, but luckily they could subrent a furnished one.

My "roper" sometimes called me in Washington on the phone at seven o'clock in the evening to make his report. But as a rule he sent me daily written reports.

After they were established in the same apartment house I told him to make it a point of getting on the same street car every morning with Mr. Scott Willets, careful of course, to attract no attention. I always warned: never to hurry and never to attract attention. But I told him to watch his opportunity to enter into conversation. After four days, the "roper" called me at my home at seven in the evening and the first thing he said was:

"I met him today."

"Good."

"It was on the street car. He got up and left a package and I called his attention to it. We got off the car together and discovered that we lived in the same apartment house."

"Cultivate the friendship," I instructed. "Have your wife meet Mrs. Willets. Don't hurry but at the first opportunity, get me a key to the apartment."

"I understand."

Both of them being musicians, the friendship grew rapidly and there was much visiting between the two. Every morning, they rode down to the Loop together.

It was only about a week later when I received a key to the apartment by registered mail. Immediately, I took train for Chicago. Again I taxied to the LaSalle Hotel and registered.

I went to the apartment of my "roper." He was very proud of his quick work.

"How did you get the key?" I asked.

"Well—it was this way. We are very friendly down there. Their apartment is two floors below. And one evening, Miss Britton's sister was sewing on the machine. The phone rang and she got up and went into the other room to answer. Then,—I saw a key lying on the top of the machine. I was sure it was the key to the apartment. Mr. Willets was not at home. I had my paraffin in my pocket—ready. So I quickly made the two impressions—and put the key back on the machine. The next day, I had one made for you."

"Good. Fine job."

My "roper" had no idea what I was after. As is my custom, I trust no one. I said to him:

"I want to search that apartment thoroughly. How can it be done? Do they keep a servant?"

"No, they keep no servant. And it will be easy, for they don't lock up anything."

"Where are they during the day?"

"They both work down-town. She never returns during the day. Sometimes, he does but not often, in the afternoon."

"We will begin tomorrow morning soon after they leave."

"Well—Mr. Means—if you can find anything criminal about these people and can prove it,—why then I've no business trying to be a detective, for I know nothing of human nature."

"All right. We will see."

The next morning we entered the apartment. It was a comfortable five room apartment, furnished in excellent taste. It was my purpose to search that apartment and when I search any place—I search it. And I did not care to have the 'roper' with me when I made this real search. It means—under mattresses, under rugs and carpets, behind pictures, in pillows, through bureau drawers—a minute search of every inch.

Very shortly, after a cursory inspection of the apartment, I found a locked closet in the room used by Nan Britton. This closet had two extra Yale locks on it—one above and the other below the regular lock. The regular lock was not used. I believed, naturally, that if there was anything that I wanted in the apartment it would be in this closet.

I made paraffin impressions of each of these locks and we left.

I had to wait two days to get the keys made. In order to save time and forestall any possible error or oversight, I spent those two days searching all the rest of the apartment, but found nothing.

The day I was to search the closet I sent the 'roper' down-town to keep a close watch on Mr. Willets to be perfectly sure that he would not return. And if he should happen to be returning,—I could be warned by phone. I told the 'roper' that I was expecting certain phone calls to that apartment and would be in there all day waiting.

I was alone, of course, when I unlocked the closet and entered. It was about four and one-half feet long by two and one-half feet wide and about ten feet high.

There were the usual dresses and coats hanging up, belonging to a woman and a child—and other paraphernalia. But what interested me most and caught my eye at once—were four black leather loose-leaf note-books lying on a shelf right by my hand.

I took them down and stepped back into the room for better light. I opened one. As I had supposed—they were diaries. Four closely written diaries. I thought they were diaries for they were exactly the kind of loose-leaf books that I use for my diaries, except these were much larger than mine.

I read snatches here and there—and then took possession of them for I believed that they would undoubtedly give me the information that I was assigned to get. I put one of these books in each pocket—two in my back pants pocket and two in my coat pockets.

I went back into the closet. There were many boxes on shelves—hat boxes, large empty candy boxes and many wooden boxes. Some of these boxes were filled with ribbons and laces and trinkets; some had hats in them.

In one of the larger wooden boxes I found letters—many letters, tied in bundles with stout pink silk corset ribbon. Again I went into the room to the light—with this box. I saw that these letters were all systematically arranged in chronological order and accurately indexed. There were also a great many souvenir postcards bundled together and tied. I knew these letters would be of interest in getting the assignment consummated.

I put them all back as I had found them in the wooden box and placed the box on the shelf and closed the closet.

I returned to my 'roper's' apartment. I went into the kitchen and found a regular ten cent market basket. I put a newspaper in it.

I made my way back to the apartment downstairs. Again I unlocked the closet and took down the box with the letters and placed them in the market basket and covered them over with the newspaper. I went back upstairs to the 'roper's' apartment. It had taken me only seven minutes to do all this.

I then took all the letters out of the market basket and the diaries from my pockets and put them in a handbag that belonged to the 'roper'.

I returned to my hotel with the handbag. In my own room, with locked door, I put the bundles of letters and the diaries on a table.

I untied the knot from the bundle that contained the latest letters, as indexed. The first one I opened was the one on the bottom of that bundle which was the very last one received. It was written on old Senatorial stationery.

I ran through a number of the letters and glanced through the diaries. But I saw that it would take several days to read them carefully. However, I knew that I had found what I wanted.

I got in touch with my 'roper', calling him on the phone when I knew that he would be in. I told him to come to the LaSalle Hotel. Before he arrived, I put in his handbag four quart bottles of whiskey.

"So—you do not feel that the Willets are in any way breaking the law? Look in that handbag," I said to him.

He opened the handbag and saw the four quarts of whiskey.

"Good Heavens," he exclaimed, "if that is all you wanted to know, I could have told you that long ago."

I paid no attention to what he said but further informed:

"As a result of being in the apartment waiting for phone calls, I have succeeded in getting the information I wanted. I have been able to make connections that can lead me to the source of law violators of the prohibition law—through the drug stores. I was not after this couple at all,—but after the sources."

That 'roper' must think to this day that I am an awful poor investigator to go to all that trouble and expense—to find some drug store prohibition violators. He was polite enough not to express himself. I further instructed:

"I have the information I came after. Now—you say nothing at all to anybody. Get out of that apartment as quickly as possible and do not meet the Willets again anywhere at any time."

He was an excellent 'roper' and obeyed orders.

I returned to Washington as quickly as possible. I began a systematic study of the letters and the diaries, trying to establish the one fact that Mrs. Harding had assigned me: exactly the time and place that improper relations had begun. It took me two or three days of intensive work. One thing that impressed me most was the fact that Mr. Harding had been sending Nan Britton souvenir postcards for a great many years, since she was a child in Marion. Evidently, she had preserved every scratch of his pen.

I compared the records in her diaries with the letters and while I was convinced that their relations had begun in Marion, just when and where I could not determine. To attempt to establish the exact facts, as directed by Mrs. Harding, was an impossibility. I could not do it.

Chapter VIII

A Storm in the White House

It was with real sorrow and regret that I had to go to Mrs. Harding, for I had not been successful with the assignment: I had not discovered when and where improper relations had begun between President Harding and Nan Britton. It is always depressing to me to fail in any assignment, no matter how important or how insignificant.

I found Mrs. Harding eager and alert for my report. She knew that I had been in Chicago on two occasions. I really believe—that she was frantically grasping at a forlorn hope that I would bring her evidence—that it was all a mistake.

I had myself been confident that if I could find letters, to say nothing of diaries—I would get for her the specific information she desired. But I had failed.

Mrs. Harding was wearing that day—it was around noon when I called—a brownish figured dress that was not becoming. As she opened the door of her apartment for me, I was conscious of an indefinable irritation, wondering why she never wore plain clothes. Why were her dresses always like upholstery goods? They confuse one's mind, to start with. This time she had also a black and red Spanish shawl over her shoulders and with wide fringe that almost touched the floor in front. Her hair was artistically arranged as always: each hair waved into its exact place. Her thin cheeks were flushed. The inevitable band of black velvet encircled her throat.

"Oh, but I am glad to see you," was her greeting. "I have been so impatient. Why on earth have you been so long?"

I removed my light overcoat. It was early Spring and even

a light overcoat was oppressive in the house. I threw it over the back of a chair.

"Long? Why I have worked with amazing speed. You gave me a hard job," was my reply.

She didn't sit on the couch as usual with a pillow arranged behind her back. With no further word, she sat down on a stiff little Windsor chair. She had not taken her eyes off my face since I had appeared. Her eyes seemed to bore right through my head. For a change, I made myself comfortable in a corner of the couch.

"Well!" she sharply prompted. "Don't tell me that you haven't found out anything—for I know you have. Madam X told me that you would bring me vital news." She spoke in short jerks.

I began deliberately:

"Mrs. Harding—I have not found out what you assigned me to. I am sorry. Perhaps—Madam X can do better for you. I was so sure and certain of success and then—I have to acknowledge disappointment."

"How? What do you mean?"

"You assigned me to get you specific documentary evidence—as to when and where improper relations began between President Harding and Nan Britton. I did find documentary evidence confirming the fact that there have been relations. You were already convinced of this anyhow. But I could not and did not find out—when such relations began."

She gulped as she said:

"What? You have actual proof? You have documentary evidence?"

"Yes."

"Tell me. Tell me quick!"

"I have in my possession—four of Nan Britton's diaries and also letters written to her by President Harding."

She gazed at me in amazement. Her eyes snapped. Her frozen countenance for the moment forgot its mask of immobility. The muscles and nerves of her face worked. She swallowed hard once or twice. She actually appeared incapable of speech.

"What!" she finally gasped. "You—you—do you mean to tell me that you have letters Warren Harding has written to Nan Britton and you did not bring them to me?"

I was uneasy. I did not like the way she looked. I spoke with studied calmness.

"They do not disclose the information that you wanted——"

She interrupted, quick as a flash.

"How dare you! Go—get those letters and bring them to me——"

Again I ventured calmness. This scene was not to my liking at all.

"Now, Mrs. Harding—please. Let us be reasonable. You did not ask for letters——"

"I did not ask for letters! You know I did. I asked for proof! I dared not think—there could be letters! I want to see them with my own eyes. I must see them. I will see them."

I went on:

"You ask for a piece of specific information. That was my assignment. I get diaries and letters and try to find in them the information you desired——"

She sprang to her feet and turned on me like a tigress. Her eyes were wild—venomous. She cried:

"Are you a machine—or a human being? Have you no heart in you? Don't you know I've got to have and see those letters? Don't you know what they mean to me? Any scratch of the pen that Warren Harding has ever written to Nan Britton——"

She was walking back and forth in the room, her Spanish shawl hanging from her shoulders,—trailing unheeded behind her. She would now and then snatch it back over her shoulders—her hands perpetually in motion, clasping and unclasping her fingers.

I protested:

"But—Mrs. Harding——"

She would not listen to anything that I might have to say.

"What do you know about it?" she raged. "You are a man! Get me those letters I say. Why don't you go and do it—now? Heretofore, I've had only my own suspicions and conclusions—but now—with *proof, proof—I'll* be master of the situation. Get me those letters!"

I made a second attempt to speak.

"But—Mrs. Harding——"

She waved her hands wildly.

"Hush. Go get me those letters. He says—I've nagged—God in heaven—nagged! I want to see those letters with my own eyes and I intend to see them. You hear? You don't know what I may do. Get those letters! You hear me——"

The woman was beside herself. I was becoming thoroughly frightened. Her voice had gradually grown louder and louder until it was almost a scream. People might hear! I began to fear that I had gotten into an awful mess.

She stormed on:

"Don't you know how any wife feels? .I don't believe there's a spark of human nature in you. You are made of iron. But—you will do what I say!"

Suddenly she stopped in front of me and looked me squarely in the face and said:

"Will you get those letters for me—now?"

I got up and stood,—facing her.

"Not now—Mrs. Harding," I calmly stated.

Her eyes flashed; she could not comprehend that I meant what I said. But she changed her tactics.

"Can't you see what all this means to me—and to the country? Do you realize—that Warren Harding is President of the United States? Don't you think we owe something to the American people who trusted him? Don't you think—he owes something to me—who put him in this place? I did it. He knows I did it. He has said—that I did it. Can't you see—the horrible position this places me in?"

I was beginning to see quite plainly—the horrible position that I was in! I had listened to her tirade in silence. But I had listened long enough.

"Mrs. Harding—will you let me say a word? I am an investigator. You sent me for specific information. You did not ask for diaries or letters. Incidentally, in working for the specific information you asked for,—I got possession of diaries and letters. I am an investigator. There are times when I must protect myself. I try always to keep myself in a position to do that."

She actually stamped her foot.

"Oh—you're talking nonsense——"

"Therefore," I went on with a determination equal to hers, "I am gladly returning to you—the assignment you have given me. I will also return it to the Department of Justice."

I picked up my overcoat and slipped it on. I was frightened. I wanted to get out of the place. I did not indeed know what she might do. She was right about that. I picked up my hat and walked out of the room, leaving her.

She had said nothing. She was unquestionably as astonished and alarmed at my conduct as I had been at hers. Before she could get herself together even to speak—I was gone.

I was glad to reach the seclusion of my home. My wife

and boy are always a panacea for the worries and hardships of my profession. But I had scarcely been in the house thirty minutes when the phone rang.

It was Mrs. Boyd. Her greeting was abrupt and to the point.

"Mr. Means—I want to see you right away. Will you take a taxi and come to my house at once? Just as quickly as possible."

"If you insist."

"I do insist. I will expect you."

Mrs. Boyd received me in her dining room as was customary. Mrs. Boyd knew that I could talk better after a drink of good whiskey. She had good whiskey and she knew that I appreciated it. It was always handy on her sideboard. She now poured me a drink and I took it and thanked her.

"Gaston Means—sit right down there now and tell me about it."

"About what?"

"Mrs. Harding phoned me a while ago—all excited and up in the air. She was almost incoherent. She said—that she had apparently hurt your feelings. I almost had to laugh. Fancy you—with hurt feelings!"

"I'm human."

"Oh—no, you're not. I venture to say—you've never had hurt feelings in your life. Whatever your feelings—they are never hurt."

"You think not? You don't know me."

"Anyhow—she begged me to call you right away quick and tell you that she did not intend to be rude and for me to tell you particularly—that under no circumstances are you to return the letters and diaries to the source from which you got them. What letters? What diaries? What is it all about?"

"She didn't tell you?"

"She wouldn't take time. She was in such a rush for me to get hold of you."

"Mrs. Boyd—you are Mrs. Harding's friend. And I believe you are my friend, so—I'll tell you."

And I told her all about the diaries and letters that I had in my possession.

I concluded:

"You must understand that, of necessity, I have to avoid scenes of any kind—even though it may be in the White House. I am an undercover Investigator. I cannot afford to put myself in jeopardy through any woman's hysteria."

"Of course, I understand," she assured.

"I have no confidence in hysterical, wild-eyed, wild-mannered, wild-acting women—or men."

She laughed.

"Did Mrs. Harding get wild-eyed and wild-acting?"

"She did. And then some! I had a perfect legal right—to take these letters and diaries, to obtain the data my assignment called for. They did not establish that fact to my satisfaction. I can't afford to be accused of deliberately stealing letters and diaries. Why—Mrs. Harding is capable of—anything!"

"Where are these letters and diaries?" she asked.

"I have them."

She was silent but a moment and then she said emphatically:

"You must give them to her."

It was my turn to be emphatic:

"No—I mustn't! I tell you,—that women will do anything! And I'd just as soon be kicked to death by a mule that intended to kick me to death, as by a fool mule that didn't intend to kick me to death."

Then Mrs. Boyd said:

"Now see here—Gaston. You know me pretty well. You've seen me under great stress. You don't believe that I lose my head and become wild-eyed and hysterical. You don't believe that under any circumstances would I allow myself to become panic-stricken as a result of what an undercover Investigator may be able to get in his possession as documentary evidence."

"You seriously think that I ought to turn all that documentary evidence over to Mrs. Harding? You really think so?"

She did not hesitate a moment.

"I most certainly do! It is her right! I feel that they belong to her!"

"Well—listen. I'll tell you what I'll do. I'll go home and get these diaries and letters and bring them to you. You can then do what you think right. But I tell you now—those documents establish conclusively just what Mrs. Harding had hoped they would not establish!"

"But she ought to know. It is her right to know. I feel very strongly about this. They belong to her."

I felt that I must further elucidate.

"Because they do establish just that,—in her venom and hate—to tell you the truth, I was afraid she might turn on me just as much as on Nan Britton—or anybody else involved in the matter."

She smiled curiously.

"Why?" she asked.

"The sin with a woman is not because of the act, but because of the discovery."

She laughed.

"Oh—nonsense! That's wrong psychology."

"I know—it's sound psychology," I quickly challenged. "I've had it tested out many times. Will you take the responsibility of giving her these letters?"

"I will. You see, Gaston—Mrs. Harding is incapable of judging—now. This involves everything that is dear to her. It topples over—all the structure of her life—as it has been —and will be. You must be patient and lenient."

She had already rung for her car and it was at the door. So I went to my home in Mrs. Boyd's private car—and returned with the letters and diaries.

When I came back into the dining room, Mrs. Harding and Mrs. Boyd were sitting at a side table. It was evident that she had phoned for Mrs. Harding the moment I had left.

I placed the diaries and the letters down on the side table and said:

"Mrs. Harding—after you have read these, you will find them self-explanatory."

Mrs. Harding had on a brown hat with a medium wide brim and the usual veils draped over it. She had already removed her coat. Now—she jerked off her hat and veils and threw them on the dining table. She jerked open a cut steel beaded bag of beautiful design,—fumbled inside a moment and withdrew her glasses and put them on.

She grabbed at random one of the letters from a bundle.

These letters were all tied exactly as I had found them: the same pink silk corset ribbon, the same knots,—and all arranged in chronological order—as indexed.

While removing the letter from the envelope, she said:

"Now—tell me in minute detail—just where you got these and when you got them and how—and how long you have had them. And why you didn't bring them to me immediately."

I replied as quietly and politely as I knew how.

"I did not bring them to you, Mrs. Harding. I brought them to Mrs. Boyd."

She was paying scant attention to anything that I might say.

"Well—well—" she murmured.

But I must try to make one point clear to her. I said:

"I really can't understand—or have dealings with anyone who cannot control themselves. I am plain so—afraid of nervous, high-strung, excitable people."

She was looking at the letter and I dare say she had not heard me, but I continued:

"As for your other questions,—my official reports will answer all of them."

I was right. She had not heard me for she floundered:

"Oh—ah—I won't let you quit working for me! You shall not. I need you. I must have your services."

She began to untie the other bundles of letters.

"I cannot afford to sacrifice myself—to accomplish your purposes," I defended.

"Oh—I'll see to it that you don't sacrifice yourself. Never fear that," she replied.

I suggested a compromise:

"If you insist that I continue to work for you, then with your consent and approval, I will hereafter make my reports to Mrs. Boyd, if she will consent to be our go-between. It is best that we have a go-between."

"Certainly—certainly—certainly. But—I must be present. I must know first, or exactly at the same time, anything you may have to say."

Mrs. Boyd motioned me to stop arguing and she said:

"Yes. We'll arrange that all right."

Again, Mrs. Harding became insistent.

"Tell me—you've got to tell me—where you found these."

By this time, she had untied every bundle of the letters and had mixed them all together. She would jerk out letter after letter from the envelope and I could not help but see that she was not reading them—at such a rate of speed. She scarcely knew what she was doing.

"Tell me—who put them in this order?"

"I brought them here—exactly as I found them. Nan Britton may not be orderly and systematic in other things but she certainly was in the manner in which she preserved Mr. Harding's letters—and in her correspondence with him."

Then came one of her sudden changes of subject.

"Have you told any living human soul but me?"

"Yes."

For the first time, I think, I attracted her attention. She looked up at me.

"What? What do you mean?"

"I mean—that no one else in the world would have known anything about these letters, if you yourself had not told Mrs. Boyd. You told the third person."

The explanation was satisfactory. Her voice changed as she explained:

"Mr. Means—I have had no experience at all with Investigators. I've had much experience with newspaper men. You have always seemed to me—like a high-grade newspaper man. And I do know—that when a newspaper man gets information he wants to publish it."

"Publishing things is not in line with my profession. On the contrary," I replied, curtly.

"I understand. But that explains my abruptness to you and my criticism of you. As an Investigator,—I realize that you have accomplished wonderful results for me. I want you to know always—that I am grateful. Will you?"

She paid no attention as to whether I replied or not. She said:

"Sit right down here now and read every one of these letters with me and tell me all about where you got them.

Oh—there are so many questions that I must ask you. I can't think of them all right now but I will—while we are reading the letters——"

"Mrs. Harding, it took me several days to read those letters and diaries and it will take you even longer."

"Oh no. I can do it in thirty minutes," she snapped.

Mrs. Harding was snatching up letter after letter, glancing at one, putting it down—opening another. I saw that her face was white as chalk and that her hands were like transparent wax.

Presently her attention was caught by something in one of the letters and she moaned:

"Oh—oh—how could he! How could he!"

That age-old cry of outraged wifehood,—that has come down through the centuries since man first stood up.—"How could he!"

I felt a sudden stirring of real pity,—but in a moment, I heard her muttering between clenched teeth:

"The little huzzy! The brazen little fool. Did you ever! —Who could believe it—who could——"

I turned to Mrs. Boyd.

"May I have another drink?"

To my surprise, Mrs. Harding paused, glanced up and said:

"And I want a drink, too. Bring me one."

Then she went back to her reading.

Mrs. Boyd served us stiff drinks. I took mine and watched to see if Mrs. Harding would drink hers. She paid no attention to it. Mrs. Boyd had put it on the table beside her. Presently I said:

"Mrs. Harding—if you're not going to take that drink—I believe I will."

But Mrs. Boyd interposed:

"No. She must have it. She needs it. I'll get you another."

She motioned for me to come over by the sideboard,—drew me to one side and said:

"Gaston—you're a good boy. But in coping with an hysterical woman you're just about as much out of place as the proverbial bull in a china shop."

She poured the drink for me.

"Here—take this," she commanded. "And then—you slip out by the kitchen. I have a dangerous situation here to deal with. . . . You have nerves of steel and you think everybody else has too. . . . Mrs. Harding does not know what she is doing and what she is saying. . . . You're a good boy—" she repeated, patting me on the shoulder, "but you don't know everything. . . . Run along——"

And as I passed out of the rear door that she opened, I heard Mrs. Harding—:

"Could you believe it. . . . Oh—oh! Fool! Fool! I ought to kill them both. . . . That's what I ought to do. . . . They deserve it. . . . They are not fit to live——"

Chapter IX

Harding Forced to Sign on the Dotted Line

On the evening of that same day, Mrs. Boyd called me on the phone at my home. She said:

"Mrs. Harding and I have spent all these hours reading those letters carefully and systematically."

"You didn't finish?"

"No. Of course, not. It will take many days. Just after you left this morning Mrs. Harding was in a nervous frenzy. I was afraid of a total nervous collapse. She was pitiful."

"I'm sorry."

"This has been an awful shock and I've called to tell you—for mercy's sake, if you have any further evidence of a similar nature—wait! Don't tell her. I know she would never stand another shock—like this. It will kill her."

"You remember, Mrs. Boyd—I did not want to give those letters and diaries to Mrs. Harding. I doubted the wisdom of it. You insisted—that it was her right."

She was quickly on the defensive.

"I know. I haven't changed my mind either."

"I had sense enough to know—it would be a terrible shock —and I put the responsibility on you."

"It was all so sudden. I should have prepared her—been more cautious. Anyhow—come to me first next time. I didn't realize myself how frightful the shock would be."

"How is she now?"

"She has gone back to the White House. She has pulled herself together. But it will take several days—to read all the documents."

"Of course," I replied. "I knew that."

Five days elapsed before I had another message from

them. Mrs. Boyd called on the phone early in the morning and told me that Mrs. Harding wanted me to come to the White House right away.

"But if you have any further documentary evidence,—don't take it," she warned.

"Will you be there?" I inquired.

"Not this time."

"Then—I'd rather not go."

"Oh—don't be stupid. She is all right now. And she wants to see you very much."

I arrived at eleven o'clock at the White House.

I was astounded—to put it mildly—to find the President sitting comfortable in Mrs. Harding's private sitting room where we always held our conferences. He was in a big wing chair between two windows. As I entered, he got up. I bowed and spoke—waiting for a cue which Mrs. Harding promptly gave. The President looked worried. Mrs. Harding seemed entirely composed.

"Mr. Means, we are discussing statistics and—oil leases and many other matters that are clamoring for attention at the Department of Justice."

The President looked at her in surprise.

"These things do not interest Mr. Means—certainly. Play around all you please in your investigations—but keep your hands off the Department of Justice, my dear."

She was not to be easily silenced.

"But you have signed those oil leases. You didn't want to do it. I've heard you say—you never would. There's something behind all this. Those men are bullying you,—why, it's getting to be blackmail. Why not tell Mr. Means and——"

His reply was instant and final.

"No."

In his eyes I caught a glimpse of that gnawing fear that must stalk with him day and night.

She became bold:

"You're afraid of Harry Daugherty."

"Silly!" he retorted. I could see that he was greatly annoyed. She rasped:

"I'm no fool, Warren. You can't fool me. They force you to sign anything they please. You are afraid of them. Tell me why. I'll find out. I always find out."

Nag. Nag. Nag. God—what a life the man was leading. I was embarrassed, but the President now put me at ease by his composed bearing. He moved toward the door and addressed himself to me.

"We all have our little ups and downs—don't we?"

He bowed himself out of the door leading into his own apartment and closed it.

Mrs. Harding looked at me with grim chagrin.

"He signed those leases. He will do anything! Anything Mr. Daugherty asks. And Mr. Daugherty doesn't ask,—he demands! I see many things now that I could never understand before. Mr. Harding did not want to be a candidate for the Presidency. He was afraid. He had reason to be! It took Harry Daugherty's cold nerves of steel—to steady and hold him! And it has taken Warren Harding's friendliness and affability and geniality—to keep Harry Daugherty going. Don't you see?"

I saw.

Again we were sitting in the accustomed places. She was on the end of the couch. Mrs. Harding's face showed unmistakable signs of the mental strain under which she had labored for the past few days. She wore the same unbecoming brown flowered dress that she had had on the last time I had seen her. And the same Spanish shawl. This costume brought back the former unpleasant scene.

She began:

"I will tell you frankly—that I have never in my life passed through such trying times. Of course,—no man can understand. I have not slept at all."

"I think I do understand."

"No. You couldn't."

She then went into a long dissertation of what love meant and what it didn't mean. I had to call her attention as quietly as possible to the fact that she had sent for me. And that we need not enter into a discussion of the letters—that I had read them and was familiar with them. I finished:

"Just why have you sent for me now?"

She sprang to her feet.

"Excuse me. One moment."

She went out of the room,—into and down the outside hall. Presently, she returned with several of Mr. Harding's letters to Nan Britton in her hand. I therefore knew that she had these documents hidden somewhere—outside of their apartments.

She sat down stiffly straight, put the letters on her lap while she put on her glasses,—saying to me while she was doing this:

"Get out paper and pencil. I want you to make a memorandum."

I did as instructed. In looking over the letters, she began to enumerate:

"A bracelet. A wrist watch. A necklace. And a ring. These things Warren Harding has given to Nan Britton."

I said nothing but made the memorandum as she dictated. She went on:

"And to the baby he has given: a solid gold heart on a chain, gold pins, gold pins with chains through them and four bib pins. Have you put those down?"

"I have."

She looked at me.

"Do you think you could get these things for me—if you went back to Chicago? As you know from the letters, they are gifts that Warren Harding has made to Nan Britton and her child. They have no right to them. Besides—I have a purpose in getting them. I must have them."

"Really—Mrs. Harding, I have no serious objections to getting for you any gifts that your husband may have made to Nan Britton,—but I can't take from a baby such little gifts. That's carrying matters too far—for a two hundred pound man to cause a tiny child needless grief and distress."

"Oh—how inanely silly!" she sneered. "That has nothing to do with it. I am determined to have these things. Why—I'd rather have the presents sent to the baby than those given to Nan Britton. I have a very special reason."

"Well—I just won't do it. I won't take those things from a baby," I flatly declared.

"Wouldn't it be possible for you to get them and bring them to me—for my purpose—and then you can return them?"

"I'll agree to that."

I had my assignment and left.

Two days later—I was back in Chicago, I was in a hurry. It was an assignment that I did not like. It seemed to me of no real importance,—but instead, it was catering to a woman's fury and venom and hysteria.

In my profession—haste always spells disaster. It did in this instance. I made a blunder that caused me several days' delay.

My sailing was not easy at best. My "roper" was gone. I had no inside contact. All I had to function with—was the key to the Willets' apartment and those to the closet.

I hung around the apartment house. Once I saw a maid

at a window in the Willets' apartment which caused me worry, for if they now kept a maid, my difficulties would be greatly increased. However, I discovered that this one was a window washer and in, only for the day.

In hanging around the apartment house myself, I attracted the attention of the policeman on the beat. He came up to me on the evening of the third day and said:

"Just why—are you around in this neighborhood without apparently knowing what you want to do?"

This meant trouble. I had to think quickly.

"I'm a bill collector," I replied.

"Where are your bills?" he asked.

"I have no bills. It's a confidential debt a man owes me."

"Who is the man?"

"Now—see here. If you want to run me in, if you think I am violating any law—I'll answer the questions before the Judge. You have no authority to ask questions. Only to make arrests."

He eyed me viciously as he said:

"Well—I believe you are one of these damn smart-aleck bootleggers and, of course, your bill is confidential and not in writing. But I'll tell you right now—if the liquor is like most other liquor being sold around in this neighborhood by the bootleggers,—and you have *credited* anybody,—you'll have a hell of a time collecting your money."

I smiled and said nothing. He made his final thrust.

"I want you to get out of this neighborhood and stay out. Don't come around here any more. I've had my eye on you for two days."

There was nothing for me to do but to obey this edict. It took me several days to get this policeman's name and Precinct and quietly have him transferred to the North side of Chicago.

But my assignment had not yet been accomplished. Then

I thought of something that should have come to my mind at first. I remembered that my 'roper' had told me that the Willets at different times had gin and whiskey for parties.

I went to a prohibition agent whom I knew well and told him that whiskey was being sold in that apartment building and he could easily confirm this by causing a regular investigation. And if it did develop and he was positive that gin and whiskey was being delivered there, not to make a move but to come and let me know. This was just a friendly tip from one officer to another.

This necessitated another wait of three or four days. Then I received word from him that it was true: gin and whiskey were being delivered to that apartment house. I requested him to get the names of all the tenants in the building and have search warrants issued and to turn the search warrants over to me.

I knew then that I was properly fortified. I availed myself of the search warrants—only in making a search of the one apartment—I had the keys. I was not looking for whiskey and if any had been there, I wouldn't have found it. I gave the apartment and the closet a thorough search again but not a piece of the jewelry did I find.

I then got in communication with my "shadow" men who had Nan Britton under surveillance and described each article of the jewelry and told them to get it if possible.

In less than a week, I had their reports and every article of the jewelry except the ring, which they said was on her finger.

I returned to Washington bringing the jewelry with me. My assignment had been successfully accomplished.

Remembering Mrs. Boyd's warning to take no further evidence to Mrs. Harding, I called Mrs. Boyd on the phone and told her of the assignment and that I had the articles.

"What shall I do with them—now that I've got them?" I asked.

She actually laughed.

"Take them to her, of course. I don't believe you know what will cause a shock and what will not. Mrs. Harding asked you to get these articles. She knows of their existence. They will not shock her in the least. On the other hand, she will be greatly pleased."

In dealing with women I find that there are always new things to learn.

I went straight to Mrs. Harding without being sent for. I knew that Mrs. Boyd would phone her to expect me. I had been told to avoid using her telephone. In case of emergencies, I had been instructed to get in touch with her personal maid service. This I did and was promptly escorted to her apartment.

She was pleased to see me and pleased at the success of my mission. I had not intended to sit down this time. So, standing, I took the articles from my pocket and handed them to her and asked:

"How long do you think you will want to keep these baby trinkets?"

She replied:

"A very short time. Don't worry about a little thing like that. They are now in my possession which is the important thing."

I had the jewelry wrapped together in white tissue paper and placed in a small pasteboard box. She removed the lid of the box and spread the tissue paper out flat on the surface of the table. All the articles lay exposed. She bent over them, lifting up one by one and putting it down again. Accursed things! Entombed within these glittering baubles were her past dreams, her present happiness and her future hopes.

"No husband has any right to give anything away without the knowledge of his wife," she spoke with an ominous mildness.

What a picture of hate and wrath was on Mrs. Harding's face as she bent over that table and looked at those articles of jewelry!

"Do you realize that it was as much my money as his? That *my* money helped pay for these things. It was I—who saved and scrimped and sacrificed through years and years and years—to save money. And—this is what he does with it."

I couldn't understand then why she did not mention the actual money that the diaries and letters had revealed that Mr. Harding had sent Nan Britton. He had been most generous with money. He had sent her large sums and frequently.

I gathered the impression, I couldn't have told how—that she did not intend to return those baby trinkets—ever,—but before I had time to speak of this, she had made one of her sudden shifts in conversation.

"I have eagerly waited for your return. I am sorry that I didn't enumerate some other things that I want you to get. There are other things that Warren Harding has given Nan Britton and her child. I have a description from these documents of a very handsome fur coat that he sent her and a fur coat for the baby. And I notice that he himself personally selected for the child—shoes and stockings and hats and dresses and a very handsome baby carriage."

I wondered—if she intended to try to send me to Chicago to steal a baby carriage and bring it to her—but no, she had that well thought out.

"I want you to get a picture of this baby carriage. But the fur coats and the articles mentioned, I want you to get and bring to me."

I never saw such fury of determination on a human countenance. But on this assignment, I took a firm stand.

"Really, Mrs. Harding, I refuse to become engaged in taking from a mother and her child—I don't care who they are—their actual clothing."

"You will do as I tell you," she snapped.

"You ask me to take the winter coats from this woman and her child. Do you want them to freeze to death? Why next—you'll be commanding me to take from them—their very lives."

"You are an Investigator, Mr. Means. I am the wife of the President of the United States. You are in my employ. I pay you well. You are ordered—to carry out my wishes."

She took a seat by the table on which was still spread out the white tissue paper with the jewelry.

"I want every scrap of evidence possible," she repeated, "so I will know exactly what to do, what I am to say and how I shall present my facts to President Harding."

This was the first intimation that I had had that she had not yet said anything to the President.

"I am not ready to act—yet. I want a confession. I must wait until I can force a complete confession. Continue the surveillance of Nan Britton and keep me advised. And come at once, if any emergency arises. My personal maids are instructed—that I am to see you at any time you may call."

"I have not accepted the new assignment," I reminded her. She continued:

"With those things in my possession, I will be master of the situation. I hold the whip hand. Warren Harding will do exactly what I tell him to do. Nan Britton will do exactly what I tell her to do."

She paused as if turning this triumph over in her mind and enjoying its exultation. She went on:

"I must consult Madam X. Mrs. Boyd will let her meet

me at her home. She will tell me what to do and how to do it. She has declared many times,—that I am a 'Child of Destiny'. Warren Harding shall do—what I say, hereafter. And Nan Britton.—Well, sometimes it's harder to live—than to die. I'll show them. I am master now."

I had not been seated during this entire interview. I turned to go and said:

"I refuse this assignment. Is there anything else?"

She looked at me and her eyes narrowed.

"Yes."

She paused and I waited. Then she commanded:

"Take off your overcoat and sit down."

A sudden shift of subject and she said:

"Mr. Means—Warren Harding is not the father of Nan Britton's child—and I shall prove it."

Chapter X

Means' Investigations Concerning President Harding

"WARREN HARDING is not capable of having a child, therefore he is not the father of Nan Britton's child. That's logical, isn't it?"

"If sure of your premise," I warned.

"We have had no children. I have demonstrated my ability. I've had a living son by a former marriage."

"Does that line of reasoning always follow?"

"How do I know?" she snapped. "Nor do I care. The thing I want you to do—is to prove for me that Warren Harding cannot be father of a child."

I waited her explanation.

"Well?"

"When we were first married, we longed for children. He was eager for a child of his own. Oh,—we discussed this every day. It was then paramount in our minds and hearts. I had thought our love might be forever cemented by the bond of parenthood. A son would have held him—to his own fireside. I believe so in any case, although my observations of other people do not confirm this as a sure hypothesis. President Harding loves children. Everybody knows that. And he was crazy for a child of his own," she reiterated several times.

"You are quite sure of this?"

I asked the question because there had flashed into my mind certain reasons that I knew why Mr. Harding might not have wanted a legitimate child. I remembered the vicious "whispering campaign" against him: that he had a taint of Negro blood in his veins. A professor in an Ohio university wrote a book proving in a scientific dissertation[18]—as he claimed—that there was this taint. I myself had helped light a bonfire that burnt up the entire edition of this book—copyright and all—bought at a price. And the plates for this book were destroyed also.

The bonfire was made in the rear grounds around the palatial home of Mr. Boyd. These books and plates had come to Washington from Ohio in a guarded express car. The car was packed full. They made a big bonfire.

Did Warren Harding really want a legitimate child? I asked myself this question again? A man might take a chance with a mistress—that was different. But at the moment, in spite of all that Mrs. Harding was emphasizing to the contrary, I had my own doubts.

"Of course, I am sure," she was saying. "Certainly! We both yearned for children—he really more than I. And—a child would have come to us—had it been a physical possibility. I am assigning you the task to prove this physical impossibility. He has been examined by several specialists. You must see their actual reports and records. Can you?"

"I have yet to fail in getting a record that I went after."

How pleased she looked at this statement.

"Get these! He told me—after the various professional visits and final diagnoses,—that the doctors had always affirmed that there was no reason on earth why he could not be father of a child. That he was a perfect virile normal man in every way. Well—now, I don't believe he told me the truth. Pride—the pride of the male alone would make him deny this truth. But you will get it. Bring all records and copies of them to me so I can see with my own eyes. Will you do this?"

"Yes. I certainly will. I think it will not be difficult. Then—what?"

How alert and eager she was!

"That's the first thing. Concentrate on that. Oh—I will

yet save Warren from this awful sword that is suspended over him. I'll save him from that bad, designing girl. She thinks—she holds him in her power—I'll show her! I'll make fools of both of them,—but I'll save him!"

Mrs. Harding was a woman of indomitable determination and whenever she spoke of "saving" Warren—there was a fanatical gleam in her eyes that made me know that she would go to any lengths to "save Warren",—she would sacrifice anybody, anything, any principle that dared obstruct her path.

"Complete this assignment as rapidly as possible,—and in the meantime I want you to make an exhaustive investigation of Nan Britton."

How calmly and incidentally she suggested this herculean task.

"Mrs. Harding, you well know, by this time, that for me to investigate any person means that I go back and begin at the hour of birth and trace their lives—day by day—month by month—year by year."

She nodded her head vigorously.

"Precisely what I want. Find out everything there is to know about Nan Britton. Begin at the beginning. It takes time—I understand—and money. Consider neither. Get your men to work—immediately."

"I have already had seventeen men working at various investigations for you. And by the way, here are the last reports of the men covering Col. Darwin's investigation. You may take these and read them at your leisure."

Col. Darwin was a friend of Harry Daugherty and was a frequent visitor at the White House. I had been assigned by Mrs. Harding to investigate his social career.

I handed the papers to her, which she took.

"I am only interested in results and conclusions so far as

Col. Darwin is concerned. Is it actually true—all that I have heard—that he had six wives and—all those rumors of his scandalous career with women? Is it really true?"

"It is."

"Then—my course is simple. Col. Darwin will come no more to the White House. That is one thing that I simply cannot and will not tolerate."

I was well aware that Mrs. Harding could not be cognizant of just what it might mean—to affront Col. Darwin: Col. Darwin's various operations and manipulations connected with Oil leases were known to no one outside the inner circle.

When I left Mrs. Harding on this occasion, she was in an apparently normal state of mind, certainly more calm than I had ever seen her before. She reminded me of an Army General,—carefully mustering his forces for battle. Deep in my heart was a great pity for the President. Little did he dream—of the storm that was soon to break over his head!

The cares of State and the responsibilities of the Presidency of the greatest Nation on earth would fall away from him like chaff before the wind,—compared to the final domestic conflict that she was elaborately staging.

The ethical question of my own position in this matter never entered my head—strange as that may seem. I was an investigator. I had been officially assigned to Mrs. Harding for special personal detective work. She was my client. That was the sum total of the whole equation so far as I was concerned. I did—what she asked, with all the skill of my profession. If I ever stopped to consider sympathies—they were not with her, certainly. Whatever sympathies I ever allowed myself indulgence,—were entirely with Mr. Harding.

I liked President Harding. Everybody liked him who knew him. He was a humanly lovable man.

It is comparatively a simple matter to get a complete physical history of anybody.

Of course, I knew that the President carried life insurance. Because of my confidential contacts and connections with an insurance association, I established the date when his first examination for insurance had been made. This gave me his physical career from boyhood.[14] It developed from this first examination that in his early manhood he had suffered from a chronic ailment. Because of his youth and inexperience, he had taken many patent medicines and had consulted quack doctors. His father, being a doctor himself, soon discovered this condition and took him in charge.

Because of my contacts with investigators of the Insurance Association at their headquarters in New York, I saw his father's affidavit with my own eyes and soon had in my possession the entire physical history of President Harding.

I found also that long after his marriage he had been examined by a very eminent specialist at Columbus, Ohio. This examination had been unquestionably inspired by Mr. Harry M. Daugherty,—arising out of the same question as to whether he could be the father of Nan Britton's child. That must have been for Mr. Harding's positive assurance and for the purpose of easing his conscience in the matter. Every test known to science had been resorted to by that specialist. All confirmed and affirmed that he could be father of a child.

For further confirmation and in connection with a throat treatment at Johns Hopkins in Baltimore the last and final examination had been made by an eminent specialist there.

Again, every method known to science had been resorted to, with the verdict that he could become a father. Under that examination, the chemical and microscopic tests were designated by a number.

The moment a man is elected President of the United

States, it is customary for the Insurance Companies to give him additional insurance at the minimum rate. This is obviously for the purpose of encouraging insurance. President Harding's insurance was increased at this time and all recent reports and examinations were attached to this last application. The actual getting of this cumulative data did not take more than fifteen minutes.

Knowing Mrs. Harding as I did, I secured copies of all these reports for her. I went to Columbus, Ohio. From the secretary of the eminent specialist there who had examined Mr. Harding, I obtained for a consideration the original records of diagnoses. I carried those records out of their office, had them photostated and returned them.

I got in contact with a nurse whom I knew very well at Johns Hopkins and there I obtained all the original diagnoses made there and had these photostated and returned them.

With all of this mass of unimpeachable documents I went to Mrs. Harding and placed them before her. She could not hide her real alarm.

"You will have to give in,—with such positive reports from such eminent sources," I declared.

She stiffened.

"Give in? To what?" was her scornful rejoinder.

"To the oft confirmed fact: that President Harding could become a father," I stated.

Her mouth became set with determination.

"I will not! I shall follow my own line of action. I shall consult with Gen. Sawyer. He is our White House physician and life-long friend. He has made numerous examinations of me. I shall get him to write out a statement that I could become a mother, which will prove that the President could not become a father."

I had never yet heard Mrs. Harding admit defeat. Her tenacity of purpose was unbelievable.

"The days of miracles are no more," I ventured with a smile.

"What do you mean?"

I laughed, thinking to ease the tension of a situation that was becoming absurd.

"In Holy Writ—Abraham's wife, Sarah—ninety years old,—had a child——"

Quick as a flash, she turned toward me. Her face was white.

"Are you trying to be funny? There is nothing funny to me. You forget yourself, Mr. Means!"

Her manner had frozen with hauteur.

"I beg pardon. But—why not admit the inevitable?"

"Never! Never! Time and again Gen. Sawyer has told me that Warren Harding could not become a father. Time and time again. If I don't know,—and Gen. Sawyer doesn't know that he cannot become a father,—who could know? And I don't care if a million eminent specialists said he could be a father,—I know it is not true."

What could a reasonable man say in the face of an argument like this?

"I've begun the investigation of Nan Britton, according to your instructions."

But she was not to be diverted from the question under discussion.

"Wait! All I want now to confirm my own proof is a good look into the face of that child! Your next assignment from me is this: bring that child here for me to see!"

I rose to go. Further conference with her now was useless.

"Mrs. Harding,—you've made a thief of me—and now you want to turn me into a kidnaper."

Her white face flamed. She was furious.

"You won't do that?"

"No. I won't."

Always, when she saw that I meant what I said, she quickly accepted.

"Then—find out for me—the very minute this baby was born. I will get Gen. Sawyer to trace back for me,—and we will know exactly when that child was conceived and where Warren Harding was at that time. He was *not* with Nan Britton."

"You are wasting my time and your money," I stated bluntly.

"You don't understand. I *know*—because Madame X has assured me, that this child is not Warren Harding's. Madame X knows."

"How? How can she know?" The conversation had drifted into the ridiculous.

She replied with emphasis:

"By the moon and the stars. They tell her. She has spent many nights studying this very question for me, before she would give me her decision. And when she did give me her ultimatum, it was final. There can be no appeal from what Madam X says! She is linked with celestial forces by supernatural powers,—and they do her bidding."

"Then—why in the name of Heaven, if you know what you want to know, through Gen. Sawyer and Madam X,—do you employ me?"

"I was hoping that you would unearth the truth. You failed."

"I—see!"

But I didn't see. Mrs. Harding was a woman of unusually brilliant mind and logical reasoning. I began to wonder—if anything could be happening to her?

This was a mere flit of a suspicion. I felt its preposterousness and dismissed it in disgust and—fear. But I could not smile at that fear.

Chapter XI

Nan Reaches Washington—and Harding

AGAIN that very night my phone rang and it was Mrs. Boyd. Her voice sounded flustered.

"Did you know that Nan Britton is coming to Washington?"

"I did not."

"Well—she is. On the train from New York tonight. She has made awful threats. She is capable of anything! Now listen: her train will reach Baltimore early tomorrow morning. I want you to go to Baltimore and get on that train. Why, I am actually afraid that she will march herself straight to the White House and demand her rights—demand that she be received—demand that she has as much right there—as Mrs. Harding. She'll do—anything!"

"Want me to kidnap and hold her."

"Listen. This is no time to be funny. Find her on the train and see where she goes when she gets here and let me know as quickly as possible. Have you ever seen her? Do you know her?"

"No."

"You'll know her all right. Will you do this?"

"Sure," I assured. "If she goes to the White House what shall I do?"

"Be there—as quickly as she. Arrest her! Use your wits! I don't care what you do. But—prevent a public scene."

I went to Baltimore that night and caught the early morning train from New York to Washington. I walked leisurely through the Pullman cars, and when I entered the car in which Nan Britton had a berth, I recognized her instantly. She was standing in the aisle and the porter was holding her coat.

She was a most attractive young woman: blonde, fresh, vital. I took a seat in that car and watched her and I also noticed that the other men in the car were watching her. She was decidedly the type to attract men.

As I sat in the Pullman seat I marveled! I was inclined to believe that President Harding was just as eager to see Nan Britton as she was to see him. In fact—it was much easier for me to understand his infatuation for her—than hers for him.

What was she getting out of it? After all, what a lonesome sort of life for her! Money? Yes. He gave her plenty of money. There was much to that. He gave her all and more than she could use and discreetly explain.

And President Harding was an unusually handsome man—to be sure—but he was thirty years older than this fresh, lovely, vivid young woman who was sitting in a Pullman train journeying to Washington to see him.

Then, sudden, I felt that I had found the solution: he was President of the United States! He had been Senator! I believed that the real reason of her continued interest lay in the glamor and glory of his position. It was the only sensible way to explain it.

My thoughts were moving at random.

I had no doubt but that President Harding suffered deeply for his philandering transgressions and the mess of a triangle in which he was now entangled. Men have always suffered for these things,—since David walked upon the housetop and saw and coveted and took—Bathsheba. And there is no hint in the record of Bathsheba's unwillingness. David was King!

And did David suffer? The Scriptural record says that for twelve long months he drank the bitter dregs of repentance. That certainly diverges from the modern current versions—

repentance is not a popular modern pastime. Not that I've heard of!

And—isn't it hard to reconcile our puritanical conceptions of ethics and theology and morality—with the Biblical statement that David was a 'man after God's own heart'.

Yes,—David was King! And Bathsheba was willing!

If I mistook not,—the delightful little modern woman who was sitting across the aisle from me in this Pullman car—three seats in front—looking demurely out the window at the passing landscape,—had her mind and heart more enthrallingly engrossed in the glamours of the "King"—than the mere romance of her young life, with a man almost old enough to be her grandfather.

Mrs. Harding had told me that Nan Britton had been 'crazy' about Warren Harding—always. She had persistently pursued him, from the time she was twelve years old. She had dangled herself tantalizingly before his restless male eyes,—a luscious bit of adolescent virgin femininity. Her attractiveness was systematically, persistently, determinedly set before him—until he succumbed.

This attractive young woman—with her bobbed blonde hair peeping from a closely fitting cloche, was really after all no more alluring than many other girls and women, in whose presence I myself have seen President Harding all aflutter. But she was young, eager, panting,—calling for sex-fulfilment, dazzled by his masculine beauty and his position,—determined, flattered, seductive. And he loved girls.

What of the woman who had been his wife for thirty-two years! A little, drab, strong-minded, self-willed woman, years older than he, clinging with tenacious ferocity to the illusions of youth,—seeing no reason at all why she was not as attractive as any young girl! Consulting a soothsayer to find mystic ways and means to enhance her attractiveness. Feeling secure—because of her mental equipment!

The faithful wife—who had made him what he was. Granted—all that! I did not believe that the President had ever wanted to hurt her. He had tried to shield and protect her. I knew that he could not feel romantic in her presence—not to save his immortal soul! I doubted if he ever had! She was not the type to inspire romance or passion. So he had assumed the very simple, popular modern attitude, in universal approval, towards the sins of the flesh.

Nan Britton may have been one of many—undoubtedly she was—a passing transport of ecstasy, except for the mammoth fact—that she had borne him a child! His only child! The pride of the male in parenthood. She had lifted the stigma! The child!

That was where the shoe pinched hardest. That was what engendered hate and more hate in Mrs. Harding's impotent breast. And that explained the President's continued interest in Nan Britton—or did it?

The President *had* to continue to make love to Nan Britton. He *had* to keep her satisfied and quieted. And it was doubtless easier and more interesting to appeal to her feminine penchant for self-sacrifice and point to his all-consuming need for her co-operation to help him hold his position. He probably had to work overtime—along these lines. And he *had* to make continuous and convincing love to her. Which probably was rather easy. She was certainly easy to look at!

During his Senatorial years, they had traveled together, sharing Pullman berths, registering in various hotels in various cities, meeting each other in any and every sort of place.

And now this very comely and alert young woman, sitting alone in a Pullman car, with the hawk eye of a Department of Justice Investigator full upon her,—traveling to Washington, might even at this moment, be concocting in her pretty blonde head—ways and means of demanding her rights and the rights of her child!

Her rights? What 'rights' has a mistress of any man in this country?. . . . What 'rights' has an illegitimate child?. . . .

Pity I thought, that Nan Britton could not have lived in the days of the Borgias, when illegitimate children had legal and social prestige, sometimes even holding precedence over those born in holy wedlock.

No social stigma was attached to illegitimacy during the days of the Borgias. Cesare Borgia was an illegitimate child and so was his sister Lucretia. They enjoyed their rank and inheritance, unchallenged on the score of their birth.

However tragic and lamentable it is that the innocent should suffer for a condition that was none of their contriving,—but merely 'accidental consequences' following the lust of their parents, civilization has moved forward since the days of the Borgias. There are fundamental laws of decency that convention has established—and convention is the accumulated good taste of the best people of all ages.

The Borgias!

I hadn't thought of the Borgias since I had studied medieval history in college. Couldn't one trace a startling parallel between those barbaric, blood-drenched days—and our own very civilized era?

We had entered the station. Miss Britton had stepped briskly down the aisle and was waiting on the platform. I was close behind her. The porter was taking off the baggage.

She stepped off the train, pointed a red-cap to her suitcase and bag—and walked down the platform and through the station.

She hailed a 'For Hire' car, had her baggage put in,

jumped in herself and slammed the door. The car moved off.

I hopped in a taxi and followed.

Was she going to the White House?

She was not. Her taxi stopped before the Continental Hotel and she registered there. I phoned Mrs. Boyd.

Chapter XII

Where an Embarrassing Encounter Is Averted

THE range of my detective activities for Mrs. Harding changed often, quickly and unexpectedly, from the sublime to the ridiculous.

The serious business of conducting the life investigations of Mr. Daugherty and Mr. Fall and Mr. Weeks,[6] in which at one time I had seventeen expert men engaged and which necessarily covered a period of many months was interrupted sometimes by urgent assignments of the most trivial character.

I recall on one occasion, when I was assembling the various written reports from my men on these life investigations, and arranging them in proper chronological order,—Mrs. Boyd put in a hurried phone call for me to come at once to her home, 'Glen Haven'.

I had to lay everything aside, and rush in my car to answer her summons. I always knew that a message from Mrs. Boyd meant business for Mrs. Harding.

I reached 'Glen Haven' in about twenty minutes and was not surprised to see the White House car parked at the side of the driveway.

Mrs. Boyd herself, however, met me at the front door. She was pale and excited. She whispered to me before she spoke a word of greeting.

"For heaven's sake— get Mrs. Harding away. Make some excuse. Any excuse. The President and Nan Britton are out here now. *They are upstairs.* Get Mrs. Harding away. *Get Mrs. Harding away!*"

I made no reply but I understood. Mr. Boyd was sponsor for the President in his clandestine meetings with Nan Britton and I inferred that it was he who had arranged this visit for them.

It was a bad situation. No doubt of that. Did Mrs. Harding suspect, I wondered? If she did,—my mission would be a difficult and a useless one.

I found Mrs. Harding comfortably seated on a couch in the library.

She had not removed her hat. I decided after a first glance that this was purely an accidental mix-up and could be handled. Mrs. Boyd left us alone. Mrs. Harding was frankly pleased to see me. I made this excuse:

"You are always so eager to get reports from the investigations of your various Cabinet friends,—I know you'll be glad to know that my men have just turned in—a large assortment."

This, as always, aroused her keen attention.

"Oh,—yes. How slow they have been though in finding things I can use. Have they at last put the proper weapons into my hands. Have they?"

I did not sit down but stood,—carelessly leaning against the mantel.

"Depends on the kind of weapons you want," I smiled.

"You know what I want," she snapped.

I must not appear hurried.

"You can best judge for yourself. Would you like to go over these written reports with me before I copy and file them? You can see the originals and judge better than I."

"Oh, yes, I would like that."

"Have you anything in particular to do this afternoon?"

"No. Didn't you bring these reports with you? We could go over them—so nicely—here."

I drawled:

"Well—no. I didn't." I lowered my voice: "I did not

know that you wanted Mrs. Boyd to know anything about your investigations of these gentlemen. Does she know?"

"No. She doesn't."

I again spoke in a half whisper:

"I wouldn't burden her with the knowledge if I were you. Can't you come on back with me now? And you can help me by reading these reports? They tell their own story."

"What will Mrs. Boyd think? I have just come."

But she stood up and was preparing to leave.

"Oh,—she won't mind. I'll make an excuse."

I pressed a button and when a servant appeared I asked him to call Mrs. Boyd, which he did.

"You don't mind—do you—if I take Mrs. Harding off on a little business?" I asked her.

Such a look of gratitude—she flashed at me.

"Why, of course not," she assured.

Did she mind? Never was there greater relief written on a human countenance.

Mrs. Harding left in the White House car—and some minutes later, I followed in my own car. I went to my office 903—16th St. and gathered together all the written reports from my men which I had not yet copied and filed as was my invariable custom. These I carried with me to the White House and Mrs. Harding and I spent several hours reading and discussing them. Another situation had been saved—or averted.

Chapter XIII

Means Investigates Nan Britton's Life

WHEN Mrs. Harding gave me the assignment to make a complete investigation of the entire life of Nan Britton it was for the definite purpose of establishing the fact that Nan Britton had other lovers, and that President Harding was not the father of her child. She had by this time exhausted every other possibility or probability. Even though Madam X, after her numerous orgies with the moon and the stars, had given assurances to Mrs. Harding that the President was not the father of the child, according to the last "ultimatum," Mrs. Harding was still determined to corroborate Madam X with other more tangible and even more convincing proofs.

As is an investigator's custom, after being given a verbal assignment, I made out a "Journal Memorandum" as we call it, and carried it to Mrs. Harding for her approval. This avoids misunderstandings and confusion.

Mrs. Harding had said to me:

"I want you to find out *all* about Nan Britton for me. I want to know *all* about her."

When I handed her the "Journal Memorandum" for her confirmation, she glanced at it. "Subject: Nan Britton. Trace from date of birth." She said:

"Oh—I don't care to know anything about her birth. I know all about that. Don't waste time on things like that."

I affirmed:

"You may think you know all about her birth but I cannot properly cover an investigation when you say you want to know *all* about anybody, unless I myself take them from birth forward,—day by day, week by week, month by month, year by year."

"You did do that with the others, didn't you?"

"I certainly did—as you must remember. With Mr. Daugherty and three other members of the Cabinet."

"Well—I'm in a hurry now. Don't waste any time on trifles. Begin at 12 years of age."

She put her O.K. of approval on the "Journal Memorandum" and I went to work.

I began at birth, however, as I always do. I sent two of my best men to Marion, Ohio. It is a much easier and simpler process—quickly and rapidly to get the facts on any life, than people imagine. If one does not get the facts quickly and easily, one can lay the foundation on which to acquire the facts.

The men went to the graded schools in Marion. They got Nan Britton's complete school record. They also acquired the enrollment of all of her school mates while she was in the graded school and in the high school. This gave us, in her parents' handwriting and in her own handwriting, her birth record, her vaccinations, the childhood diseases she had had and so forth.

We had a list of her friends and acquaintances among her girl school mates.

We quickly spotted two girls who had gone through the schools with her and who were working in Dayton, Ohio. My men went to Dayton. They became acquainted with these two girls. From them they learned the names of several boys who were friends of Nan Britton and who had had 'crushes' on her.

These girls knew little or nothing at first hand of Nan Britton. They said—she was a prude, a stick, a frost. That she didn't care for boys.

My men interviewed the boys who had had 'crushes' on Nan. They separately and candidly stated that Nan Britton never allowed any boy to take privileges.

One of these girls in Dayton confided to one of my men,

that one of the printers of the *Marion Daily Star* had told her some "stories" about Nan Britton and President Harding. The man went back to Marion and talked with this printer.

He was told that when Nan was fourteen or fifteen years old, about twice a week, she would come to the *Star* office after everybody had gone,—Mrs. Harding also. He had to stay to clean up and straighten things around. And he said he used to stand on a stool and peep through a partition transom window—and that Nan Britton would be sitting on the President's lap and he would be fondling and caressing her——

But this information was not leading us along the lines of our client's wishes and demands!

All of her friends and acquaintances during her years in Marion insisted that Nan Britton was a good and virtuous girl. Occasionally a boy might have kissed her, but that was all.

After she left Marion and went out into the world to "paddle her own canoe" my men went with her in their investigation,—from the moment she stepped off the train until she left each place.

They would ascertain where she lived. They would talk with her landlady. They would find out what her expenses were, how much she paid for board, where she bought her clothes and what she paid for them. They would find out where she had worked,—what her salary had been.

In the first city to which she went after leaving Marion, my men were able to check up her earnings and her expenditures,—almost to the penny.

Then they traced her to another city in the same way and used the same method of checking up.

They reported that Nan Britton was a very careful and prudent young woman. Her laundry bills were meager.

Once or twice they found she had had tilts with her landlady because she did washing in her room. They found where she had her shoes half-soled and mended and where she bought her drugs. The latter is always important in any investigation. Nan Britton bought only the barest necessities.

Nan Britton stood high among her acquaintances whereever she lived.

She was bright and vivacious and popular, but cared nothing for men. Many young fellows had sought her favors,—in vain.

One landlady reported that she had but one picture of a man in her room and that one picture was always on her dresser. We made a quick deduction.

Still we were not making much headway.

We also found that everywhere she lived or happened to be, she was always in more or less frequent correspondence with Mr. Harding. He sent her a great many souvenir post-cards.

During this investigation we enlisted the help of several women.

To make the story short, Nan Britton had no lover *but* Mr. Harding. We traced her life day by day, month by month and year by year—every detail, with the object of establishing, if humanly possible, that she was not a virtuous girl. In this we failed completely.

No man ever gave Nan Britton money except Mr. Harding. She did her own washing; she had her shoes mended; she had a winter coat dyed; she bought sparingly. She paid her bills irregularly sometimes but a very little at a time. She had the respect and admiration of everybody who knew her.

These reports, as they came in to me,—I would pass on to Mrs. Harding. Her chagrin and consternation grew with each report until at last she abandoned hope.

Chapter XIV

Mrs. Harding Confronts the President with Proofs

SEVERAL weeks had passed. I was busy completing the work of the life-investigations of the several people to which Mrs. Harding had definitely assigned me. She was so eager to get reports on these investigations that she wanted me to see her almost every day and tell her all that I had found out. Especially was this true, of course, of my surveillance of Nan Britton.

A change had gradually, almost imperceptibly, come over Mrs. Harding. I knew in what direction her activities were being focused. She was playing a bold hand—for power. The actuating motive of her entire life had been a consuming thirst for power. Her ambition knew no bounds. She visualized herself as ruler of the land, which as a matter of actual fact she was, in larger measure than anybody would dream.

I was at home, in my office at 903—16th Street, working over and copying some detailed reports on the Nan Britton investigation which was not yet quite completed, when my phone rang and Mrs. Boyd was on the wire. My appointments to meet Mrs. Harding at Mrs. Boyd's home had been so regular and definite recently that it had not been necessary to 'phone. This call, therefore, from her, whatever it might be, I knew instantly was something unusual and important.

She said: "Mrs. Harding wants you to come to the White House and as quickly as possible. She has just 'phoned here."

She paused. I waited.

"Well?" I queried.

"She is greatly excited—" her voice trailed.

"Thank you. I'll go."

Had the fatal moment arrived? Had Mrs. Harding confronted the President with her proofs of his relations with Nan Britton?

I did not hurry. I sat at my desk—thinking. I had a premonition of evil,—an uncanny presentiment that always portends trouble.

Swiftly my mind reviewed the conditions of the predicament in which I found myself. Mrs. Harding was my client. I had been working for her.

I knew that Mrs. Harding felt that she was the divinely appointed arbiter of her husband's destiny. Had she not helped him up step by step and placed him in the highest office in the gift of the greatest nation on earth? All that she had wanted me to do for her had been done for him.

She was a "Child of Destiny". Madam X had told her so—and that settled it! A Child of Destiny!

How could such a man as Warren Harding ever have been captivated by her, I wondered? He was a prince of a man—an Apollo—an Adonis. He was a likeable sort of a man, as both men and women agreed. It was said by his friends that no woman could resist him or would ever try to. He had indeed a fatal charm with women. And she? Her best friends would readily admit her lack of beauty or even a semblance of it. She was not quick-witted. She was not even attractive, notwithstanding her pitiful attempts in that direction. A little drab woman, strong-minded, self-willed, older than her husband by nine years, 'twas said—clinging with tenacious ferocity to the illusions of youth, deceiving nobody but herself. Ambitious, worldly, greedy for power.

And now what was going on up there in their rooms at the White House whither I had been summoned?

Naturally, the vicissitudes of my profession have brought me many times into unpleasant scenes between husband and wife and such scenes were never to my liking. I always avoid

"Had she not brought him up, step by step, and placed him in the highest office in the gift of the greatest nation on earth?"

scenes if possible. That is one important rule for an investigator.

I had a hunch—I was confident that such a scene awaited me now. Subconsciously I had been expecting this summons for a week or more, always with the forlorn hope that it would not come.

However, after Mrs. Harding had in her possession as complete and detailed data as I had ever handed to any one for whom I had conducted an investigation, I feared that there was no escape for me.

If only Mrs. Harding could have had the sense to leave the President alone! She never did; she never would. I felt sure that she had always been nagging him concerning appointments and statistics and other public matters—nagging, nagging, nagging.[9] She was always at it: "Why was that, Warren?"—"Strange you had to do that. You didn't want to." "I've heard you say you never would." "There's something behind all this bullying—it's getting to be blackmail." "Why don't you say something?" "What woman is at the bottom of it?" "I'm no fool, Warren. You can't fool me. What I know, I know." "You can't call your soul—your own." "You're afraid of these men!" "Why? Tell me, why?" "I'll find out. I always find out!"

Nag! Nag! Nag!

If only she would let him alone. He had always been loyal to the Party. That was the most important factor in his career. A model of Party discipline. Always at the Party's call.

A private life that ignores the demands of conventional society with regard to marital fidelity does not necessarily preclude the possibility of a public life devoted to the service of the country. Does it,—I asked myself? Such dual personalities are by no means unknown in our 20th Century civilization.

And yet, I knew that—whatever President Harding's private life may have been, however thrilling, however romantic, it was now to be brought forth to light—in agony. And I was also forced to admit from what I knew—by undisputed evidence, that his public career had not been entirely devoted to upbuilding the dignity and honor of the country. All the gang knew it—all of my superior officers knew it. What could and would be the final outcome?

He was now being hoisted on his own domestic petard and Mrs. Harding was holding that petard in her own relentless hands. What expiation would she demand of him? God knows? Heaven help him. I felt sorry for him.

Before the concrete evidence Mrs. Harding had confronted him with, I surmised that naturally there would have to be an admission of guilt. Would he make this forced confession or would he show defiance in the face of all the evidence? But—what man is not guilty I mused? And how many men in such an hour of reckoning have cried out that they were being unjustly punished by the wrath of God, for the sins that no man is without.

Would the grace of an indulgent Providence save him? I hoped so.

Why should I have to get mixed up in the affair at all? The evidence was there: his letters to Nan Britton, her diaries, the jewelry he had sent to her and the baby—all the mass of data. Mrs. Harding had them.

I had merely done my duty. I had performed my office. I would be loyal to my client, as the ethics of my calling demanded,—no matter what my personal preferences or feelings might be. My loyalty and services belonged to her, but our sympathies are our own. I reasoned that it was not likely that I would be called upon to take sides—one way or the other. Why should I? She had all the stuff in her own possession. Little did I know!

My real sympathies were with the President. I could visualize his mental suffering. I knew that he did not want to hurt Mrs. Harding. He would never have hurt her intentionally.

Abruptly I got up and put on my hat and started out to obey the summons.

As I slowly covered the short distance from my home to the White House,—I felt a weight of lead on each foot. My sympathies were given freer play than was expedient. I could not afford the human luxury of sympathy. Whatever scene was before me must be met,—professionally.

I recalled my first summons from Mrs. Harding to come to the White House. It had been in the fall—October. I remembered the men on the lawn raking dead leaves and carting them off. I recalled the leaf I had picked up: withered, wrinkled—that reminded me of the face of an old woman.

It was early Spring now. I knew that all over the country the freed earth was suddenly bursting into life. There was a fragrance in the atmosphere of the hawthorn, faint and elusive—like the sweet smell of the English country-side in May. There was a first robin red-breast hopping over the newly brightening grass of the White House lawn. The old dead leaves had decayed and new fresh life was germinating.

But Mrs. Harding would never let herself be replaced—by a fresh young girl. Not she! She would cling to her Warren with her last withering gasp. As she should do—of course. Of course! She was his wife! And yet,—suddenly, my thoughts veered,—for I was getting deeper into philosophical ramifications than the occasion warranted.

What had I let myself in for I asked myself? Mrs. Harding had sent for me. She was excited. Again, I knew that she had undoubtedly confronted the President with all the proofs of his infidelity. Where did I come in? What could she do to me? Why need I be a party to this upheaval?

I realized fully that the scene toward which I was inevitably headed would be between the President of the United States and his wife, the First Lady of the Land, and that it would have an historical setting,—in the White House, the Executive Mansion.

The frailties and weaknesses of human nature are no respecter of persons. I must forget their eminence and regard them as two regular human beings. This would simplify things for me. I would be on familiar ground. It was the practical, sensible thing to do.

As usual I entered the 'viaduct' way, and went directly to Mrs. Harding's apartment. I was indeed a familiar figure by this time and the guards, servants and maids paid no attention to me, except to nod a greeting.

As I approached the door of her room, I saw that it was open, and I heard loud voices:—a jarring unfamiliar note in that place. Through the open door,—I saw the President stride across the room and out an opposite door.

The atmosphere was charged. I felt the thing,—even before I took cognizance of Mrs. Harding, in her inevitable flowered dress, with pale, set face, and determination written all over her countenance. She was standing in the middle of the floor, her hands were straight at her side—feet set wide apart,—like a General on the field of battle.

Her eyes were gleaming in her white, wrinkled face,—dilating, expanding, like those of a cat or a panther. I saw that her hands hanging straight at her side were clenched until the knuckles were white. She was trembling all over. And withal, her excitement held a triumphant challenge.

Without a word of greeting, she began:

"I've had a scene with Warren.[15] He knows now that I know—everything. I hold the whip hand,—and don't you

"I must forget their eminence and regard them as two regular human beings."

forget it! You will receive a letter from him soon. He will condemn you—unmercifully."

"What have I done?"

"He'll tell you. And what I want to know now from you is this: what is your attitude going to be? Are you going to stand by me, or by him?"

Chapter XV

President Harding Fires Means

EVADING a direct reply to her question, I said:

"You say the President will write me a letter. Letters have never bothered me, Mrs. Harding. Sometimes, a personal contact will put me on the defensive—but really I prefer personal contacts.

"You would not choose personal contact with—the President?" The last word came, with bated breath.

"The President is a man,—at the moment,—no more, nor less,—from my point of view. Personally, I never hide behind letters. I am not in the least afraid of people who write letters,—especially when one can talk face to face. Why write?"

She came back abruptly to her chief point of interest.

"Would you give him any information that you have or any copies of documents?"

I put her mind at ease immediately.

"You are my client, Mrs. Harding. What has taken place between you and me so far as I am concerned is confidential. You can tell him what you see fit. It is my intention to tell him nothing."

She was not yet fully assured.

"Don't you know that he can have you discharged and indicted?"

I shrugged uneasy shoulders.

"There are other ways to make a living—in that contingency."

She took a step toward me and lowered her voice. She said:

"Warren Harding can be aroused, you know!"

Using the parlance of the street, I replied:

"The bigger the man, the harder he falls."

"What do you mean?"

"I mean—that Warren G. Harding,—your husband, is President of the United States. He has been a musician and he has been a printer. I shall view him from the standpoint of any other average human being,—say, as a typesetter. At the moment, in a crisis like this,—his being President of the United States is—incidental."

From what followed, I have always believed that there was a dictaphone in that room,—that the President had had it put there to hear our conversation. I had scarcely finished my explanation of how I was viewing the President, when suddenly he appeared in the door, through which I had seen him pass just before I entered.

At a bound, it seemed, he was standing directly in front of me, with extended arm, and pointing his finger straight at me. His infuriated face was crimson: he was trembling all over.

But this attitude gave me reassurance, incongruous as that may appear. Had he entered the room with clenched fists, I would have expected a physical blow,—or had he held clenched fists at his side,—I would have feared the possibility of physical encounter, but the fact that he pointed his finger indicated conclusively that he was not going to attack me. A pointed finger signifies accusation and not combat,—reproach, not a fight.

He said:

"I've instructed the Department of Justice to discharge you. By what authority have you put the President of the United States under surveillance?"

"You ask two questions in one. Which do you want me to answer first?"

I was entirely composed and smiling.

Mrs. Harding was still standing as she was when I came

in, looking first at the President and then at me. She kept her composure. Her thin lips were pressed together.

He snapped back:

"Either you prefer."

I replied:

"I allowed the Department of Justice to publicly discharge me on one occasion, to prevent the House of Representatives from impeaching your friend,—Mr. Harry M. Daugherty, Attorney-General of the United States. This enabled me to steal from Congressman Woodruff and Congressman Johnson [29] all the documentary evidence that would have impeached him. By this public discharge, these Congressmen assumed that I was antagonistic to Mr. Harry M. Daugherty and to you and your clique. This enabled me successfully to rope these Congressmen. This little incident is entirely familiar to you. Have you—perhaps—another—similar—job?"

This reminder may have been in bad taste,—doubtless it was—but to save my soul, I could not forego the satisfaction of it. I paused and waited for a reply—but he made none. The red in his face had slowly turned to white. I continued:

"In reply to your second question, I didn't have you under surveillance—but I did have your mistress and the mother of your child under surveillance."

He staggered backward a step or two, but caught himself by holding to the side of a couch. A small end-table overturned. Mrs. Harding darted behind him, picked up the table and carefully set it upright again.

"Calm yourself, Warren. Now calm yourself. Don't make a scene. Calm yourself," she pleaded.

He apparently neither saw nor heard her. I saw his racked face change from gray to livid green, and I watched his hands twitching in the damp quivering of torture. His voice was thick. He said:

"Well,—you'll find that you have been summarily discharged—and your discharge paper is now at your home, 903—16th Street," he answered.[16]

I am but a human being myself. To get angry is another forbidden human luxury. But it was all I could do at the moment to control myself. However, I did. I spoke in the most casual conversational tone, as I replied:

"Will you allow me to confirm that statement by using the phone? I'm an investigator. That will enable me to talk more intelligently to you. May I?"

"You certainly may."

To his surprise, I think—I walked over and picked up the phone on Mrs. Harding's desk and called my home number at 903—16th Street. Mr. Patterson, my father-in-law and also my confidant, answered, and before I could ask any question, he told me that a most important letter had just come for me from Mr. Harry M. Daugherty, telling me to turn in my badge and credentials as an investigator for the Department of Justice—that I was forthwith discharged.

I hung up the phone and turned back in the room. I spoke to the President: "Your statement is correct, sir. If I know the interpretation of the law,—I must turn over my badge and credentials to the first higher official with whom I come in contact. And so—not to violate the law, I herewith turn them over to you."

I extended my hand with the badge and credentials. He took a step backward.

"You refuse?"

"I do."

I then offered them to Mrs. Harding. She made no move to take them.

"You—also?"

"That's none of my business."

"Very well. I shall place them here."

I laid them on the top of her desk. I said:

"Gaston Means—citizen—is now talking to you—and not Gaston Means, Agent of the Department of Justice. Either of you—or both of you—can go as far as you like."

It was the President who spoke:

"Don't you know that you have violated the law and that you are going to be indicted? Don't you know that the Congress of the United States has provided that the Secret Service of the United States shall guard the President,—and not the Department of Justice?"

"I understand that. I have not guarded you," was my quick defense.

He was equally quick with the challenge:

"What have you been doing with Mrs. Harding?"

"The law says nothing whatever about anybody guarding the President's wife. I guess the law assumed that she is a nonentity. At least that is what Col. T. B. Felder told me when I sought his legal advice in connection with the work for Mrs. Harding. He assured me that I was within the law."

His face flamed crimson.

"Oh, you've been consulting lawyers about what you've been doing—have you?"

"No. I consulted them before I began what I was doing,—just like you did with Mr. Daugherty. As I understand it, according to Col. Felder, the Secret Service is designated under the law to guard you day and night. Expenses are provided. If there is any conflict between the Department of Justice and the Secret Service in connection with this,—I suggest that Mr. Harry Daugherty seek an opinion from his close and personal and professional friend—Col. T. B. Felder,—always, in fact,—on any matter of importance."

"You have the reputation of being a good investigator, Mr. Means. I guess that means—you seek legal advice before you proceed."

"Always. I'd be a fool, not to, on any matter of importance."

"Well,—what I want you to get down to and get down to right now,—is this: where are those papers and letters and documents and articles—all those things that you got for Mrs. Harding. She tells me that you have them."

This gave me a very disagreeble surprise, but I was powerless to deny.

"She's your wife. What she tells you, you wouldn't question, would you?" I parried.

"I want you to produce them right away. Bring them over here—to this place—to me. And if you don't, I'll have you indicted regardless of what Col. Felder told you,—or anybody else. The Secret Service is the only branch of the Government that has any power to attend to any Presidential matters,—in any connection whatever."

"According to Col. Felder, that is entirely correct. But the law does not mention anything about the President's wife. Mrs. Harding was my client."

Again, he charged toward me with his pointed finger.

"By God, I want you to know,—and Col. Felder to know,—that you are not going to get away with a matter of this kind. I want all those letters, diaries, photographs and articles—all material you have gotten together—and I intend to have them. Mrs. Harding tells me—they are in your possession. You will bring them to me. And I want you to sit right down there now—at that table, and I'll bring a stenographer in here,—and you'll sit there and dictate every detail exactly as it has transpired between you and Mrs. Harding and all concerned."

During this long tirade, with voice choking with rage and chagrin and the words falling over each other, the President had been striding back and forth—back and forth across the room,—like an infuriated lion. Mrs. Harding had sat down in a low, old fashioned rocker, and was rocking violently back and forth.

I said:

"You might have told me to do this—two hours ago,—but not now! For I am not with the government and I don't take orders from you or anybody else. By what authority are you trying to give orders to me now?"

His reply was,—and almost as though speaking to himself:

"I don't believe you realize the purport of what you are doing."

"I can't help or prevent any opinion you may have but the results speak for themselves. I am not going to sit down at any table and dictate any statement to you—or anybody else. Mrs. Harding can tell you whatever she cares for you to know. That's her business and regardless of what she may tell you I am not going to contradict it. I've got too much sense, under any circumstances to say to a man that his wife is not telling the truth. Neither am I going to produce any letters or diaries or photographs or articles—or anything else for you. Neither will I tell you anything about where they are."

Still he was pacing the floor—back and forth—back and forth across the room. Now facing me and then with back turned toward me.

She played her game well, as all women do under such circumstances. She had kept entirely silent, except now and then to say to the President:

"Calm yourself, Warren. Calm yourself. Don't make a scene."

She felt safe for she now realized that I would not betray her.

With my statement to him that I did not intend to produce anything, or dictate any statement, the interview was over.

Unwisely perhaps,—I made one final thrust:

" 'Get the facts!' That's your own life slogan. 'Get-the-facts.' Well,—you've got the facts! What is your complaint?"

He turned and strode out of the room. Just as he was disappearing through the door, he whirled on Mrs. Harding and shook his clenched fist almost in her face and said:

"You have ruined me. You have ruined me! You and your contemptible detectives."

His gesture of shaking his clenched fist in her face was really the biggest surprise the interview had given me.

Then he turned to me with these parting words:

"And as for you, you have been discharged and you'll be indicted in twenty-four hours. You will never again put your foot in the White House. And—I'll have those papers. I'll have search warrants—and you'll be under surveillance for the rest of your life——"

I made no response but I looked him straight in the eye. He had pointed his *finger* at me, but oh, how he did shake his *fist* at Mrs. Harding.

The President had said that I would never enter the White House again. To be sure, that was my last visit to the White House during Pres. Harding's life, but it was not so very many months before I entered its portals again.

And then—President Harding was there,—lying in magnificent grandeur—in his gorgeous casket amid banks of flowers in the center of the East room: a commanding figure even more regal and kingly looking in death than he had been in life. And the nation was in mourning.

I was there—at Mrs. Harding's very urgent and special written request—standing at the head of the casket with four of my strong-arm men behind me. Mrs. Harding had very good and sufficient reasons of her own for having me there.

Chapter XVI

Jess Smith Warns Means

As soon as the President left the room Mrs. Harding ran toward the hall and opened the door. Then as if her strength had failed her, she sank down in a chair. She was breathing hard.

I picked up my hat where I had thrown it on a table as I entered and turned to go through the opened door. By the time I reached the door she had jumped up and was standing by it.

As I was passing through the door, she slipped into my hand three one thousand dollar bills. I glanced at them and had I followed my first impulse, I would have thrown them back into her face. She had said no word in my defense. She had not even told the President that she had employed me. She had said that I held the papers in my possession,—had calmly placed the responsibility of everything on my shoulders.

Well—my shoulders are broad,—that's true,—and in this instance they proved broad enough to reach eventually all the way from the White House in Washington to the Penitentiary in Atlanta, and to carry on their accommodating breadth a pack-load of sins of numerous other people!

I retraced my steps to my home 903—16th St., N. W.

I was out of a job—fired! Had I made a political *faux pas?* Perhaps. I had been summarily dismissed by Mr. Harry M. Daugherty, Attorney-General of the United States, by direct command from President Harding. I could no longer draw my weekly salary of $89.33-1/3. But I thought—I would continue to live at 903—16th Street. N. W., paying $1,000.00 a month rent. I would continue to be driven by my private chauffeur in my private $5,000.00 car. The routine of my daily life would change in no way whatever,—except that I would be relieved of the tedious make-believe work at my desk at the Department of Justice.

All this would continue,—I reasoned—unless—unless—? Oh, well, I would sit pat and wait for the next move.

It was not long in coming. That night between twelve and one, after I had retired,—there was one long ring,—one short ring,—one long ring, two short rings on the confidential electric button from the rear entrance of the yard of the house, that set the buzzer going in my bed room. I realized that my rear entrance caller was familiar with the confidential signals.

Pursuing my usual methods, I went to the window and with a flash light in my hand pointed it down to the entrance gate, thus letting the ringer know that I would be there.

I dressed and went to the rear gate. One of Mr. Douglas Boyd's secretaries, who was a close confidant of Mrs. Boyd, stood outside. He handed me a leatheroid sample case and said:

"When you have examined this, you will know what it is. Keep it until you hear otherwise."

Without making any reply, I took possession of the sample case, closed the door, went into my office and opened the lid.

I saw at a glance what the case contained: the letters from President Harding to Nan Britton—her diaries—the articles of jewelry and all the data Mrs. Harding had collected through my agency.

Mrs. Harding was a fast, efficient worker, with no regard whatever for anything but the accomplishment of her own designs and purposes.

I realized that it was up to me—to be a fast worker also. The next morning, after having put in a long distance call to Col. Felder in New York,—I boarded the train around nine o'clock at the Union Station. I carried the sample case with its contents in a larger suit case. On arrival in New York, I hopped in a taxi and went directly to Col. Felder's office at 165 Broadway. It was very early morning but he was expecting me and was there, waiting. I delivered the case to him.

I explained the entire situation. I told him that undoubtedly I would be served with some kind of court papers and search warrants and so forth, and that I wanted to be in a position to say that such documents that had been in my possession, were not in my possession now. I wanted him to hold them—as evidence for my defense, whatever that defense might happen to be. As such, no power or process of law could get them from him.

I returned to Washington, and on my arrival at my home the next night, Mr. Patterson told me that the phone had been ringing continuously every moment all day long: messages from Mr. Burns at the Department of Justice, and from others, and that any number of alleged messengers had come to the door to ask my whereabouts.

Jess Smith came to my house that afternoon. He slipped in through the back gate entrance as usual. I was stretched on a couch in my office,—comfortable in shirt sleeves and reading the *New York Times*.

Jess was so excited he could scarcely speak.

"Good God—man—how can you lie there and read a newspaper?"

I threw the papers down and sat up.

"Got nothing else to do," I smiled.

"You're damn right, you've got nothing else to do. Everybody knows—you're fired!"

"I've been fired before."

"This is different and you know it. You were in with

the clique then,—doing their dirty work for them. And now—who knows where you are?"

"Don't worry Jess,—I'm right here and I'll stay right here."

"Don't you realize what a serious mess you've gotten into? Don't you know—they are not going to let you do any talking. They'll silence you, Gaston,—if they have to do it with a Maxim Silencer."

"Sit down, Jess,—and relax and tell me what it's all about."

He sat down facing me.

"It's reported that you talked to the President as if he were a day laborer."

"It might be so interpreted," I affirmed.

"And furthermore, they say,—you got scared and ran away."

"Got scared, eh?"

"That's another thing nobody will ever be able to do. Get scared! The first man that gets scared and they think will either run away or talk,—zip! He'll blow out! I tell you, Gaston—you're in a dangerous fix. And I mean it!"

"Just what sort of danger do you think I'm in, Jess?"

"Plenty! They are not going to have anybody talking. They'll make away with you—I tell you,—and I know what I'm talking about. Nobody shall talk. Dead men can't talk!"

"Whoever said—I was going to talk. They know damn well that I'll never do any talking."

"Well—you've crossed swords with the 'Big Boss,'—understand? They'll get you! You know too much. My God—man,—you could blow the lid off of Washington! Don't you suppose they know that? And don't think they'll sit quiet and wait for you to do it either."

"What will they do?"

"Send you on some mission,—somewhere,—some important mission and lead you into a trap! Slip some little white powder in a drink—maybe,—that white stuff that eases one off,—quickly and gently. You can be shot down—from ambush. You can be railroaded to prison. Don't you worry about what they can't do!"

"This fortress they've put me in—is a pretty safe place, don't you think?"

"No. You can't stay barricaded in here forever. Don't you know—tyrants always make away with the instruments they've used? The moment you've outlived your usefulness—look out! Or—the moment you become a danger, —look out!"

"How about yourself?" I asked quizzically. As I had suspected he was beginning to be afraid for himself. Jess was never noted for bravery.

"You've said it! Don't think I don't know how much they love me! I'm not blind and deaf and dumb. Pretty soon, it's a-gonna be—every man for himself! I'm telling you. But you're in danger now, Gaston, take that tip from me."

Of course, I knew that Jess was not telling all that he knew, and I saw that he was sincerely and honestly alarmed for my safety. He went on:

"You remember that girl that was hit on the head with a bottle in the H Street house? Remember that? All covered over. Nobody knew a breath."

"Yes."

"Remember that young reporter who somehow got wind of the truth and dared think that the story of a girl hit on the head with a bottle during a party in the "Little House of Mystery" was news for his newspaper? He was a fine young fellow,—a good reporter whose duty it was to get news. You remember what happened to him—don't you?"

"Yes."

"And you remember how this young chap inquired of

me—about what had taken place at the party? I tried to throw him off the track. But I didn't. He dared still further. He went for confirmation and details to the 'gang'. Didn't take long to slap him into an insane asylum,—did it?"

"What on earth can that have to do with me?"

"Think it over. You're in danger, Gaston. And—*I'm in danger.*"

"Didn't take that young reporter long to get out of Saint Elizabeth's either, did it?" I reminded still further.

"But you haven't got a rich and powerful Daddy to come along and get you out,—and fix everything—have you? I know I haven't."

And neither did Jess Smith know what I knew,—that it was not Gaston Means that had always been considered the weak link in our chain,—but it was *Jess Smith.*

"Now see here, Jess,—you look out for number one."

I read approval to this suggestion in every line of his face.

"From now on,—I've got a feeling that that's what we've all got to do," he replied.

"Well,—you do that,—and don't worry about me." After a moment's silence, I asked:

"Who said I ran away?"

"Everybody knows that you were not here," he informed.

"Now, listen. I was accused of murder one time and I ran back to the scene at sixty miles an hour to meet those charges. I may be guilty Jess—of everything in the world,—but two things: no one has ever been able to say or will ever be able to say; one:—that I am a coward,—and the other, no one will ever dare say that I am not a good investigator."

"That's right, too."

"If I ran away,—I certainly ran back just as fast as I ran away,—with the same speed and in the same conveyance that carried me away."

Jess lingered around the place—was extremely nervous

and seemed loath to go. He jumped at every little sound. I invited him to stay to dinner with me and he did. We ate together in the basement dining room.

It was quite dark when we had finished dinner. We came back into the office and still he did not go. Slowly—it began to dawn on me that Jess was actually afraid to leave—to go out of the house.

"For the love of Pete,—Jess,—I swear, I believe you're afraid to get out of this house."

This made him mad but he said:

"That's silly, of course! Gaston, I tell you I know they're going to get you—somehow."

"You're afraid,—if you leave,—somebody might mistake you for me?"

"It's reasonable, isn't it?"

"All right. Get your hat, Buddy,—and I'll go out first,—and they can get a first shot at me. Or—I'll walk out with you—and take you all the way to the Wardman Park Hotel,—and fix your milk bottle and nipple."

He flushed and slapped his hat on his head.

"It's damn funny,—ain't it? You'll see. You'll see I'm right!"

He was pathetic in his physical fright at any mention of danger. And in warning me, his thoughts had worked themselves around into an actual terror of what might and could happen to himself.

I went with him all the way to the door of the Wardman Park Hotel and left him there. His parting words were:

"There's a crash coming, Gaston. I feel it! Things are heading up,—and when it does come,—every man for himself. But, you and I ought to stick together. We must stick together."

"Of course, Jess. Of course," I assured, as I left him.

I walked leisurely back to my home. And—I wondered how far right Jess Smith might not be, after all!

Mr. Patterson, my father-in-law and confidant met me at the door of my home and told me that a visitor was in the office. I went in immediately.

One of Mr. Boyd's secretaries was waiting for me. I recognized him as the man who had brought the leatheroid sample case to me the night before and which I had taken to Col. Felder in New York.

"What can I do for you, sir?" was my greeting. He said:

"It is understood that a complaint is to be sworn out against you,—to enable the issuance of a search-warrant for this house."

"Sit down," I invited with a degree of cordiality that was sincere, for I felt that this man might give me valuable information. He sat down. I availed myself of the swivel chair at my desk.

"Well?" I encouraged.

He informed:

"I am instructed to ask you if you are prepared to meet such a contingency?"

I knew without inquiry that he had been sent by Mrs. Boyd—from Mrs. Harding.

"That depends—on what the search warrants call for and how far they search?" I hedged.

He clarified.

"So far as I know—the interest centers in the leatheroid sample case I handed you last night."

I made his mind easy on that score.

"Oh, they can search here all they please for that. But let them specify what floors are to be searched. No use to tear up the whole house. Or—if they wish—they can go the limit."

I knew that he would report to Mrs. Boyd, who would report to Mrs. Harding. I also knew that this man hung around the Department of Justice and overheard many important conversations. I said casually:

"Well—what do you know?"

His reply was frank and to the point:

"There are high influences that are going to cause you trouble."

"Think so?"

"I know it."

"How? Where did you hear?"

He smiled: "Not on the streets. It is generally rumored around among those 'in the know' that you've been discharged from the Department of Justice."

"That is perfectly true."

I was acutely aware that what I said to this man would be repeated and would get back to those same "high influences" he had been talking about. I would be careful—but also it was my opportunity. I said, weighing each word:

"When anybody in the United States sees fit to move against me,—actuated by any motive that is manifest on the face of the complaint or warrant,—and with the charges plainly made, why I will meet them at the proper time, at the proper place and in the proper way. Now—listen! If any framed-up charges are made against me,—for the purpose of search-warrants—as a defense for myself, I'll give out to the members of the Press all over the country, the entire history of the Col. Darwin matter."

He looked puzzled, for I knew that he could not understand the full purport of what I had said, although I believed that he would remember. He inquired:

"Are you saying this to me—confidentially,—to go no further?"

I'd make that clear.

"No. I'm saying it as a warning,—and as a defense."

Forty-eight hours after this conversation I was tipped off that I was under constant surveillance. Seventy-two hours later, I discovered that this was a fact, from my own observation. Also that my mail was being tampered with and that my telephone wires were tapped.

Had Jess Smith been right?

No search-warrant was ever issued. They had sense enough to know that I wouldn't keep any papers or documents where any search-warrant could reach them.

A day or so later,—I had another friendly visitor with a friendly warning. This time, it was Col. Miller.

He said: "Gaston—you're a man of sense and—perception. You stay off the streets of Washington. Don't go into any hotel lobbies—or into any public buildings. You understand?"

"I do."

"There are several reasons. You don't want to be cornered by any newspaper man. The papers may be tipped off. In fact,—they are beginning to ask pertinent questions. Somebody has already talked—too much."

"They know—I don't talk," I said to him.

"They know—*nothing—now.* Watch your step."

His instructions followed along nicely with the very plan of action that I had marked out for myself: to stay quietly around the house and watch eventualities. Also, it gave me opportunity to avail myself of the pleasure of devoting a little more time to my family.

Every day,—my wife and boy and nurse and some close relative would all go with me in my car—starting very early in the morning—for a long trip, down into Maryland and the Eastern Shore or into Virginia, visiting interesting historic battle-grounds. Once we made the trip to Harper's

Ferry. We would return usually about midnight. This proceeded along for days.

Months previous to all this, I had conducted an investigation of Col. Darwin for Mrs. Harding. After this investigation, Mrs. Harding had refused to entertain Col. Darwin and he had been dropped by all of them.

And now, while I was hibernating and rusticating with my family and under surveillance, important newspapers all over the country, began to ask important questions. The *Chicago Tribune* was the first. Rumors—insistent rumors, were being picked up by the Associated Press and the United Press and the Universal Service. Prominent editors of leading newspapers throughout the country were coming to Washington to ask pointed questions.

Who was tipping these newspapers? My skirts were clear, for I was under surveillance. In the meantime, I knew that an attempt was being made to build up a case against me either in Washington or in New York. They were preparing to sacrifice me to placate public rumors. I also knew that it was hard to build up a case against me—without drawing Jess Smith and others into it—even if I should show a disposition to keep quiet. The very thought and first hint of this threw Jess Smith into a paroxism of fear and terror,—for me and for himself.

"They'll not do it. Calm yourself, Jess. They can't do it," I repeated to him many times, as he would come to my home for comfort and I believed in my heart,—for the sense of protection that the place gave him.

"It's war,—I tell you. It's war!" he gasped.

"Stop and consider this one thing, Jess. As long as this house—903—16th Street—stands as it is—nobody will dare do anything. If the newspapers but knew it, an investigation into this home of mine,—would land most of the clique into jail for life!"

Jess was ready with a fresh horror.

"They'll burn down this house, first thing you know. Why look! Didn't they burn down all of those tanks that had been full of liquor and which they had first emptied? Every last one of them? And nobody knew that they had been emptied. Millions and millions of dollars worth?"

"They'll not burn this house," I reiterated with what assurance I could muster.

Just then,—my phone rang. My phone had been strangely silent all these weeks.

I answered. A voice said:

"I want to speak to Gaston Means."

"This is Gaston Means."

I had recognized the voice before he said: "Mr. Means,—this is President Harding. I know—that there are differences between us,—but I believe in a crisis, we can both forget those differences for the moment, for the good of all concerned."

"I know that I can."

"I want you to do a very special piece of work for me."

"What is it? I am at your service."

"Somebody is talking to the newspapers. I want you to put Col. Darwin under strictest surveillance immediately. Do you understand?"

"I do, sir."

"That is all."

"Thank you."

We hung up. I did indeed understand. And I had to laugh when I looked at Jess Smith standing in the middle of the floor,—his mouth hanging open,—his face white as chalk,—and his big eyes almost popping out of his head.

"Jess. I've an important assignment from President Harding."

"Good—God—Almighty!"

Chapter XVII

Jess Smith Threatens to "Tell Everything"

"It's a trap! I told you! It's a trap, Gaston. Don't you do it. It's a trap," Jess Smith sputtered.

"This is no trap. This is business, and don't you forget it."

"You're under surveillance, yourself," he warned.

"Probably. But I shall investigate our friend Col. Darwin. Watch me."

Jess was not to be convinced. He made a last thrust.

"You can do what you damn please, but I'm gonna look out for number one. Watch *me!*"

I was glad when he was gone, for I needed to be alone and assemble my thoughts.

Col. Darwin was one of the most magnetic men that I have ever come in contact with. Before the Harding Administration, he had been playing around Washington for years—was an Oil Promoter representing Western interests. When, under previous administrations, the Tea-Pot-Dome and California oil fields belonging to the government were turned over to the Navy and thus taken out of the possibility of development by private corporations, Col. Darwin realized that his greatest ambitions had been thwarted—that is, for private corporations to get control of the supposedly wonderful oil fields.

The Oil scandal of the Harding Administration is old stuff, but even so,—it has yet to be excelled in criminal annals for sheer thievery and deviltry. It has been thrashed out and over in public trials and through the Press. I shall not rehash it, although the real truth has never been told.

Col. Darwin was a frequent visitor at my home 903—16th Street, N. W. He was a very shrewd and clever man. He was equally captivating to both men and women.

His career with women had been spectacular. He had married six wives, and it was said that $300,000 was the minimum that he had gotten from any one of them. He was a wonderful believer in the Bible and the literal interpretation of it—"that woman was made for man." I've heard him say: "Give a little telephone switch operator three flowers and a piece of ribbon, and she's your slave. Never under any circumstances give her money. She will think you commercialize her."

In one of his love affairs, he slipped up. He courted, and successfully, the daughter of a great hardware merchant in Washington worth millions. He managed to get from the girl all the wealth her mother had left her and was scheming to dip into her father's money-bags when the father stepped in and kidnaped the daughter and claimed that she was insane.

"Sure, she's insane," said Col. Darwin. "Insane with love."

The man actually behind all the scenes in the Sinclair and the Doheny Oil transactions was Col. Darwin. Of course, the Executive Order from President Harding, about three months after his inauguration, and the transfer of those oil fields from the Navy to the Department of the Interior had been later declared illegal by the Supreme Court. Mr. Daugherty knew at the time that the transfer was illegal and President Harding must likewise have known it,—and hence the significance of the message that I indirectly sent to the 'higher powers' via Mr. Boyd's secretary. They knew what I meant and they knew that I was on the defensive.

The one way to obtain tremendous blackmail money was the threat of the possibility of selling to some newspaper a sensational story backed up by documentary evidence easily confirmable.

Col. Darwin was proceeding along those lines, spurred on by a sense of outrage and injustice at his social ostracism. He handled the Presidential clique's end of the graft, —from the Oil leases. Mr. Fall never passed them anything that I know of. Many other high officials in Washington were also afraid of Col. Darwin.

Through Col. Darwin's tips, that acquisition of these oil fields had been gained by private companies, a marvelous advance was brought about on the Stock Exchange on those stocks. All those 'in the know', including many high officials, derived enormous profits by buying the stocks. All of these transactions and intrigues were discussed and decided at 903—16th St. N. W.

Col. Darwin had been a regular visitor at the White House. Through an anonymous letter, Mrs. Harding was first informed of his career with women. This was one thing that Mrs. Harding could not and would not stand for. She demanded that President Harding investigate the matter. The President did not believe the reports, but at Mrs. Harding's insistence, I was assigned to that investigation.

I had conducted the investigation single-handed and the reports and rumors were confirmed. Mrs. Harding invited Colonel Darwin no more to the White House. Mr. Daugherty was forced to drop him also. Colonel Darwin bought a magnificent estate up in Pennsylvania and retired to it, living the life of a country gentleman of great wealth and leisure, with fine horses and fine dogs.

When we began to hear the first rumblings of a gathering storm it was evident that somebody was tipping off the newspapers. And now—from the message received from the President over the phone, I knew that Colonel Darwin was the man under suspicion. And it was my business to find out.

I went to work with a vim, but try hard as I would, attacking from every possible angle, I could get hold of no tangible documentary evidence that Colonel Darwin was giving out tips to the Press.

Several times, however, we had turned over to our clique anonymous typewritten articles conveying information in this manner, so definite and specific that they could not fail to impress and convince. These I did succeed in tracing to Colonel Darwin's typewriter. But there are too many typewriters exactly alike in the world to be absolutely positive.

The situation was becoming appalling. Where would it end? We heard rumors of Senate investigations. The word "impeachment" was not infrequently mentioned by many leading newspapers.

The clique again assembled at 903—16th Street,—holding daily conferences. Col. Felder came over frequently from New York to advise.

All the time I was working on the Col. Darwin investigation, Jess Smith was hanging around 903—16th Street day and night. At each visit he seemed to have worked himself up into a new frenzy of imagining—the terrible things that might happen to me,—and to himself.

One day he spoke in a hoarse whisper:

"You remember C. F. Cramer,[17]—don't you? He died, suddenly in his own bath room in his own house. They called it—suicide."

I myself had done some wondering about Cramer.

"He had domestic troubles a-plenty," I informed. Jess continued:

"They were a devoted couple when they first came to Washington, you remember? Cramer had troubles enough. Yes, that's so."

"Let him rest, with his troubles."

"He eased off,—with that 'little white powder' stuff. He may have done it—and he may not! His going was terribly convenient and opportune."

"Cut it out, Jess. That's enough."

"I tell you, Gaston, it's war—to the finish. I'm looking out for number one and for God's sake, Gaston—you be careful too. You're so reckless. You never sense danger."

"I've nothing to fear. They all know—I do no talking."

"You may be forced to talk."

"Hardly. I never have been, if I didn't want to."

Jess was ready with another horror:

"You know Harry M. Mingle, don't you? You remember him. What sort of a menace was he? You'd better listen to me."

Harry M. Mingle was Attorney for the Japanese bankers, Matsui and Company. He was mixed up in the Standard Aircraft Case.

Jess went on:

"You investigated the Standard Aircraft Case yourself.[18] You know all about it. You built up a strong case. It was never prosecuted. Remember, they passed one hundred, one thousand dollar bills to you in the Bellevue Hotel and you passed them on to me, two hours later?[19] You remember?"

"They passed $500,000.00—all told," I stated grimly.

"You remember—Lawyer Thurston—of Boston, don't you? The Independent Attorney for the Alien Property Custodian Office. He died—suddenly—didn't he? More 'little white powder'. I'd stake my life on it."

"The moral is Jess: steer clear of the 'little white powder'." I laughed.

But Jess was not through. His imagination was working at fever heat.

"Remember 'Mickey'—poor little underdog? He outlived his usefulness. Well—he died, too—didn't he?"

"For Heaven's sake, Jess—think of something more cheerful. We've all got to die."

"Well—I don't propose to die until my time comes,—

not to accommodate anybody. I tell you that! I'm already getting my ducks in a row."

"That so? How?"

"To begin with,—I've got something you or nobody else knows I've got. I've got a detailed account of every transaction of every kind—that has passed through my hands!"

I was astounded and he saw it.

"What!"

I knew that a knowledge of this little fact would be a bombshell and a boomerang in the camp of the entire Harding clique.

"Did you think I'd be fool enough not to keep books?"

He was in dead earnest.

"Nobody keeps books, Jess, in this sort of business."

He nodded his head emphatically.

"Well, I do! In any sort of business. I always have. I always will."

I was turning this new development over in my mind.

We all knew that Jess Smith was the weak link in our chain. But this was a different phase of weakness—against which we had not calculated. And—the most dangerous one!

"Do the others know about this?" I asked curiously.

Jess went blandly on:

"I told them last night—and they had a million fits, cussed me all over the place and demanded that I give all my papers right over to them. Fat chance!"

I could well imagine the consternation that this bit of casual information had thrown into the souls of certain men. That Jess Smith had a minute and detailed written record of every transaction that had passed through his hands! *Everything* had passed through the hands of Jess Smith! What a record that must be! And how it could be verified and checked up!

"Just for curiosity, Jess,—where do you keep these records?" I inquired.

"A-ah. Wouldn't they like to know? Well—they won't."

"You wouldn't tell me?"

"Yes. I'd tell you, Gaston, only I want you to be in a position to say to them that you do not know, in case they ask you."

"That's better," I conceded. Jess was growing in acumen.

Many councils of war were held by all the clique together at 903—16th St., in the absence of Jess Smith, concerning his book-keeping habits and those fatal records that he had prepared and preserved with so much care and pains.

"Those records must be destroyed!" One of my superior officers said to me. "Means—you've never yet fallen down on getting documents when you went after them. I assign you right now—to get those records from Jess Smith."

"It can't be done," I stated bluntly.

"Why?"

"I believe—he carries them on his person, that's why."

"Did he tell you?"

"No. But that's my guess."

One spoke:

"Pity—an automobile can't run over him on the street—eh?"

Another retorted:

"And have those statements fall into the hands of the police. Are you crazy?"

"That wouldn't do—would it?" was conceded.

"Pity he didn't die under his appendicitis operation."

"Great pity!"

"He tells me he's getting better and better every day, and the wound has long been healed. He plays golf," I asserted, assuming that a man who plays frequent golf must be in fit physical condition.

"If he weren't such a careful driver he might run his car over a precipice?" was suggested.

"Not Jess."

Indirectly, by implication every known method of possibly getting rid of Jess Smith was discussed. "How fortunate if he should fall off a boat—on a trip." "Or—get hold of poison liquor." "Or—fall down an elevator shaft." "Or—fall off a swiftly moving train." And on and on!

"By God—he's a traitor to his government and should be treated as such," was boldly introduced.

This idea was a new and pleasing one. Traitor to the Government! If he wasn't that—what was he? But—oh, say—this was too dangerous a way to talk!

I put in a quick word of defense:

"Now see here. We don't know what Jess has in mind to do with his statements and itemized records. Don't brand him a traitor, until he shows his hand. He will probably do nothing. What could he do with them, without putting a noose around his own neck."

My reasoning was logical. But someone interposed:

"He's such a damn fraid-cat! He'll do anything to save his own hide. We've got to destroy those papers of his!"

"Give him the benefit of the doubt. You don't know—I don't know," I pleaded. I was sorry for Jess. He had lost his nerve completely. And, maybe, his terrifying sense of impending, threatening danger was not all imagination!

Some one was speaking:

"But when we do know—the beans will have been spilled! We've got to watch him—put him under surveillance every second—day and night."

I foresaw easy complications. I warned:

"That's difficult—unless we ourselves do the work—the watching and shadowing."

Who could be trusted to shadow Jess Smith? Nobody outside the clique.

"We'll have to do it, then—turn about. We'll all nursemaid him until we get those papers."

* * * * * * *

At that time I saw that my indictment was approaching,—I also saw that it was becoming necessary to appease the public. We all saw it. We had to make a sacrifice. Finally, I spoke to the assembly.

"Oh—Hell,—if that's what you want,—*make me it!* I'll plead guilty. I don't want to go to the 'Pen' though."

All leaped quickly with assurances:

"Oh—that's out of the question altogether,—your ever going to the 'Pen'! That shall never happen! Never! Never!

I was assured and reassured over and over again.

I came to a final and definite understanding. I was to plead guilty to any charge, and I was solemnly promised by all—that I would only be fined. This was agreeable to me. It would hurt me less than any of them, as I had already stood trial for my life.

Jess lingered that night after the others had gone. He was all nerves, wouldn't sit still a moment and looked on the verge of a collapse or hysterics,—I couldn't tell which.

"Gaston, don't you know that their agreements and intentions may all go up in smoke? Suppose it gets out of hand! Suppose it is lifted out of the hands of the District Attorney,—and the friendly Judge?"

"Jess—the Government of the United States has promised me—these things. I'm safe."

"Who's the Government of the United States?"

"Don't you know?"

"I know too well."

"Then watch your step and don't be a traitor. That word traitor has an ugly sound, Jess."

"Traitor, Who's traitor? They'll traitor you, if you don't look out! And they'll traitor me! They're looking out for number one,—every last one of them! And suppose—you go to trial—and there's a mix-up,—something goes wrong?"

"It can't go wrong. The Government of the United States is defending me."

Could one have a more powerful defender—than the highest legal tribunal on earth? If they cannot do anything they want to do—who can?

"I say—what if something slips a cog,—in this cut and dried Court procedure,—what,—I ask you, *what* might happen to *me?*"

I smiled.

"So—that's what's really troubling you most, eh, Jess?"

But Jess had no smile these days.

"I tell you—it's war. And every man for himself! You can make your grandstand play all you like,—with all the frills on it, but if you take my advice, Gaston, you'll drop this sacrifice business and do what I'm going to do."

"What's that?"

"Jump clear over the fence! *Turn State's evidence.*"

"So that's your racket."

"If needs must and the devil drives."

"Let him who can save himself," I quoted, but it went over his head.

Jess was left alone with me, and as per my agreement with the others, I had to keep him in sight until another member of the clique had him. So once again, to his great delight, for he was terrified now always to go alone on the streets, I got my hat and walked with him to the Wardman Park Hotel. There I left him. Jess Smith was under as strict surveillance as any man had ever been, or ever could be.

Well I knew then that Jess Smith was a traitor to his government and as such,—*he must cease to be.*

Chapter XVIII

Means Collects Prohibition Graft

It is very difficult really to protect anybody in crime. The human equation is so uncertain. So many unexpected things might happen. There might be so many swings around!

I may be sent to New York to protect a certain crowd,—allow them certain privileges,—say for two months. I might become suddenly ill,—or some accident happen to me, and another man put in my place. This man would know nothing about these special privileges. If I am off the job even for two days, anything might happen.

However, the big bootleggers in New York City wanted to pay for Federal protection and they were allowed to do this.[20] It became known in the underworld that they could pay this protection money to me. I was then stationed at the Vanderbilt Hotel first, in a gorgeous suite of rooms.

Our method there was simple. We had our runners, twenty-five men,—tipsters of the underworld. They were to keep us posted as to how much money different bootleggers were making. From their reports, my superior officers would estimate how much each one would pay, for protection. These bootleggers were then notified of the amount they would be expected to pay.

We did not want these bootleggers to be handing this money to any individual. I then had another room engaged,—on another floor of the Vanderbilt Hotel—we will say number 518. The register would show that this room had been engaged by another man. In similar manner, the room next door, number 517 was engaged.

In room 518, I took a big round glass bowl that one could easily see through, a big gold fish aquarium. We made a peep hole in the door connecting 518 and 517. This big glass bowl was conspicuously placed on a table in 518.

Our purchaser of protection was told to be in this room at a very definite hour, and he would find a place to put the money. One man would be instructed to enter the door of 518 at ten-sixteen (10:16) o'clock standard time; another say at eleven forty-two (11:42)—always on an odd minute, making sure of promptness and accuracy.

He would enter 518,—would see nobody, but he would see the glass bowl, which always had bills of money in it. From 517, through the peep hole in the door, I would see him all the time. They were instructed never to bring a bill less than $500.00. He would throw into the bowl so many $500.00 bills,—or so many $1,000.00 bills. I watched for two reasons: to make sure that he put his money into the bowl and to be sure that he took none out. As soon as he would step out, quick as a flash, I'd unlock the door between and lock the outside door. I'd check up. Never once was I short-changed! Then, I would leave the money,—say $10,-000.00 in the bowl, unlock the outside door again and wait for the next man. Each man was told to have his watch set exactly right by standard time and to come on the second.

Bootleggers are straight shooters in matters like that. Seeing money in the bowl gave them assurance that others were paying for protection also.

At night, after business was over—we generally observed union hours; all government employees are strict about that—and my day's work was done, I would go into my cash register—the glass bowl—and count up my sales for the day. Usually from $55,000.00 to $65,000.00 per day.

By this process,—at the Vanderbilt Hotel, we covered in territory besides New York City and New York State,—Massachusetts, Connecticut, Rhode Island, New Jersey and Eastern Pennsylvania.

A conservative estimate of the sum total of each visit I made, I would put at a quarter of a million,—$250,000.00.

With my bowl as my cash register, I was at various times at the Vanderbilt Hotel, the Pennsylvania Hotel, the McAlpin Hotel, the Imperial Hotel and the Herald Square Hotel.

Fully $7,000,000.00 passed through my glass bowl and through my hands.

After all collections had been made each day, I generally took the money to John T. King's office and put it in the safe there. Then, when the visit was over,—I carried the money to Washington to my home 903—16th St. and turned it over to Jess Smith, with my statement. He would take the money and the statements away and carefully check them up, and then he returned the money to 903—16th St., where it would find a safe resting place in the metal box buried twenty feet in my back yard. There it would stay until it was convenient for Jess Smith to place it elsewhere.

In similar manner, we collected protection graft in the city of Chicago and in St. Louis, Cincinnati, Detroit and San Francisco.

Jess Smith always kept detailed accounts of every transaction. He did this for his own protection and from habits of a life time. He had been a merchant. His accounts had to balance every Saturday night. Jess never took a nickel that did not belong to him.

My overhead expenses at the Vanderbilt Hotel were enormous. I have paid many a dinner check there for $50.00. I lived like a king. All "overhead" expenses were taken care of by Jess Smith. And Jess Smith had accurate written detailed records!

II

Handling the graft for the Alien Property Custodian was a very simple matter.[21] That also was part of my job. Attorneys from various places would come to the Alien Property Custodian's offices to file claims for the return of certain properties. At the office they would ascertain at what hotel these attorneys were registered. The attorneys were advised that there would necessarily be tremendous delays, —probably twelve or sixteen months before their claims could be considered: so many ahead of them, so much red tape and so forth.

Then, I was notified who these attorneys were and where they were registered. I would go to the hotel. If I did not already know them, or could not get a proper introduction, I would manage in any way possible to make contact,—to get into conversation with them. Eventually, I would ask them how they got along with their claim and they would reply that they hadn't gotten anywhere—so much delay. They were discouraged. I would ask them if they had ever handled any government departmental work before. Usually, they had not. Then I would suggest that they get in touch with a Mr. Thurston, a lawyer, in Boston. I would write down for them his full name and address. I told them that Mr. Thurston was an independent attorney. This was just a friendly tip to them to get quick action.

They would give Mr. Thurston a forty or fifty thousand dollar fee. He would split with Col. Miller. I handled no funds for them. I'd get a little *cut-in* gift—some two or three thousand dollars.

Every Alien Property claim case that was expedited came through Mr. Thurston. However, all matters of importance pertaining to the Alien Property Custodian's offices had to pass throught three hands: Mr. Daugherty, President Harding and Col. Miller.

Mr. Harry M. Daugherty was a man of iron and steel. He was a very handsome, striking looking man: cultured, finished. Whenever he entered any room,—he dominated that room. When he sat down at any table,—he was the head of that table. He walked with firm regular step as though his legs were pursuing a purpose rather than an objective. It was the stride of a man who knows that people fall in with his walk: that the strong vibrant rhythm of his living and his stepping swept lesser bodies into his pace.

During any council of war at 903—16th St., when the question would arise about the withdrawal of whiskey and alcohol,—or delaying prosecutions,—or shipping board controversies—the one weak link that we had in our entire chain and the only weak link was—Jess Smith.

All of our other men were men of more than normal nerve and physical bravery. And they were men who could take punishment if need be. Jess Smith was not lacking in intelligence of a sort, but he was lacking in nerve. He was quick as lightning on some things. From his retail store training he was as eager to make a profit of eighty cents,—as of $80,000.00. All the rest of us realized that we were selling privileges and not merchandise. Jess was suspicious of everybody,—everything. He was afraid of his own shadow. He was suspicious of a taxi-driver, a waiter in a café—a telephone operator,—a bell hop.

Those were hectic days in the Department of Justice in Washington, while national oil lands were being juggled from the government.

Back in the consciousness of each of us was a growing wonderment—as to what Jess Smith would do,—if a real crash should come. But not even in our wildest imaginings did we picture what was even then taking form in his brain, as a final desperate measure for self-protection. It was not long before we knew.

Chapter XIX

Daugherty and Fall—"Master Salesmen"

IT WAS said that during the Harding administration, everything in Washington was for sale,—except the dome of the Capitol. This—in a spirit of wit and as a joke, of course. It was further elucidated that it was not the intention to sell the dome of the Capitol, because later they might want to throw high dice for it. The winner would then have it removed and placed on top of a mansion home, as a monument befitting the exalted position of the master-mind of high finance in America.

This was not such a joke indeed as might have been intended. Mr. Daugherty and Mr. Fall were, without question, the crack salesmen of the Harding Administration, and they surrounded themselves with carefully selected assistants.

Mr. Fall and Mr. Daugherty were not friends. There was strong feeling between them as business competitors in the commodities and privileges belonging to the Government that they had to offer for sale. And they were constantly stepping into each other's reservations, which proved embarrassing to the subordinates who were conducting the sales for them. Efficient salesmanship was not depended upon so much as a disposition to cut prices,—undercut each other for the same privileges.

The line of merchandise directly under Mr. Fall's control was not altogether privileges and opportunities but actual physical tangible property assets. It involved such little matters as:

Power sights on Indian Reservations and Government lands,—worth billions of dollars.

Timber lands on Indian Reservations and Government lands worth billions of dollars.

Pasturing Privileges on Indian Reservations and Government Reservations—let to cattle raisers of the West, worth millions of dollars.

Alaskan and other U. S. Government territorial privileges and opportunities to be retailed somewhat under the system of the 5 and 10 cent chain of stores, namely: to make as many sales as possible and as quickly as possible at a short profit. The big profit to be derived —from the great number of sales made.

In 1922 and 1923, our lady-fair purchasers of furs were especially indebted to Mr. Fall for the opportunity of bedecking themselves in fine and costly and rare skins,—at a minimum cost. Mr. Fall lifted all barriers and restrictions in connection with killing and trapping on Government reservations.

But it was not in connection with the commodities above named that Mr. Fall was an expert. These were trivial side issues. It was Oil—in which he found his element! Whether the Oil was in Mexico or Texas or Wyoming or Montana or California or Alaska,—or anywhere else, it mattered not. The Oil men had been his friends and bosom companions from his boyhood. The Privileges of Oil—the luscious "flowing gold"—was the impetus that gave birth to his ambition to become a Cabinet member. And once installed,—these Oil Privileges he preempted entirely for himself,—to be sold over his own individual counter, without the aid or assistance of any of his salesmen. And right here,—was where he tripped up! He could not make a scapegoat of any subordinate for he had handled all the deals himself.

Mr. Daugherty was more far-seeing and astute. With lynx-like eye, he watched Mr. Fall as Mr. Fall proceeded with his sales. These sales required the O. K. signature of President Harding. Mr. Daugherty was closest to President Harding,—and so it was a simple matter for the President's signature to be so manipulated that both Mr. Daugherty and Mr. Harding could get a considerable "cut-in". Here Col. Darwin played his master game. Mr. Fall believed that the President was signing these papers because of his personal friendship,—while in reality, he was signing because of Mr. Daugherty and Col. Darwin.

And in order to cut through the red tape and the possible delay in getting Mr. Harding's signature, the purchasers of Oil lands were willing to listen to Col. Darwin's siren song: —funds to replenish the exhausted campaign coffers,—the necessity to pay off campaign debts. Party loyalty and honor demanded that these deals be made.

II

But it was his master mind in ordering prosecutions delayed and later quashed, and civil actions in behalf of the Government withdrawn,—that Mr. Daugherty displayed his greatest gifts—as salesman. Mr. Daugherty had been the lobbyist and the go-between and the undercover man for many of the great industrial plants of America,—for many years. When he became United States Attorney General, the samples with which he was most familiar,—were already in his hands and assets of this nature were quickly and deftly converted into cold cash by his experienced and accustomed fingers.

Our big Industrial and Mercantile and Department Store magnates operate on the idea that 33-1/3 per cent is ample profit. Not so—Mr. Daugherty. He believed that to do business and take care of all overhead charges and provide amply for his assistants, at least 50 per cent profit was necessary.

Of course, there are many gigantic Industrial plants in the United States. They are constantly running afoul of some of our numerous Federal laws. In fact, before Mr. Daugherty came into power as Attorney General, many of these Industrial plants were already afoul of the law. The records can speak for themselves. It is public information and available.

Ask for the number and names of such actions, really begun prior to Mr. Daugherty's Attorney Generalship,—and dismissed by Mr. Daugherty,—against great Industrial enterprises in the United States during his administration. From this official record, you will discover that more actions were dismissed by Mr. Daugherty or never brought to trial than the total of all similar actions dismissed during the entire history of the United States Government.

His official statement in explanation of this was a masterstroke in mob-psychology. He said that he wanted to clear the dockets of the Federal Courts in order to enable the Courts to proceed with the thousands of indictments that had been brought against violators of the Volstead Act. This was vastly pleasing to the church crowd,—always an important and deciding factor in any American political equation,—or in any bid for popular approval. This also tickled the Anti-Saloon League followers. It placed Mr. Daugherty in a position of security—and lined his pockets with gold.

Also, it enabled the clique to know who were the monied bootleggers. This put us in a position to collect our tribute from these bootleggers. This enabled us to discriminate. When one of these real monied bootleggers happened to be convicted,—we could,—for sufficient tribute, see to it that he got a short sentence, or was paroled,—or even pardoned. This sort of service—came high!

Also,—it enabled us to make the necessary contact with these bootleggers. Mr. Daugherty was never a piker! He wanted to know the bootleggers who were capable of handling large quantities of whiskey,—that is: in 5,000 barrel lots; or 5,000 case lots. He wanted to know the men who could make the necessary arrangements for the removal of such quantities from bonded warehouses as often as it became necessary to satisfy the bone-dry thirst of the American people.

And so from all of this you can see that Mr. Daugherty was not killing two birds with one stone,—but a dozen or so.

Shall I summarize a few of these privileges: [22]

Modified decrees of Federal Judges.

Dismissal of Civil and Criminal actions against great Industrial plants.

Entering actions,—or threatening to enter actions, to force collection of tribute.

Modifying prospective prison sentences.

Selling of paroles.

Selling of pardons.

Selling of Federal Judgeships.

Selling of U. S. District Attorney Offices.

Removal of whiskey from bonded warehouses.

Privileges to sell whiskey under Federal protection.

Threats to any and all Departments of the Government,—whenever opportunity arose,—as the Chief legal adviser of the Government.

Disposition of seized property in connection with the violation of Federal laws.

Minor and numerous other matters, as brought out during the Senate investigation of Mr. Daugherty,—such as:

The exhibition of the Dempsey-Carpentier Fight Film pictures which netted us around seven or eight million dollars.[23]

Of course, Mr. Daugherty had not placed himself in the position of Attorney General of the United States with his own carefully and personally selected assistants,—to play marbles. We did not play marbles. The harvest was ripe and we knew that we were there as reapers.

In selecting his assistants, Mr. Daugherty evinced a knowledge of human nature that was almost uncanny. He liked intelligence and bravery and mortally hated anybody —to use the parlance of the underworld—who would "knock down" a penny because the opportunity presented itself. Mr. Daugherty chose men who took great pride in their individual honesty,—and his entire selection of men was based on this idea. In reviewing and analyzing any and all complications and embarrassing situations that arose,—it was apparent, satisfactorily to my own mind, that it was Mr. Daugherty himself who invariably created the condition by an attack on some man's self-respect.

It was a fatal day for me when I dared take offense at his direct insult to my one pardonable pride: that of being a good and skillful investigator.

Chapter XX

Jess Smith "Passes On"

Mr. Harry M. Daugherty's health had been very uncertain since the preceding January. He was extremely nervous. Many threatening rumbles based on too positive facts had come to light and were being hinted and discussed in the newspapers. Many of his friends had made tremendous blunders and errors. They had neither the brains nor the nerves of steel that Mr. Daugherty had. He was in reality a sick man from these swiftly accumulating worries. He remained the larger part of his time in his apartment at the Wardman Park Hotel where he made his home with Jess Smith. They lived together in the apartment.

Very soon after the conference related in a previous chapter, it was a relief to everybody concerned when it was announced that Mr. Daugherty had decided to take a trip to Columbus, Ohio, and to Washington Court House, Ohio, and was going to take Jess Smith along with him. What secret plans or schemes or intrigues the trip may have portended, no one will ever know.

While at Washington Court House, they visited "The Shack", a country place where many important conferences had been held.

They returned to Washington, D. C., on the 27th of May. Jess came to 903—16th St., N. W.—on the Monday evening following.

The moment my eyes fell upon him, I saw a changed Jess Smith! There was a resolute air of determination about him that had not been perceptible before. I was sincerely glad to see him. He was the weak link in our chain all right, —but I was personally fond of him.

"Say—you're late, old boy. Why haven't you been around before?"

"Been too busy."

"What doing?"

"We'll get to that later."

"Have a pleasant vacation?"

"Aw—it was a hell of a pleasant trip! It's a nightmare. But I saw my wife. I enjoyed that."

His harassed face brightened as he spoke of his wife.

"You love your wife—don't you, Jess?"

His answer was quick and to the point.

"Always have. Always will. And I've made plans too. I'm going to get out of all this mess, and take her and live in peace the rest of my life."

I laughed as I replied:

"I reckon we'd all like to get out of this mess. That's not the point at present. You can't get out!"

"Can't I? You watch me. Harry Daugherty treated me like a dog all the time we were gone, and I don't intend to stand for it any longer. I've worshiped that man,—but I'm done! Through."

He looked it. He was a man with a final and definite purpose in view. Jess didn't throw himself down on a couch as was his usual custom, but sat erect and stiff in a straight chair.

"You wanted to know what I've been doing—that I haven't come around here before? Well—I've made a new will—for one thing. Wrote it all out myself and I want to tell you right now,—Harry Daugherty's name is not mentioned in that will. Neither is his brother's,—Mal Daugherty. I'm off those two for life. *I'm going to give this will to Mrs. Harding to keep for me.* I can't trust it in any vault. Vault? What's a vault—to the gang? Nothing! Nothing at all. She'll keep the will for me. And I'll tell you, I've left everything I've got to my wife. Yes, sir. She will get everything,—but a few bequests to some blood kin."

"I see you're as cheerful as when you went away," I remarked.

"Much more so. I know now exactly what I am going to do and how I am going to do it."

"That's interesting."

I kept silent, hoping that he would further elucidate, which he did.

"I've—decided! *I am going straight to Mrs. Harding and I'm going to tell her the whole business from A to Z,—and I'm going to turn over to her,—all my papers and accounts and records,—and she will protect me!*"

Had a bomb exploded in my face, I could not have been more shocked or astounded. He went on:

"You know, Mrs. Harding likes me and I like her, Gaston. I've helped her select most of her dresses and wraps and hats since she has been in the White House. We are very congenial,—and she's sore at Harry Daugherty anyhow."

I was thinking hard and fast, but I said:

"Is she? Why?"

"Chiefly because one day, when she got after him for appointing some man Federal Judge,—when he knew she didn't want that man to get the appointment,—he said to her: 'You attend to your business and I'll attend to mine. Do you know where I think women belong:—back in the kitchen. They have no business interfering in Governmental affairs!' That was insult supreme to Florence Harding. She's hated Harry ever since."

"I know about that. I was present when he said that to her, and it did make her mad. But do you know of any other reasons why she should hate him?"

"No. What other reasons could there be? Well—anyhow, I'm going to *her*. *She's* my friend."

I then asked the pertinent question:

"Did you tell Mr. Daugherty of this little intended move for self-protection?"

He exploded:

"Did I? Yes! I told him and he knows I mean it! You take it from me, Gaston, Harry's getting scared too. Out in Washington Court House, he had me go into a hardware store and buy him a pistol."

I knew the antipathy that Jess Smith had for any sort of fire-arms.[24]

"And you did it?"

He shrugged his shoulders.

"I did. I hate a pistol. I'm scared to death of a pistol. I never shot one in my life. I never touch one, if I can help it! And do you know, after I bought it for him, he didn't take the damn thing and its still in my suit case!"

"Where is Mr. Daugherty?" I asked.

"He's visiting up at the White House. Been there since the hour we returned."

"Spent the night there?"

"Yes."

Were things more threatening than I had realized? Jess went on:

"I phoned Mrs. Harding today but I couldn't get her on the phone. I'll get her tomorrow."

I was beginning to see a great light! Would he get Mrs. Harding tomorrow? *Would he?* I thought not!

I had never before seen Jess Smith with such sure and settled determination. He had reasoned his way out,—and had adopted his course of action. What that course of action might mean to anybody else—he didn't care. He said it was war. Every man for himself!

With all those records and accounts in front of her—what would Mrs. Harding do? She would do a-plenty, and she would protect her Warren! No obstacle would stand in her path in protecting her husband. Could she protect him, —and how? I couldn't figure it out but I knew that she would find a way. Trust her for that.

While we were talking, one of Mr. Burns' trusted men came in, and sat around a while gossiping about nothing in particular and he and Jess left the house together.

I next saw Jess Smith at six o'clock on the evening of May 30th. He came again to 903—16th St., N. W.

Quickly, I asked:

"Have you seen Mrs. Harding yet?"

He was troubled, but had lost nothing of his determination. In fact, he was even more determined! He replied:

"No. I did get her on the phone and what do you think she said to me? She said she was so sorry that she couldn't see me,—quite yet. But that Mr. Daugherty was there and he had said to her—that *he was sick and tired of my company for the moment and was so glad just to rest quietly there—and not have me around*. Can you beat that?"

Jess sat down at my desk and began to write a letter. He said: "I'm writing my wife and I'm telling her all about the new will and everything."

I sat in silence until he had finished his letter and addressed and stamped it and put it in his pocket.

He resumed the conversation just where he had left off:

"Well, Harry Daugherty's no more sick and tired of my company than I am of his. And Gaston,—sure as you're born, he's camped up there—*to keep me from getting to Mrs. Harding*. Sure as you're born! They're going to get me, Gaston—and they're going to get you."

I was doing some fast thinking, but I said nothing. He continued:

"Well—he can't roost up there at the White House forever—can he? This is Wednesday. I'll bide my time. It's such a relief to me to know exactly what I'm going to do and how I'm going to do it. And—then—wife and happiness and peace——"

How simply and clearly he had worked it all out! He went on:

"I'm not going to be anybody's scapegoat,—and that's what it's going to head up to, for both you and me. I've warned you and you won't listen! You think you know better. You don't. I'm going to be made no sacrifice for anybody! *Mrs. Harding will protect me!*" [25]

"You think she will?"

"Sure. I know she will," and in this I, too, believed that he was right. She would protect him.

"Can't you see—it's war? Don't you know that Hell is popping in every direction? Soon as I can get to Mrs. Harding—I'll be all right. Harry Daugherty can't stay up there forever—barring me out! That's what he's doing. Don't you see that?"

Poor Jess. He was showing the white feather again—more clearly than ever before. He was plastered all over with white feathers. Oh—well—this was not my fight and I'd keep out of it.

He went off on a fresh tangent.

"Gaston,—why won't you join with me and go to the Judge with Mrs. Harding—that's what she'll have me do, I think—and be State's Witness? What do they care about me or you? Nothing. I'm telling you. They'd bump us off in a second if they could get away with it. You're a fool to let them throw you in the dump heap. That's where you'll land,—in the 'Pen'. Mark what I say!"

"I'm taking chances on it. And I don't agree with you." That was all the answer I made.

Jess left my home that night, alone. I was extremely busy at the moment and had expected some one to come for him. But as no one came, I assumed that they had adopted other methods and I would not interfere. I had been informed that I need not take the time or trouble to nurse-maid him again myself. They all knew how very busy I was, working up on my own indictment and defense.

Very early the next morning—it must have been around four o'clock,—in the month of May, it is getting light by four o'clock,—my confidential phone rang and a voice that I recognized, told me to come immediately to the Wardman Park Hotel, and into a certain apartment.

I dressed as rapidly as possible and hurried around there and slipped up the fire-escape staircase to the apartment I had been told to go to.

I was evidently expected. The door of the apartment quietly opened just as I reached it.

One of my superior officers confronted me.

"Gaston,—Jess Smith has committed suicide. He has shot himself." [26]

I said nothing. I was incapable of speech. A silence, deep and black as the grave and eternity, hung between us.

"Well?" I finally asked.

His voice was short and tense:

"You know your business: *do as you are told and ask no questions*. He is down in his own apartment. Nobody is there —yet. You go down there and search his body and bring to me,—every scrap of paper that you find. *Get those papers.* The key is in the latch."

"Am I deputized for this job?"

"Yes, you are! Go and guard the body, and bring those papers to me. Search the apartment if you do not find them on his body."

I said nothing—made no reply whatever, but turned and went down the steps again and opened the door of Jess Smith's apartment where he lived with Mr. Daugherty, stepped inside and closed the door.

In the eerie light of that early May morning, I could see but little at first. I was in the long hall, leading into the living room. The bed rooms were on each side of this hall. I stopped at Jess Smith's bed room door. It was slightly ajar.

I gave the door a steady push,—and it opened. I stepped inside and closed the door and turned the key.

I have always been known as a man of iron nerve, but as I stood with my back against that closed door, and tried to accustom my eyes to the even dimmer light in the bed room, and gradually saw and took cognizance of each article of furniture and of each object in that room, for the first time in my life, my iron nerve threatened to break.

To my trained eye,—that room was too manifest! God—Almighty—what had happened—in this room? I stood for several minutes. My mind and imagination refused to assemble any kind of order out of the wild speculations that flooded and blinded me.

Jess Smith—a suicide?

Never on God's green earth!

That one fact held in my mind—to the exclusion of all and every other.

Jess Smith had been called—traitor. Traitor to the "gang"? Had he been executed—as such? Had it been done, not merely for the protection of three or more individuals—but as an unpleasant executive patriotic duty—"the greatest good to the greatest number"?

Once those papers of his,—revealing every crooked transaction since the inauguration in accurate detail *had gotten into the hands of Mrs. Harding*, which was his expressed and avowed intention, who would without a question—*have turned them over to the proper authorities*—what would have happened?

Why—the Government would have fallen—blown up! There would have been almost no Government left!

It was unthinkable. Had Jess Smith been sentenced to death and executed as a political casualty? A traitor?

Was a similar sentence suspended over my head? I did not know. How could I?

However, I felt even then a measurable assurance of personal security, for I was—as yet—too useful to the whole clique and furthermore they knew I would never talk and they knew I had no—accounts—records like Jess Smith.

This reminded me of my mission in that room. I had to get those papers—and ask no questions!

But my mind went on trying to follow their possible reasoning.

They knew that Jess had determined to place all his written evidence before Mrs. Harding and seek her protection. He had outlived his usefulness! He was a menace! Should he have been allowed to follow out his plan,—wouldn't chaos have been the order of the day? For, in the explosion that would follow,—many leading high officials,—many Cabinet members, even the President himself would have blown up with it!

The Government must be saved. It was logical! It was a patriotic duty!

Hadn't every Government on earth since the days of Acaan in the camp put to death its traitors? Why—in the 15th and 16th Centuries—look what happened? When necessary, they slaughtered in wholesale lots. They annihilated nations. Would our little noise of an advanced civilization become puny and weak and futile,—when only the execution of one man was necessary to preserve the Government? What is one life—in the balance of universal benefit to our millions of citizens? The Government had to be saved!

Thus, I calculated—had run their thoughts——.

Then, with an effort, I went about the task to which I had been assigned.

Again, I surveyed the room. As I have said, the physical evidences of suicide were entirely too manifest,—too obvious. It appeared to me a stage setting.

The body lay on the floor some four feet from the bed. It was crumpled up—face downward. A pistol was several inches from his extended hand and arm. Pistol? The pistol he had told me he had bought for Mr. Daugherty,—and which had remained in his suit case, because Mr. Daugherty had not yet taken it and he—Jess—had been afraid to touch it.

I turned the body over. I examined the wound in the temple. Had he died from this pistol wound? I did not think so! Why, a pistol shot in that hotel would have awakened everybody in it! I remembered all Jess had said so many times,—about the "little white powder".

I tried to reconstruct and retrace his movements after he had left my home at six o'clock,—but I was all at sea and could do nothing in that direction.

I searched the body carefully. I removed all papers from the pockets,—but I found no papers of any importance in his pockets. I went further. And under all of his clothing next to his skin,—I found a sort of belt,—a harness suspended around his shoulders and hanging just under his arms. On this harness was securely strapped,—a legal size extension envelope,—packed full of papers.

This I removed, for I knew that it was what they had sent me to get.

I arranged everything again exactly as I had found it, opened the doors and returned to the apartment upstairs.

I delivered the envelope to my superior officer and returned to my home as I had come.

As I walked home,—I began to think more definitely of the personal equation that interlaced all this affair. Was Jess Smith's new will of which he had told me and of which he had written his wife in my offices that very evening,—was this will among those papers in that envelope? I tried to conjecture what would be done with this will? It would be interesting to watch developments. Did they know that I knew about the will?

I went home and lay down on a couch in the office.

About six o'clock my phone rang. Again a familiar voice said: "Jess Smith has killed himself. Come and take charge with the hotel detective."

I went again to Wardman Park Hotel. The house detective and I took official charge. The coroner was sent for. There was no autopsy. It was not deemed necessary. Everything so clearly proclaimed—suicide.

Again, I went home around eight o'clock. At eight-thirty my confidential phone rang. A voice said to me:

"You get your car,—and your chauffeur and wife and boy,—and at nine-thirty—stop on the corner of———A man will be waiting for you on that corner. Pick him up and drive him to Harper's Ferry. Understand?"

"I do."

I did as ordered. I took my chauffeur and wife and boy and nurse, and at this certain corner, we found a man standing—waiting.

We drove the car to the edge of the curbing and he got in. No word was spoken, until after he was seated and we were outside the city and in the open country. Then we talked about the weather and the scenery. He boarded a West bound train at Harper's Ferry.

I had never seen this man before, and I have never seen his since.[27]

Chapter XXI

Covering Up the Trail

DRIVING home from Harper's Ferry, I bought a Washington paper at a Railroad Station and read the full account of the suicide of Jess Smith.

As related in the papers,—Jess Smith was seen in the lobby of the Wardman Park Hotel around eight o'clock the previous evening. He did not take dinner at the hotel. Around eight-thirty o'clock, he went to his apartment. About six a. m. the paper said one of Mr. Daugherty's secretaries had heard a pistol shot, which he thought was the slamming of a door. He investigated and found the body.

Of course, I well knew the inaccuracy of newspaper accounts. It was further stated that Mr. Daugherty had phoned his apartment from the White House at seven a. m. and had been told the news.[28]

All the way home in the car that day, I tried to retrace the actions of Jess Smith after he had left my home at 903—16th St., N. W., at six o'clock the previous night. I inferred that he had taken dinner out—down-town somewhere, mailed the letter to his wife and had then gone to the Wardman Park Hotel.

The papers said he was seen in the lobby about eight-thirty o'clock.

Probably—he sat down in the beautiful lobby to watch the people and listen to the music. Jess loved music. There was a big dance in the ball-room that night. Everything was gayety and laughter,—light and happiness!

If there ever was a being in the world who loved life and dress,—the beautiful and artistic—it was Jess Smith. I could picture him sitting in the lobby of the Wardman Park Hotel and watching the beautifully gowned girls and women and the elegantly dressed men,—coming in and passing through to the dance,—and listening to the music.

But he did not tarry long in the lobby. His mind and soul were too harassed. Did he then go on up to his apartment? Was the apartment empty? If so,—I did not believe that Jess would have stayed in it. Jess could not bear to be alone. He could not sit in an empty room. He would see terrifying things on the walls. Had he found his apartment empty,—and had he then gone out into some friend's apartment to find comradeship?

What had happened?

Again and again, I turned over in my mind every possible angle of speculation. I did not believe that I would ever know the truth. But nobody could keep me from forming my own deductions.

Had he perhaps taken a drink in some friend's apartment? Jess loved to take a social drink—for the sense of companionship it brought. He never drank—just for the effect of the drink. Was Jess after all a victim of the fatal "little white powder" which he held in such mortal fear and terror? Had he stayed in his own apartment? Who had been in there with him? I paid scant attention to the newspaper account. Of course,—there would be no blunder in the story given out to the Press!

How had Jess Smith died?

This question beat into my brain all that day! In his room had been no evidences of a struggle. There were no empty glasses—no evidence of drinking! How he would have fought for his life—had he been given even half a chance! This—to my mind—settled the point of his having died of a pistol wound. Was Jess Smith dead,—when that pistol was fired into his head? How else could it have been done?

That Jess Smith took his own life was so entirely outside

the realm of possibility in my mind, I did not even consider it.

Well, Jess Smith had died as he had lived since the beginning of the Harding Administration,—with peals of thunder clapping around his head one moment, and at his feet,—the next moment, and not knowing when the torrents might break down on him. He knew that he was fooling with T.N.T., but he didn't know how to handle it,—and it finally exploded in his face.

Again, I asked the question: what had happened in that room?

I was told later that some one—Mary Roberts Rheinhart, I believe it was,—had written a story based on the room at the Wardman Park Hotel where Penrose had lived. She had gone into this room alone and had sat down—and waited to be psychically inspired. I thought to myself just then: "Lady—if walls can talk to you—and you want a story, you've gone into the wrong room!"

Jess Smith take his own life?

Never! It was inconceivable to those who knew him intimately.

And the new will? What would become of that new will written the Monday before he died on Wednesday?

When we returned to my home that evening, I found two important messages: one was to come immediately to the Wardman Park Hotel, and the other,—to phone Mrs. Boyd as quickly as possible. I knew that the latter message meant that Mrs. Harding wanted to see me.

Once more, I went to the Wardman Park Hotel. There I was told of everything that had transpired. Mr. Daugherty had taken complete charge, of course. They had been puzzled to know, just whom to notify of Jess Smith's sudden death, and after much discussion, they had decided to notify

Mr. Daugherty's brother—Mr. Mal Daugherty of Washington Court House, Ohio.

Why had they not notified his former wife,—Roxy Stinson? They knew her.

"Too damned adroit!" was my mental comment. Wouldn't it have been the natural thing to have notified the next of kin?

In her sworn testimony on the witness stand at the Daugherty Investigation, Jess Smith's wife said that Mr. Daugherty had hastily shown her a photostatic copy of the new will that Jess had written her about, and Mr. Daugherty had told her that it was illegal, for it had no witnesses. She only saw it hastily the day after the funeral. It appeared to be similar to the one that was probated, anyhow,—his estate to be divided into five parts: Mr. Harry Daugherty,—Mr. Mal Daugherty,—the two St. John kin, and his wife.

Jess Smith's estate was appraised at $250,000. From my personal first-hand knowledge, I could have sworn that he must have left an estate of between two and three million. And from the very nature of things, this money was all in cash, in bank safe-deposit boxes.

I seem to have been born without any sense of personal fear. After Jess Smith's death, there was a great lessening of tension all around—everywhere. A crisis was passed! We had no weak link in the chain. The Government had been saved. Providence was kind!

But the public clamor did not cease. The rumblings continued.

It was the following day, before I could phone Mrs. Boyd, and I was asked to come to her country estate "Glen Haven" that afternoon at three o'clock. Mrs. Harding would be there.

Since the painful scene with President Harding, Mrs.

Harding had been ill. I had not been able to see her for weeks. But she was better now,—and was arranging for their proposed trip to Alaska. I was instructed to come prepared to stay until evening, as she had many things to go over with me.

Chapter XXII

Mrs. Harding Catches Nan Britton in the White House

"Did Jess Smith shoot himself? Where is Nan Britton?"

Without a word of greeting, Mrs. Harding fired these two totally disconnected questions at me,—the first moment we were alone. I had gone out to "Glen Haven" and had sent my car and chauffeur away, with instructions to return in two and a half hours.

I found Mrs. Harding sitting on the lawn talking to Mrs. Boyd. As I approached, Mrs. Boyd went into the house.

"Haven't you read the accounts in the papers?" I asked, seating myself in one of the big comfortable lawn chairs opposite her.

Her keen intelligent eyes searched my face.

"Every word. But you haven't answered my questions. I haven't slept a wink these two nights. I couldn't sleep. I have been wondering—wondering! Now—tell me—tell me everything about it."

As she paused,—I looked into her face. For a full minute, we gazed thus. She was trying to penetrate my innermost thoughts and I had an uncomfortable sensation that she was doing it. I spoke as convincingly as I could:

"I have nothing to tell. The newspapers seem to have covered the story."

Suddenly,—she shifted to the second question:

"Where is Nan Britton?" she snapped.

Without replying, I removed from my pocket, the last reports that she had not seen, from my shadow men who were keeping Nan Britton under constant surveillance. They had accumulated during Mrs. Harding's illness. They were arranged in chronological order. She adjusted her glasses and read each report with concentration. This required some little time.

I then noted many changes in Mrs. Harding. How much grayer—and older—and more haggard she was! I recalled my first visit to her:—I thought she looked like an old woman then, and she did, but not—as she now was!

My mind went back in swift review.

During the Harding campaign and the first months after the inauguration, Mrs. Harding had gone quietly along, studying the ways of the remarkable Cabinet and of Washington from her new high vantage point of observation,—listening, questioning, scheming and biding her time. Beneath her calm exterior was a haughty and violent soul,—but to the eye, her demeanor was as placid as a blue crystal lake at sunset,—held in by a fragile and picturesque dam. The dam had broken—when she had held in her nervous hands indisputable proofs of her husband's infidelity.

I knew that her keen analytical mind took frank cognizance of the disparity between President Harding's powerful physical make up, with handsome, classic beauty,—and a mediocre intelligence to which the loftiness of rank alone gave a fitful importance.

And in spite of her own limitless ambitions she could not quite accommodate herself to the eminence of her position. Therefore, she assumed a general air of hauteur, which camouflaged an inferiority complex that refused to let her be at ease and natural, and which was far in excess of the requirements. In spite of her delusions of grandeur she lacked that perfect self-possession, that pliancy of refinement, that sparkling wit and penetration that should have been a counterpart to the President's banal heaviness. He looked the part,—a king, though his fitness for that exalted position ended right there—with his looks.

To be compelled to occupy the social throne of the nation,

although it was sweet and glorious,—unquestionably caused her real mental anguish. To be the First Lady of the Land, —and the potential Ruler,—was an elixir that she drank eagerly, greedily,—and yet, its taste was bitter and its dregs were gall. She suffered, and these reactions were gradually sapping nervous forces and resistance.

Fear had stalked with her, day and night, since she had first entered the portals of the White House. Fear—of Nan Britton, of Nan Britton's child with the terrifying vision of possible exposure.

She finished reading the reports at last, and, as was her custom, she folded them up and put them in her beaded bag. She held in her hand a crumpled handkerchief.

"Well—these are very satisfactory, but keep it up,—more carefully and rigidly now than ever. There are vital reasons why I must know where that girl is—at any moment."

There was an air about her that told me to keep quiet and to let her do the talking. Wisely, I did.

"I have so much to tell you, Mr. Means—so much! There is no one else to whom I can talk freely. And I shall leave nothing unsaid."

As she paused a moment, I wondered if I could possibly imagine all that I knew she would leave unsaid. She continued:

"You had a violent scene with President Harding. That scene was nothing compared to what I have gone through."

I could readily believe this,—for I remembered how he shook his clenched fists in her face.

"I have been ill. I prayed for death. No one has ever prayed for death harder than I. Nobody ever wished for death—for that rest of oblivion that is my only hope of a future, after death—more than I. I reasoned it all out. The triangle had to be broken and could be broken only by the death of one of us. I had chosen this—for myself. Fate decreed differently. I consulted Madam X. She told me—that I would not pass on—until after President Harding had died. She reminded me—that I am a 'Child of Destiny'."

As she paused a moment, I wondered to myself what can be the fate of a country that is governed by a ruler who is governed by a wife who indulges in such beliefs and is actually ruled by an old soothsayer?

"I have surprising things to tell you, Mr. Means. I've been doing some good detective work myself—on the side. Your reports of Nan Britton and her movements are good—but incomplete."

"How is that?"

Well, I knew they were incomplete. I had reached the point long before, where I dared not make them complete.

"I can tell you—that Nan Britton has been slipping into the White House,—repeatedly. Clandestine meetings—here in *my* home. These are sponsored by Mr. Boyd. I found out—no matter how, but I found out. And I saw,—with my own two eyes."

Of course, I had known this for months. There were others who knew, but I could not help being curious as to who had brought this information to Mrs. Harding. Maybe she would tell me. I waited.

"I always place fresh pink roses in a vase on the President's desk downstairs in the Executive offices. I have done this—oh long ago, longer than I can remember,—even before we ever thought of Washington. It was just a little gesture of love and adoration. While I was ill,—I had one of my personal maids attend to it for me."

One Sunday morning, I had been tipped off that Nan Britton was at that moment downstairs in the office. Why, I could have gone down right then and surprised them,—but I didn't—oh, I'd passed all that—but I was watching from an upper window. It was nearly time to start to church.

And I saw—I saw Nan Britton slip out of a side door of the White House. And—she was wearing—pinned on her coat—one of my roses! What vicious triumph must have been in her treacherous mind! I saw this—Gaston Means—with my own eyes!

"And then—a little later the President met me in the hall downstairs: stately, correct, respectful,—courteously assisted me into a waiting limousine—and we attended church—worshiping God in His sanctuary! God! Gaston Means—there is no God! Mockery! What sort of God would permit this thing!"

Her color was not pale. It was greenish. All the lines of her face deepened.

"We have had terrible scenes!" she said.

She carried the scars of these scenes on her face and over her entire person. Not physical scars—but the cut pride of insulted womanhood,—the wounds of a despised heart.

I could well believe that they had had scenes. I said nothing. Her eyes gleamed from half closed lids like those of a cat. Her voice was clear and firm:

"My love for Warren Harding has turned to hate. You might as well know that now. In the beginning of what I am going to tell you.

"It is no light thing to tear human beings apart by bleeding roots, deeply buried under thirty-three years of rich soil in which these roots have grown. Transplanting is impossible. Yet—what would he do? Tear them apart, ruthlessly, cruelly,—in order to try to graft himself on younger blooming growth."

What was she leading up to, I wondered.

"Oh, we had terrible scenes!" she repeated.

"I've watched his head grow a little whiter—day by day—his form stooping a bit more noticeably—day by day—lines of sorrow and anguish marking his handsome face a little deeper—day by day, yet steadily, inevitably moving toward the final denouement that destiny has ordained, and from which there can be no escape. What a figure of tragedy!"

Not a trace of sympathy was in her words or voice, however. No feeling. Cold, bitter, calculating.

"No one knows better than I the links in the chain as they have been forged one by one—through the years, and that now hold him—helplessly, hopelessly bound. It's as clear as day to me. I've traced it back over the years.

"Until I heard of Jess Smith's death, I was in a panic of fear. What could be the end of all this? I am no fool. I've known what was going on. And Warren Harding dared not oppose if his supposed friends suggested anything. They held the whip hand. They are using him to feather their own nests—with millions. Graft. Graft. Graft. Bribery. Treachery. Conspiracies—and why? All because he was just a plain fool and lost his head—to a girl who had no real claim upon him, but their mutual sinful lust."

What could I say? She expected no comment from me and I made none. She went on:

"God! That I should have lived to see it! He *has* to assent to anything they suggest! The world may think it is because of weakness of character. It is not. It is because of his lust for that girl. . . .

"Oh,—we have had terrible scenes! So many blows have struck me, I hardly know from which I suffer most. Think of his expenses—giving Nan Britton more money than he spends on his own home at the White House. Eight hundred dollars,—one week—a thousand the next week and on and on—for her luxuries and the support of his supposed child."

She was coming to some grand climax, but I could not follow her lead. I was puzzled. She continued:

"Oh—we have had terrible scenes. After one of these scenes, one day, I said to him:

'Warren—I can feel it coming!'

'What?'

'Complete exposure!'

"Then he just seemed to go all to pieces. He said: 'Damn it. Let it come! Let it come! God,—I'll be glad to have it come and over with!'

'You will be impeached.'

'I will tell the truth!'

'You will be disgraced!'

'I will tell the truth!'

'You may be imprisoned.'

'I will tell the truth. The exact truth. There can be no jury of twelve American men or women who would send me to jail. But even a jail—a prison, would be peace compared to this! I am no criminal. Let them impeach! God knows—I'm sick and tired of it all. I'll be glad to have it over. Glad! Glad!'

"I could only stare at him and gasp:

'Are you crazy?'

"How he raved. He was insane!

"He thundered at me:

'No, I am not crazy! That too—would be a relief:—to go crazy!'

"I could not speak. I had never seen Warren Harding like this. He went on:

'If they impeach—then—then do you know what I'll do? Do you want to know? I'll tell you! The world is a big place,—and—I'll take my child and go away. No one shall keep me from my child. You shall not. You hear me. You shall not.'

"I could only gasp: 'Warren—Warren——'

'Now—I've said it and I mean it!'

"I wondered then why I didn't cry like other women. I am sure any other woman would have cried. I never cry any more. I used to—long ago. So I calmly said to him.

'What will you do with me?' My voice was as firm as if I were inquiring the time of day. He said:

'You can do—what you damn please——'

"Then I did begin to plead. He was crazy and I knew it. I said:

'Warren—Warren—think of our young love——'

"He would not let me finish.

'Young love,' he hissed, 'our young love! *Love!* I never loved *you.* You want the truth. Now you've got the truth. Young love! You ran me down! God in heaven—young love—You ran me down——'

"Mr. Means,—those are the very words that President Harding said to me. The very words—to me, his wife,—for thirty-three years. Oh—it was a terrible scene. He was insane that night.

"Well—the next morning,—he was humble and penitent as usual, for he always had a kind heart, and he begged my forgiveness. . . . I told him that I forgave—how many times I've had to forgive. But I knew that nothing could ever be the same again. What I had heard that night, I shall never forget. He pleaded that he had lost self-control. It had happened. It would happen again. Sometimes loss of self-control is a means of self-revelation.

" 'I had run him down!' 'He would take his child and go away!' Well—we would see about that! Those two sentences have churned back and forth, back and forth in my brain to the exclusion of everything else. I registered a vow,—a solemn vow, that—never, *never, never,* should he take his child and go away!

"From that night, in spite of a spoken word of forgiveness, there has been deep hidden war between us. The devotion and idolizing love that had ruled my heart and brain and body for my husband was changed into something bitter and dull and hard. This was the birth of hate! It crystallized into my consciousness. I hate Warren Harding with a hatred greater than my former love and affection. A hate—remember—that surpasses the accumulated adoration and worship of thirty-three years. Was there ever so fierce a hate—kindled in a woman's soul!"

No one could have seen Mrs. Harding at that moment and have doubted the exact truth of what she was saying.

"A woman cannot hold a hate like that where she has once loved," I ventured, although I had small faith in my own words. I had to make some comment.

She was quick to flare:

"What do you know about it? Nothing at all. And I know nothing of a man's theories on such matters. I know—*facts.* Warren Harding shall never have that child—never!

"There was a time, when—for his sake, to silence his friends who were persecuting and blackmailing him, I considered plans by which I might arrange to have some member of my family—my son's wife, perhaps,—adopt the child. So he could have the child—here. Had that been done, it would have silenced his enemies. I knew a woman once who adopted the child of her chamber-maid. It was a similar case. And even Josephine took Napoleon's child—the little King of Rome—to her heart and wanted to adopt it. But—after he said what he did to me—that was thought of no more!

"When I was ill—they thought I would die. Well—I didn't die! And I am not going to die as long as things are as they are. *He* is the one who deserves to die. He is not fit to live. . . . I made him what he is—and he knows it.

"Think of the poor weak fool—the President of the United States willing to be disgraced and impeached and made a laughing stock of the whole world and go down in history in this way,—because he had determined to get hold of and to keep—his illegitimate child, born out of wedlock, —whose mother is thirty years younger than he,—a vain, flattered silly little fool, who loves his money and the thrills of his attentions and the excitement of their rendezvous. Which brings me to a piece of personal detective work that even you don't know about."

"What is that?"

Suddenly, in her excitement, she stood up and faced me.

"Their rendezvous! You found out for me how they trailed together in Pullman berths and in hotels in almost every city in the land,—from one end of the continent to the other. But I myself, found out—how she has been slipping into the White House, which is *my* home and also the home of the nation,—how they have been desecrating this home of the people by using a coat-closet downstairs, emulating the standards of a low-caste scullery maid with a gardener. Even a scullery maid would have had more pride and self-respect."

A-ah! This was the work of an inside man or woman. And it was news to me!

"Think of that, Gaston Means. It was I who found that out. Disgusting! Fool! Fool! Fool!"

She was trembling so violently, I became alarmed. I feared collapse. I got up and stood behind her chair and put my hand on her shoulder to steady her. She shook my hand off.

"Oh—let me alone," she shouted. "What do you know about it! You are a man. You take his part against me, like all the rest of them. His friends? Crooks,—thieves,—liars! All of them. Laughing at me,—knowing all the time about his child, and using that knowledge as a whip to force him to sign any papers they put before him, so they can steal and pillage the nation. Laughing at me,—so smart they are. Fool!"

There was a lawn table near,—beside her chair. She staggered against it, and again I put forth a hand to catch her, should she fall.

The crumpled web of a handkerchief was slowly turning red in her nervous fingers. I called her attention to it. Again, —as once before, she had clasped and unclasped her hands so tightly that her rings had cut into the flesh and made it bleed. She wrapped the handkerchief tightly around the finger, paying no attention to the crimson wound and went on:

"Well—well—they have done it! They will all come out rich—multi-millionaires,—and so cleverly have they hidden behind him, there is no law that can touch them. But he laughs best who laughs last! They are not through with me yet. We will see. We will see."

The poor woman had to sit down at last from sheer exhaustion. Her brain was on fire, I well knew, and she scarcely realized what she was saying. And yet—even then, I felt a cold, uncanny fear,—an icy breath of clairvoyance warned me,—that this might indeed not be the end, but rather the beginning of the tragedy.

Suddenly,—as was characteristic of her, she made a quick and sharp turn in the trend of her thoughts and conversation. She said:

"And now—tell me,—who killed Jess Smith and exactly how was it done?"

Chapter XXIII

Mrs. Harding—"The Child of Destiny"

I HAD always known that it was useless to try to satisfy Mrs. Harding by evasions in any matter. But I was not mentally prepared to do anything else, at this time. So I began:

"The newspapers——"

She would let me go no further.

"I know all about the newspapers. I'm asking you—who killed Jess Smith—and how?"

"How should I know?"

"You do know."

"I do not," I could quickly retaliate, in all truth and honesty.

"I say—you do!"

Could she possibly think that I would be fool enough to tell her, even if I did know?

"I may have my theories and deductions, that's true. I know nothing," I said quietly.

"Do you happen to know—why he wanted to see me? Jess Smith was trying day and night—to see me to tell me something important, he said. What was it? Could I have prevented this thing?"

"You could not have prevented this thing," I was glad to be able to answer one question candidly.

"I wish I had seen him. I could have tried. I might have helped him. Poor Jess!"

Apparently she had not noticed that I had failed to answer her first question.

"Did he shoot himself?" she asked suddenly. I always kept myself prepared for her sudden questions.

"I don't think so. Jess Smith never fired a pistol in his life. He was mortally afraid to touch a pistol. But, Mrs. Harding—that is over and done with. Jess is—gone. Haven't you enough troubles with the living—to forget him?"

But she was not to be diverted from the directness of her own conclusions. She spoke with finality:

"Then—he was poisoned. I thought so. I knew it all the time. Something told me. I knew it."

I would not contradict. It was useless. I said:

"He was forever talking about a deadly 'little white powder' that eased one off swiftly and painlessly."

"Yes. I have heard him talk of this 'little white powder'—myself. Jess is gone. And—I was right! And now, Mr. Means, we will concentrate on the living. I have not yet told you of my plans. I have a very definite—decided—settled schedule of action. No power on earth can divert me from it. I want you to know."

She was indeed a resolute woman. Everything about her proclaimed decision of purpose: keen, daring action. "Child of Destiny."

"I am determined that the improper influences, each and every one of them, surrounding and absolutely controlling the President shall be severed. With all the cunning of a seducing demon, Nan Britton rules President Harding. And through her,—his friends control him with a rod of iron. The tears of an innocent woman have always been impotent against the seducing smile of a beautiful girl. In another age,—I could have bought *lettres de cachet*. That would have ended it!"

Yes, I thought to myself,—and if America had a Bastille to pitilessly devour human beings, Nan Britton would certainly be in it. And—Mr. Harry M. Daugherty—and several others,—and eventually—myself, was my mental footnote.

"From the moment I stepped into the White House this thing has been a weight that weighs as heavily on my breast as the infernal rock upon the shoulders of Sisyphus. It shall be lifted off!

"There is no length, Mr. Means, to which I will not go—to bring this about. I've held many councils of war with Gen. Sawyer. He stands solidly with me. We can feel the icy chills of onrushing menace. We see ahead of us—terrible possibilities. And strange—irrelevant as it may seem to you, —Jess Smith's death removed the last vestige of hesitation and fear.

"I am determined that Warren Harding shall be completely under my control. It is because of this—and this alone—that the trip to Alaska is being planned.

"Even against my will, the prophetic words of Madam X have dinned constantly into my ears. I am a 'Child of Destiny.' I must fulfill that destiny. *The President is to die first.* He will die in honor: the stars have so decreed. There can be no appeal from this verdict.

"I—and I alone—shall fulfill Warren Harding's final destiny. Which means exactly what is happening: that the real Power rests in my hands. Warren Harding will be helpless to do anything—ever again—without my knowledge and approval. The greatest, richest, most powerful nation on earth shall know the rule of a woman. Harry M. Daugherty will be hoisted on his own petard. The lash of the whip that he held over the President shall fall on his own shoulders. It is going to tax my ingenuity and every resource of brain and cunning,—but I will find a way. Mark that! I will find a way!"

Had the woman gone stark crazy, I was asking myself as she was talking? But no crazy person could follow such concentration of determined thought.

"Every oracular word that Madam X has ever uttered has come to pass and been fulfilled. I am—a 'Child of Destiny!' From this day—Gaston Means—from this moment,

I want you to know that I begin to live that destiny. I am Ruler—supreme,—of my husband,—the President of the United States and his Cabinet,—Congress, Senate,—all the powers that function in Governmental machinery. It is I—Florence Kling Harding—who will control and guide that machinery by the touch of my little finger. Just you wait and see! He laughs best who laughs last!

"In my position now, there is nothing more to wish for. I stand at the summit and see before me, the brilliant glorious goal of Power—toward which the path lies open. I shall stand on that summit! Mark what I tell you. The world may never really know what one woman with a will of iron has accomplished. But you—Gaston Means—you will know!"

Already there gleamed forth from her face the smile of victory. How certain she was of the future! Hers was to be undying fame and victory's brilliant crown! What was she talking about? The woman must be crazy, I thought, but yet I knew that she was not.

"What you say, Mrs. Harding, may all be true,—but I can't make head or tail out of it. I talk a plainer English. Just what do you mean? Talk my language,—please."

Her lips tightened. Again she clasped and unclasped her fingers. She repeated:

"You will know. You will know."

"Maybe so. But if there's anything you want me to know now, please tell me, so I can understand. This 'Child of Destiny' business means to me—exactly nothing at all!"

"Of course—but it will! You want my concrete plans?"

"Yes."

"Very well. We are going on this trip to Alaska. Those who go with us on this trip are solely of my selection. The active campaign for renomination will begin very, very soon. This is a crisis.

"On this trip, I, and I alone, will serve as secretary to the President,—just as I used to do—years ago. I will then be able to intelligently understand the dangers and pitfalls that confront him. Every letter or telegram or paper that gets into his hands,—will go through my hands first. This gives me the opportunity that I have never had since I've been in the White House,—the opportunity to know exactly what Warren is doing, every moment of the time, day and night. If the dangers surrounding us are surmounted, it will be solely because of myself."

God in heaven—what a devil's brew this sort of arrangement would stew up! And Mr. Daugherty had not been invited to be one of the party,—I remembered.

"I have reached the point where I dread any contact with Senators' wives, or any friends and acquaintances. There are so many ugly rumors flying around like wild-fire. You know it. Washington is sitting on the edge of a volcano.[29] I do not know what it is all about,—but I *will know*. From the moment we start, I will be the President's secretary,—and his only one."

How quickly—in a flash—I visualized the potential dangers of this secretaryship. How could the President have consented to such an arrangement? Had he been so beaten down—that in desperation,—he cared no longer?

"I shall be able to learn—very soon—exactly what all these dangers are and how far-reaching they are. I am determined that I shall not be thwarted. If for one moment, I think that I am going to be thwarted,—then, the penalty will not rest on Warren Harding or on myself. If there is an intimation—or I get a suspicion—of any kind of imminent exposure,—they will never reach their culmination."

"I really do not know what you mean."

She made herself clear at last:

"I mean—that Warren Harding shall not be compelled

to bear on his shoulders the evil deeds of the crooks surrounding him."

"How can you help it—if a crash comes?"

Her reply was instant:

"A crash will not come! Don't you see that what I said is true. I,—and I alone,—am Ruler."

The tension of the moment was almost unbearable. I thought to break it. I remarked with a laugh:

"You still have faith in Madam X. I see."

The tension did not break. It tightened. Never had I confronted a woman of such determination. She retorted:

"Didn't a soothsayer tell Josephine that she was destined to be Queen of France,—when it could then appear only as a silly joke! Too improbable to consider. Yet—she was!"

Mrs. Harding had talked much about Josephine and Napoleon. She went on now:

"Josephine worked for Napoleon with all the wit and cunning and charm in her power. The true history of Josephine is the history of a perfect woman,—until her last ignominious submission to Napoleon. She was a fool. She should never have submitted to the divorce. Her acceptance of what appeared inevitable was, of course, a relic of the dark ages of woman's submission. A discarded wife! No man can begin to comprehend the ignominy of it. The hot sense of degradation. The injustice. I shall not emulate her example in this regard."

Never had I or anyone else supposed that she would. Had the recollections of her early struggles and sacrifices for the furtherance of the Harding ambitions,—of her husband's infidelity and continued philandering,—of crimes committed by those in power surrounding him,—of the many gathering and threatening dangers of exposure—of imminent impeachment, sure disgrace, and possible imprisonment,—had all these things seethed and churned through the brain and heart of this unhappy and dishonored woman,—until, in her desperate half-mad, fanatical reasoning,—her brain was snapping under the strain? I wondered!

But no snapping brain could give expression with clear-cut intelligent continuity,—as Mrs. Harding had done. From the entire interview, I gathered one supreme impression, that she was now controlled by powerful driving impelling emotions.

Inclusive of all, was her grim determination, no matter what the hazard, no matter what obstacles might present themselves—to fulfill her fate as 'Child of Destiny' and rule the Government. This meant that she would not be thwarted in any of her plans and ambitions. This meant that her husband, Warren G. Harding, President of the United States,—no matter what might be the eventuality, should never be forced to bear on his shoulders the sins and "the evil deeds of the crooks surrounding him." This meant that Warren G. Harding should never be placed in any position that would make it possible for him to "take his child and go away." Would she succeed—or fail?

She was saying:

"Was ever a woman confronted with such a situation, in the history of the world? I shall not falter or waver. I will not be thwarted!

"And Gaston Means,—whatever news may come to you, —either here in Washington or from us, during this trip to Alaska,—remember I look upon you—as my friend and protector. Do you understand and will you stand by me?"

"I will."

How could I know what must have been, even then, in the mind of this heartbroken but determined woman?

Chapter XXIV

The Journey to Alaska—and the End

Several weeks later I was sitting in my office at 903—16th Street, N. W., on the evening of August 3rd, when Col. Miller suddenly entered. I had not heard him until he stood before me.

"President Harding is dead," he announced.

"What!"

"We've just received first information that President Harding is dead. Extras will be on the streets in a few moments."

"It isn't possible. It isn't possible," I kept repeating, but subconsciously, all the time, there were racing through my brain the wildest speculations and conflicting deductions, and back of all—a ghastly sense of fear.

"It isn't possible," again I repeated.

"My God,—I tell you, he is dead," almost shouted Col. Miller, for the fact appeared not to have registered with me.

"I can't believe it," I replied shortly, reaching for my phone and calling a friend connected with the Universal News Service. He would know—to confirm or deny. But the wires were all busy and I could not get him.

Col. Miller sat down.

"Gaston,—ptomaine poisoning doesn't kill—a week later. He had ptomaine poisoning at Vancouver."

"Five days ago—to be exact."

"Well, five days! Besides—why did he have that ptomaine poisoning? He didn't eat anything that all the rest of the party were not eating? Was he subject to violent indigestion?"

"I don't know."

"Did he have any organic trouble of any kind?"

"I don't know."

"By God—what do you know? You've been shuttling back and forth up there to the White House—frequently enough to know something. Does this news surprise you?"

Was Col. Miller trying to draw me out or pump me? Was he trying to make me betray something?

"I said—does this news surprise you?" he repeated.

"What news? That the President is dead? Yes, it surprises me far more than you know. I was never more surprised in my life."

Just then I heard my wife open the door at the head of the staircase leading into the basement. She ran half way down the steps. She called:

"They are crying 'extra' out on the street—that the President is dead."

I unlocked the front iron-barred door and stepped to the pavement. The newsboys seemed to fill the streets, all screaming that the President was dead!

I eagerly read the very limited dispatches. Col. Miller returned to the office and sat with me there all evening,—buying every paper as it came out. Around midnight, I said to Col. Miller:

"Haven't you some friend in San Francisco that you could wire to get the 'low down' on this?"

Col. Miller replied:

"Yes. I know just such a person. Good idea."

We walked together over to the nearest telegraph office and Col. Miller wired this friend an official government dispatch. The reply was prompt. It read:

"Circumstances of his death appear shrouded in mystery." [80]

And then,—suddenly and vividly there appeared before my mental vision the figure of the white faced determined woman I had seen and talked with on the lawn of Mrs.

Boyd's home. I could hear her say: "I am determined. I will not be thwarted." What had happened,—I asked myself? Great God—what had happened! Col. Miller was saying:

"I suppose the papers there are giving the same accounts as the papers here."

Once or twice, Col. Miller and I walked over to the Army and Navy Club. I listened to all comments with an eagerness and interest that it was almost impossible to curb or control. What had happened? What had happened? I asked myself a hundred times. And every time, the answer came to me,—in the vision of a white faced determined woman. I could not shake myself free of this vision.

I recalled our conversation word for word and then I remembered that she had asked me,—no matter what news I might hear,—to be her "friend and—protector". And I had promised that I would. Did she realize then that she would need a protector?

I read and scanned and reread every word in the papers, and I followed the body across the continent through the newspaper accounts. I noted with keen and anxious interest all that was said about Mrs. Harding. They gave considerable space to reciting how wonderfully well she was bearing up under the tremendous shock.[32]

I was not unmindful of the fact that for once in her life she was occupying the center of the stage of the world, with full world-spotlight on her. I wondered—if she had also reached that high pinnacle of supreme Power that she had talked about—and if the Nation had indeed felt the touch of her finger—as arbiter of its destiny. If only—for a moment!

I was forced to concede—that she must be getting some considerable degree of satisfaction—from the world spotlight—no matter how it was brought about,—or for how short a period of time.

"I will not be thwarted!"

Well—she had not been thwarted. There had been no exposure. Had President Harding lived—? Oh, well, I would not formulate deductions and speculations until I knew something more definite.

When President Harding's body arrived at the Union Station in Washington, the usual curiosity seekers among the high and the low, were there. I was not. I sat in my office at 903—16th Street, N. W.

It was not more than thirty or forty minutes after the train was due to arrive, when my confidential telephone rang:

"This is Mrs. Boyd,—Mr. Means."

"Yes?"

"Mrs. Harding is here at my home. I have taken charge of her. She wants you to come here—at once."

"I'll be there."

I covered the distance just as quickly as my high powered car could make it. Mrs. Boyd was evidently watching for me. She met me at the door. In the entrance hall, she said:

"Mrs. Harding has asked me to leave you alone with her. Of course, I accede to her request. If you need or want me,—I will be close at hand."

She then opened the dining room door and I stepped in.

Mrs. Harding sat beside the dining room table—as usual. Her hat had been removed and she had on a loose dark colored kimono—I inferred that it was borrowed from Mrs. Boyd.

Her hair was whiter,—her face was whiter,—her thin blue-veined hands more restless in their nervousness. She sat with her hands on her lap, clasping and unclasping the four fingers of each.

The moment I saw her—I leaped at conclusions, not surmises. Her eyes were uncanny in their brightness: alert, cold, hard. There was no touch of sympathy or hysteria, or feeling. A bitter, calculating, determined woman sat in front of me.

Her very first words were a surprise:

"Mr. Means,—I think you would like a drink and I know I need one."

A decanter had been placed on the table—with two glasses. She poured me a drink first,—and then one for herself. Her next words held an even greater surprise. She said. "You did not do as I asked you."

"What do you mean?"

"I asked you—to be at the station. You were not there."

What was she talking about?

"You asked me to be at the station? I've had no such request from you."

"Didn't you get my letter?"

"Letter? What letter?"

"I wrote you a letter—a most important letter—from San Francisco. You have been my only adviser."

"It has not come——."

She seemed to ponder this with a far smaller degree of apprehension and alarm than I did. What had she written—in a letter—that might even now be in the hands of the Secret Service!

She then said: "Where is Nan Britton?"

"In Europe."

There was a long pause and a silence as deep as eternity. She finally broke this silence with:

"Mr. Means,—I have no regrets. None. But I do need your advice."

"Then—you must first tell me, Mrs. Harding, exactly what happened."

She then rehearsed, as if talking to herself, in staccato terms, and with a voice that was half repressed, what she had so often told me concerning the President—how the "gang's" hold upon the President had been getting tighter and tighter, and ever more merciless; how he was being compelled to sign papers that were put in front of him for signature; how she was finding it more and more difficult to check up her husband's official activities; how the President seemed to be losing his jovial, confident demeanor, and was looking and acting more and more like a hounded animal, tracked, and with his back against the wall; how she became more and more convinced that disaster was impending and inevitable, and that only she, the "Child of Destiny" could frustrate the infernal machinations of the "gang" by putting it beyond their power further to carry on their nefarious practices.

She continued: "As you know, everything was closing in. As his secretary—I learned of dangers of which I had not dreamed. From all directions,—they came."

Nor were her fears altogether unfounded. Official Washington had been in a ferment. Ever since Congressman Keller [29] started his accusations and rumors concerning the Department of Justice, an explosion had been expected at any moment, and the President's trip to Alaska had not succeeded in abating discussion.

She continued: "And then one day, he was writing a letter. I casually asked him—to whom he was writing. He replied that he was writing to his old father—in Marion. He lied. That letter was to Nan Britton. I intercepted it . . . No—I have no regrets."

Silence again. I watched her face turn even whiter and for a brief moment her lips quivered. But her voice was clear and firm, as she said:

"I was alone with the President . . . and . . . only about ten minutes. It was time for his medicine . . . I gave it to him . . . he drank it. He lay back on the pillows a

"The President seemed to be losing his jovial, confident demeanor, and was looking and acting more and more like a hounded animal, tracked, and with his back against the wall."

moment. His eyes were closed . . . He was resting . . . Then—suddenly—he opened his eyes wide . . . and moved his head and looked straight into my face. I was standing by his bedside."

As she paused I could not refrain the question:

"You think—he knew?"

"Yes. I think he knew. Then—he sighed and turned his head away—over—on the pillow. . . . After a few minutes,—I called for help. The papers told the rest."

She continued, "You have read all the newspaper accounts?"

"Yes."

"Are they clear?"

"No."

"Convincing?"

"No. Not to me, after an analytical study of them." [80]

"Will they be confusing to the average person?"

"I don't think so."

She continued, "You realize that there is nobody that I can consult with or talk to—but you. You have been my friend—tried in the fires. I trust you. You alone know the whole inside truth of conditions. I want to know to whom his body really belongs."

"To you."

"Do I have first claim on it?"

"Yes."

"Can I prevent an autopsy?"

"Yes."

"Where is Nan Britton's child?"

"That—I do not know. With Mrs. Willets, I presume."

"Can Dr. Harding order an autopsy?"

"I think not."

"Who can say when and where he shall be buried?"

"That is your prerogative."

These questions came in rapid-fire order and I answered them as quickly as possible.

"How do I know they won't perform an autopsy without saying anything to me?" she asked.

"That can be overcome."

"How?"

"By guarding the body. For you to notify anybody that you are not going to allow an autopsy would be the height of absurdity."

"Yes, I see that, and I have seen to it that no death mask was made of the President, notwithstanding this was contrary to all precedent." [31]

"Should anyone inquire, you have but one objection to an autopsy, of course—and that is—your seriously object to having the body cut up. That's your reason. Many people are bitterly opposed to autopsies."

"Of course, of course."

Was that woman made of stone, I wondered? Never a tear.[32] No emotion. Hard logic—and—*self-preservation.*

Again she paused. I said nothing and she went on:

"You know—how in every way and at all times, in trying to protect my husband—I ran into a solid wall of opposition. Every way I turned—I was balked and laughed at . . . Warren Harding died—in honor—as Madam X said he would. Had he lived twenty-four hours longer—he might have been impeached. . . . Nothing—nothing could stem the torrents that were pouring down on us.

"I have not betrayed my country or the Party that my husband loved so much. They are saved—I have no regrets —*I have fulfilled my destiny.*"

Then, out of the deep—almost oppressive silence that followed, and as if in answer to my unuttered question, in a stiff, frozen voice, without a tremor, she looked me full in the face and said:

"Mr. Means—there are some things that one tells—nobody."

To which I replied, "Mrs. Harding,—there are some things—it is not necessary to tell."

And from that instant, we understood each other.

THE END

EPILOGUE

Epilogue

Explanations and Inferences

After the funeral I was walking through the lobby of the Washington Hotel, when I heard a low timid voice call:

"Mr. Means."

I stopped and looked around. There were groups of people standing about and many sitting on the couches and chairs. Apparently, no one had spoken my name. I turned and started to pass on through, when again as if coming from space, I heard a faint:

"Mr. Means."

Once more, I stopped. I wondered if I were beginning to hear things, when my attention was attracted to a little man standing over in a shaded corner between two windows. He was jerkily making motions. I realized then that this man was trying to attract my attention. I strode over to where he was but did not recognize him until I was beside him.

"General Sawyer! I didn't know you—without your uniform."

"Are you—busy?" he tremblingly inquired.

"I am always busy. Anything I can do for you?"

"N-no. I guess not. I was—just so kind of lonesome, I thought maybe you could sit and talk awhile."

There was something wistful and appealing about this little old man.

"I'll be glad to, General."

We sat on the couch between the windows.

He looked neutral and drab—in a dark business suit. I could not think of General Sawyer without his shiny buttons. Everything about him had been shiny, now—all was dull and lifeless. Even his once shiny false teeth looked yellow.

What could he want from me? His first sentence shed some light:

"You hear everything that goes on. You haven't heard anyone expressing any—suspicions—have you?"

I was glad to be able to give him assurance of safety.

"Oh,—just an intangible hint or so,—now and then. Nothing to speak of."

"I am glad to know that. I—I feel all broken up. I can never get over this thing. I'm hanging around Washington, sitting around like this in hotel lobbies mostly,—for no reason at all. I can never get over this thing."

"No. I suppose not," I agreed.

"I had no active part in it at all, you understand. None. You know, there were rumors that—he would have been impeached?"

"Of course—I know the rumors."

"Nothing could have stopped it. Nothing. I believe myself—he himself would have chosen—this way out,—for every other avenue of escape was blocked. Every one."

"Do you mind, General, telling me exactly how it happened?" I asked. I felt that it would be a relief to him to tell it and I really wanted to know. He went on: "Well—we, she and I, we sent the guard away: the Secret Service man that stood outside the door. She told him that the President was so much better—she wanted him to feel as much at home as possible that afternoon,—she wanted everything to seem natural and homelike and that she and I would take entire charge of the President. She then sent the nurses to their rooms to rest."

He paused as if considering how to continue. I knew better than to try to prompt. I made no comment. Finally he said:

"I then went out for a walk."

This was a surprise.

"You left her alone——?"

He nodded his head as he spoke:

"Yes, I did. You know—in Vancouver,—things did not go along at all. I thought it best to leave. She will never forgive me for it though. He wasn't caring whether he lived any longer—he felt that he had made a botch of—everything."

"So—she won't forgive you—eh?"

He shook his head.

"I can't help that. I walked down through the lobby and the clerks and newspaper men saw me. It was well known that I was not in the room. But I hadn't walked the length of the hotel downstairs before—they called me. It couldn't have been more than ten minutes. I'll never get over this thing. I can't think about anything else. I've nothing to reproach myself for. Nothing at all. Death is not so bad. There are a lot of things in this world—worse than death. Don't you think so, Mr. Means?"

"I do, indeed."

I left him sitting alone in the lobby, for no reason at all: a broken little old man,—trying to soothe his conscience with banal platitudes and with apparently but one interest left in life: that of self-preservation.

II

"Mr. Means—I have no regrets."

Mrs. Harding repeated these words to me, after she had returned from the funeral of President Harding at Marion, Ohio. She had tarried only a few days in Marion.

We were sitting on a bench in the rear grounds of the White House. I had been informed that Mrs. Boyd and a friend were calling on Mrs. Harding—I fancy a formal call of condolence and sympathy—and that they were all in the

White House yard. I was instructed to be around and watching and, as soon as the callers had departed, Mrs. Harding wished me to join her there in the yard.

I saw Mrs. Boyd and her friend leave. Mrs. Harding was watching for me. She was standing beside a flower bed: cool, calm, composed.

"You are always so prompt," she greeted.

We strolled around a driveway and found a bench between two trees. As usual, I was silent and waited her lead.

"I want to tell you, Mr. Means,—how much I appreciate all that you have done for me. It seems now like a hideous dream—all of it. But—it had to be."

I thought it might help her to know:

"I've talked to General Sawyer and he has talked freely to me."

"You then know—everything?"

"I believe I do."

"Did he tell you about—Vancouver?"

"He hinted."

"That came near being fatal. . . . It passed. . . . But nothing—*nothing* can impede the carrying out of one's destiny,—as that destiny has been decreed!"

Would I have to listen again to an exegesis about the moon and the stars? I intercepted, with a bold stroke:

"General Sawyer tells me that you visited Madam X before starting on the trip."

"He should not have told that."

"He went for a walk——"

"I was alone,—with the President. And—only about ten minutes. Oh,—well it had to be! And now,—I must reconstruct my life and continue to fulfill my destiny."

"You have plans?"

"Yes. I want to take the trip through Europe that has always been the goal toward which I climbed. I will have to go alone. But—I shall begin to make plans. I have—plenty of money. The only obstacle that stands in the way—is Nan Britton! Nan Britton—even yet! How do I know what she may do? Dare I leave this country—and then have her come out with a great exposure [33]—even accusation? That girl is the curse of my life."

She paused—clasping and unclasping the four fingers of her hands. I said nothing. So far as I could see, my professional work for Mrs. Harding was finished—and I was not sorry. It was then she said,—almost between clenched teeth.

"Mr. Means—I have—no regrets."

"There is nothing else that you need me for, is there?" I asked.

She got up suddenly, as if to say goodby.

I said:

"Now—about all the data that I collected for you: The letters of President Harding to Nan Britton, her diaries,—the articles,—what shall I do with these things?"

"Keep them for me. Or—better still—I give them—to you. They belong to me. They are legally mine and I give them to you. Keep them—keep them—safe."

"I understand."

That was the last time that I ever saw Mrs. Harding. She left the White House within a few days and went to Mrs. Boyd's home "Glen Haven". After a visit there, she returned to Marion.

III

President Harding died August 3rd.

I was indicted the following October.

It had been arranged by the "gang" that with the opening of the Fall term of the Federal Courts, to appease public clamor, and, as a sacrifice,—I was to be indicted.

I was to assume all responsibility for acts that had been committed. I was to do this—supposedly—independently and on my own initiative without the knowledge of any "higher-ups".

In order to handle the matter in exactly the right way, a thorough investigation had to be made,—not so much for the purpose of getting necessary material before a Grand Jury,—but to keep the most important testimony from getting before the Grand Jury. That was the paramount problem.

So I was fully aware that an investigation was proceeding and in fact, I was helping it along.

The plan was simple and satisfactory to me. If the agreement was lived up to.[84]

This agreement was: that I would be indicted and give the newspapers a chance to spread themselves. Later—I would go before the Judge and plead guilty and listen to a "Review", for the benefit of the press, of all my acts. I was to be severely condemned and advised that sentence would be passed in ten days or two weeks, thus giving the Press a longer time to spread themselves.

On the day of sentencing, the Judge from the bench would call attention to the fact that it had been his intention to give me the absolute limit of a penitentiary sentence. But owing to the fact,—that I was more familiar with certain governmental intrigues than anyone else, and that my further attention would be required in the Courts,—he therefore suspended sentence, and put me under probation.

This suspending of sentence was given,—not at all to be merciful to me, but out of consideration for the people and the Government. However, he was to give me the limit of the fine.

Mr. Daugherty and Col. Felder sent for me to come to

the Waldorf Hotel in New York, where all of these plans were gone over in detail. They were satisfactory to me. What did I care about words?

In the meantime, I was working for Mr. Daugherty, and conducting investigations of Senator Wheeler and Senator Walsh,—in order to find out for Mr. Daugherty, what, if any, real or documentary evidence they had against him—to be used in the Senate investigation.[85]

I learned, to my entire satisfaction, that they had no documentary evidence,—but Mr. Daugherty insisted that they had and that I must get it.

Senator Wheeler and his Committee began taking evidence and examining witnesses. They were impotent so far as I was concerned, for I could not be subpœned, as I, myself, was under indictment.

They could not force me to testify.

One day, Col. Miller came into my office at 903—16th Street, N. W., and said:

"The Attorney General says,—for you to go to Hell! That you've lost your cunning. That you are not the investigator that you once were,—that you are no good any longer as an investigator. That you are discharged."

"Did Harry M. Daugherty say—for you to tell me—*that?*"

"He did!"

No man can insult me in my most vulnerable point: as to my being a skillful and thorough investigator. It is my only pride!

I saw red!

I jumped up and went to the telephone and called Senator Wheeler. I said:

"Issue your subpœna. Send it here. I am ready to testify." [86]

I hung up without waiting to hear his expressions of satisfaction and pleasure. I turned back into the room. I confronted Col. Miller.

"Now—you can go and report to Mr. Daugherty. And you can add,—for his further information that I say to him—that I am not—a Jess Smith!"

As I put the telephone receiver back on the hook, after talking to Senator Wheeler,—had my clairvoyant powers been functioning in a discerning way,—I would have heard, then and there, the click of the lock of the Atlanta prison door, as it closed behind me.

I had crossed swords with Mr. Harry M. Daugherty.[37] Attorney General of the United States, and my fate was sealed.

Mr. Daugherty well knew that in spite of all the millions of dollars that had passed through my hands, I did not have sufficient funds to conduct a proper defense. I went to prison, penniless.

I entered Atlanta Penitentiary on May 10th, 1925.

Thereafter, Col. Miller was indicted, tried, and convicted by a jury in connection with certain transactions to which he had been a party in the capacity of Alien Property Custodian during the Harding Administration.

Attorney General Daugherty was indicted and twice tried by a jury upon criminal charges for alleged acts of malfeasance in office. The juries failed to agree upon a verdict.

Senator Fall, another member of President Harding's cabinet, also was indicted and faced a jury for accepting bribes in connection with the transfer of oil leases during his tenure of office. The United States Supreme Court had already pronounced these transfers illegal and tainted with fraud; and the jury completed the job by finding Fall guilty of the crime of accepting a bribe while in office.

I emerged from prison on July 19th, 1928.

Jess Smith
"Harry Daugherty's 'Man Friday'."

C. F. Cramer
"Attorney for the Veterans' Bureau."

"Jess Smith committed suicide in the Wardman Park Hotel."
"C. F. Cramer committed suicide in his Washington home."
"John T. King died suddenly in New York."
"Col. T. B. Felder died suddenly in Savannah, Ga."

But—I emerged! There have been so many others silenced forever:

C. F. Cramer, Attorney for the Veteran's Bureau, committed suicide.[17]

Lawyer Thurston—the Boston *independent attorney* who expedited all Alien Property Custodian cases and collected enormous graft—died *suddenly* in Boston.

Jess Smith died *suddenly* at the Wardman Park Hotel, Washington.[26]

Mr. John T. King, Politician and Lobbyist, indicted with Col. Miller and H. M. Daugherty in connection with transactions involving the Alien Property Custodian, in whose safe I kept the collected graft, bootleggers' money,—died *suddenly* in New York.[38]

C. F. Hateley, expert undercover Agent for the Department of Justice in Washington, and especially close to Harry M. Daugherty, died *suddenly* in the Burlington Hotel in Washington.

Warren G. Harding, President of the United States died *suddenly* in San Francisco.[30]

Gen. Sawyer died *suddenly* in his home in Ohio about one year after Mr. Harding. Mrs. Harding was visiting him at the time. His manner of death was strikingly similar to that of President Harding.[39]

Mrs. Harding died—some months after Gen. Sawyer.[40]

Col. T. B. Felder, Attorney and Adviser for the Harding clique and my defense attorney, died *suddenly* in Savannah, Georgia.[3]

I, alone, remain.

APPENDIX A

Appendix A

Publisher's Notes

Note: The following notes have been collated by the publishers in order to enable the reader more fully to grasp many of the points that may otherwise escape his attention.

NOTE 1 (a)

United States Senate
Jan. 21, 1921

Dear Mr. Burns:

I have become possessed of information which I regard as of greatest importance to the Government and especially to the Department of Justice, and in order that I may make the best use of it, I would like to be put in touch with the cleverest investigator in your Bureau.

I would much prefer Mr. Gaston B. Means, because of my scant personal relations thus far with him have led me to think that he is as sincere as he is energetic.

George H. Moses
(Senator)

NOTE 1 (b)

Department of Justice,
Bureau of Investigation,
Washington, D. C.
March 10, 1922

Hon. Roy A. Haynes,
Prohibition Commissioner,
Treasury Department,
Washington, D. C.

My Dear Mr. Haynes:

I received a request from your office the other day asking me to let you know something about Gaston B. Means. I immediately called up your office when I returned to Washington, but was told you were in conference. I then told your secretary to tell you that Gaston B. Means was absolutely all right; honest, intelligent, straightforward, and would make a first class man for you.

Of course, I do not want to relinquish the services of Mr. Means and if there is any specific case you have in mind that requires the aid of a resourceful courageous intelligent man, Mr. Means is the one you want.

Mr. Means has been suspended in our service by the Attorney General through a complaint of some kind which the Attorney General has not explained to me, but I know it cannot be anything serious, and only a question of giving Mr. Means an opportunity of being heard.

As you know, no man can do his duty without making enemies, and Mr. Means has made some very powerful enemies by the courageous manner in which he has gone after crooks who have robbed the Government, and therefore, I expect to have Mr. Means reinstated. In the meantime, I will be very glad indeed to have him go with your organization.

Very truly yours,

William J. Burns,
Director.

NOTE 1 (c)

March 10, 1922

Maj. R. A. Haynes,
Federal Prohibition Comm.,
Treasury Dep't.,
Washington, D. C.

My Dear Major Haynes:

I take great pleasure in indorsing and commending to your kindly consideration Mr. Gaston B. Means, who has been connected with the Bureau of Investigation here under Mr. William J. Burns. Mr. Means will be of the greatest assistance to you in the work in which you are engaged if you can find a place for him. My advice to you is to find a place for him because you can rely upon what he does. He is able, experienced, industrious and he is not afraid. He will carry the message to Garcia, and what is better yet, he will come back with the answer.

Very cordially yours,
GUY D. GOFF,
Ass't to the Attorney General
Acting Att'y General in the
absence of Mr. H. M. Daugherty.

NOTE 1 (d)

Department of Justice,
Washington, D. C.
June 28, 1922

MR. RALPH A. DAY,
Federal Prohibition Director,
New York City, N. Y.
DEAR MR. DAY:

This will be handed to you by Mr. Gaston B. Means, a special investigator of the Department of Justice, who is conducting a special and confidential investigation of great importance to the enforcement of prohibition and my department.

I earnestly request that you accord him every possible co-operation and assistance for which this department will be greatly indebted.

Mr. Means has working with him Mr. James E. Watson, Jr., who is a son of Senator Watson of Indiana and also a special agent of the Department of Justice. I trust that you will also cooperate with him.

Very truly yours,
MABEL W. WILLEBRANDT,
Ass't. Attorney General.

NOTE 1 (e)

Treasury Department,
Washington, D. C.
June 22, 1922

MR. GASTON B. MEANS,
c/o Director of Special Agency Service.
Sir:

You are hereby appointed a customs agent of this department

without compensation or allowances of expenses to take effect June 22, 1922, on oath of office to be taken.

By direction of the Secretary.

Respectfully,
ELMER DOVER,
Ass't. Sec'y. of the Treasury.

NOTE 1 (f)

Department of Justice,
July 5, 1922

MR. WILLIAM C. HECHT,
United States Marshal,
New York City, N. Y.

MY DEAR MR. HECHT:

This will introduce to you Mr. Gaston B. Means who is in New York City on an investigation of importance to the Department of Justice. Will you kindly accord Mr. Means every cooperation possible from your office.

If he requests it, I suggest that you give him the authorization of a deputy marshal.

Very truly yours,
MABEL WALKER WILLEBRANDT,
Ass't. Attorney General.

NOTE 2

From John W. Davis' speech of acceptance. Reported in the New York Times, August 12, 1924.

DAVIS DECLARES HONESTY THE ISSUE INDICTS REPUBLICANS AND EXECUTIVE

"I speak with restraint when I say that it has brought forth corruption in high places, favoritism in legislation . . . impotence in government and a hot struggle for profit and advantage which has bewildered us at home and humiliated us abroad . . . the time demands for plain speaking. It is not a welcome task to recount the multiplied scandals of these melancholy years; a Senator of the United States convicted of corrupt practice in the purchase of a Senatorial seat; a Secretary of the Interior in return for bribes, granting away the naval reserves so necessary to the security of the country; a Secretary of the Navy ignorant of the spoilation in progress, if not indifferent to it; an Attorney General admitting bribe takers to the Department of Justice, making them boon companions and utilizing agencies of the law for purposes of private and political vengeance; a chief of the Veterans' Bureau stealing and helping others to steal millions in money and supplies provided for the relief of those defenders of the nation most entitled to the nation's gratitude and care. Such crimes are too gross to be forgotten or forgiven.

NOTE 3

New York Times, March 13, 1926.

"Thomas B. Felder, lawyer, convicted last year with Gaston B. Means suffers heart attack.—Had sought vindication.—Planned to renew fight in the Supreme Court in effort to clear himself in bribery case. . . . He announced in Jacksonville on Wednesday that he would ask the Supreme Court to reconsider its refusal to grant him a writ of certiorari in the conspiracy case and that he would publish the complete records of the case in a Georgia paper he intended to buy in order to vindicate himself in his home state. . . ."

NOTE 4

* *Investigation of Hon. M. Daugherty.* P. 2155.

Senator WHEELER. I see. That is what my understanding was. That is my understanding of it, Mr. Burns. He kept you advised as to his activities all of the time that he worked for the—I don't know whether it was the German Government or the German——

* This note and the others that follow under the caption "Investigation of Hon. Harry M. Daugherty" are taken from "Hearings before the Select Committee on Investigation of the Attorney General, United States Senate, Sixty-Eighth Congress, pursuant to S.Res. 157, directing a Committee to investigate the failure of the Attorney General to prosecute or defend certain criminal and civil actions, wherein the Government is interested."—Government Printing Office, Washington, D.C.

Mr. Burns. Well, now, if you will permit me I will tell you the history of it, and you will understand, and it will clarify the matter perfectly. Mr. Means came to me one day and stated that he had been authorized to pay me a $100,000 retainer to do work for the German Government, and I stated that I wouldn't do it; my sympathies were with the Allies.

He then stated that if I did not do that all right, but that his sympathies were with the Allies, that they were against England; and that if I did not accept it he thought he would resign from our agency and go to work for them.

I told Mr. Means at that time that the only work we were doing that was in any way interested in or connected with the war was protecting munition factories. I advised Mr. Means against going to work for them, but I stated that if he did go to work for them I wanted him to advise them that if any munition plants that we were guarding were blown up, or tampered with, I would go to Washington to get the people responsible for it. I told him that I wanted him to convey that information, which he said he would do.

Mr. Means also stated to me "I want you to distinctly understand that I am just as patriotic an American as you are, and while I may go to work with these men it will have nothing to do with, and nothing will interfere with, my loyalty to my country."

Senator Wheeler. When was that, before or after we entered the war?

Mr. Burns. Oh, that was long before we entered the war.

NOTE 5

Investigation of Hon. Harry M. Daugherty. P. 1024.

Senator Wheeler. How long did Gaston B. Means work for you down there in the department?

Mr. Burns. It seems to me he started in some time the latter part of 1921. I would not be sure without looking it up, however.

Senator Wheeler. You went into the liquor situation somewhat, did you not, or did he for you? That is, to investigate the liquor situation?

Mr. Burns. Well, a number of our agents from time to time

have been called upon by Mrs. Willebrandt, who has charge of the liquor situation in the Department of Justice.

Senator WHEELER. And she requested that Mr. Means be put on the liquor investigation, is that correct?

Mr. BURNS. Yes; I think that is correct.

Senator WHEELER. And Mr. Means was put on there, and you recommended him, did you not?

Mr. BURNS. Yes.

NOTE 6

Investigation of Hon. Harry M. Daugherty. P. 2543.

Senator WHEELER. What, if anything, did those things concern? What did he tell you he wanted Means to do, if anything? Were they about investigations?

Mrs. DUCKSTEIN. They were about various investigations with Mr. Means. *He was investigating, I think, General Sawyer* at one time.

Senator WHEELER. He was investigating him?

Mrs. DUCKSTEIN. Yes; he was investigating General Sawyer for Mr. Smith at one time. I think Mr. Smith was sending those reports to the President, from the way the reports read.

Senator WHEELER. You think Smith was sending them on to the President?

Mrs. DUCKSTEIN. Yes; I think so.

Senator WHEELER. You say that was General Sawyer?

Mrs. DUCKSTEIN. Yes; and oh, there were several others.

Senator WHEELER. What General Sawyer was that?

MRS. DUCKSTEIN. I guess that was the General Sawyer.

Senator WHEELER. I do not know what you mean by the General Sawyer.

Mr. CHAMBERLAIN. He was the White House physician, did you not know that?

Senator WHEELER. Oh, I thought he was some Army officer. I have not got acquainted with all these people yet.

Let me ask you this, Mrs. Duckstein: Who else did Jess Smith have Means investigating, do you know?

Mrs. DUCKSTEIN. Well, I remember a Mrs. Cross.

Senator WHEELER. A Mrs. who?

Mrs. DUCKSTEIN. A Mrs. Cross, and E. H. Mortimer, and Colonel Darden. I think that is all I can remember. It is hard to remember back so far.

Senator WHEELER. Did he ever have him investigating Senator Caraway?

Mrs. DUCKSTEIN. Oh, yes, oh, yes. I forgot about that. And Congressman Woodruff, I think he had him investigating.

Senator WHEELER. Did he have him investigating Congressman Keller, if you know?

Mrs. DUCKSTEIN. Yes; because that was about the time the agitation was getting up in the House.

Senator WHEELER. That was about the time of the impeachment proceeding, that they were being started in the House?

Mrs. DUCKSTEIN. It was about that time.

Senator WHEELER. That was the impeachment proceeding of the Attorney General?

Mrs. DUCKSTEIN. Yes, sir.

Senator WHEELER. Do you know about his investigating Senator La Follette?

Mrs. DUCKSTEIN. No; I do not know anything about that. You understand, Senator, these were only occasional memoranda Mr. Smith would give me, possibly two or three times a week. He must have had others to take other things at times.

Senator WHEELER. They were only occasional memoranda he gave you?

Mrs. DUCKSTEIN. Yes, sir.

NOTE 7

From "Presidents I've Known," by C. W. Thompson.

"They meant to control the Presidency and with that aim I knew of no better gun for them to point than Harding 'They could shuffle him and deal him like a pack of cards.'

"Harding did not take himself too seriously and was really surprised to find himself a Presidential candidate. He knew himself pretty well, and neither expected to be President nor very much wished to be. Left to himself he would not have tried. But for the persistent insistence of Harry Daugherty he would not have kept on trying. Often he used to tell Daugherty he was no statesman and that it was time to stop the nonsense and close the show. Daugherty always told him he was wrong about himself and at last, events seemed to confirm everything Daugherty said he began rather dubiously to believe."

NOTE 8

New York Times, November 22, 1924.

Charles E. Hughes said on hearing of Mrs. Harding's death:

"I am inexpressibly saddened by the death of Mrs. Harding. We can never forget the dignity and charm with which she presided as the mistress of the White House or her fortitude when she was suddenly bereft of all that life held dear. She was a woman of extraordinary strength of character and her husband's most faithful counsellor. When he was taken she felt that her mission was ended. She had borne her part most nobly."

NOTE 9

In "Secrets of the White House," by Mrs. Jeffray, published by the Cosmopolitan Book Corporation, a great deal of light is thrown on Mrs. Harding's idiosyncrasies. Mrs. Jeffray, the author, was a housekeeper at the White House during six administrations and she was able to study Mrs. Harding at very close range.

NOTE 10

Investigation of Hon. Harry M. Daugherty. Page 2541.

Senator WHEELER. After you became his confidential secretary did you see Mr. Jess Smith in Mr. Burns's office on frequent occasions?

Mrs. DUCKSTEIN. Yes; on various occasions.

Senator WHEELER. He and Mr. Burns were very close friends?

Mrs. DUCKSTEIN. Well, they did not seem to be friendly particularly. It seemed to be more or less a matter of business. Mr. Smith would come in and transact his business, say what he had to say to him, and go out.

The CHAIRMAN. Did Mr. Burns follow Mr. Smith's directions the same as everybody else?

Mrs. DUCKSTEIN. I believe he did.

Senator WHEELER. Burns took orders from Smith?

Mrs. DUCKSTEIN. I would not say that he took orders. I think if he suggested anything he would follow his suggestions.

Senator WHEELER. In fact, everybody around the department, when Jess Smith spoke they took it for granted it was the Attorney General speaking, did they not?

Mrs. DUCKSTEIN. I suppose they did.

Senator WHEELER. And whatever he said around that department went?

Mrs. DUCKSTEIN. Well, they supposed it was to the interest of the Attorney General, and therefore they followed his orders.

Senator WHEELER. They took it for granted when Jess Smith spoke that he was speaking for the Attorney General and that that was something desired by the Attorney General, did they not?

Mrs. DUCKSTEIN. Or in the interest of the Attorney General.

Senator WHEELER. Or in the interest of the Attorney General, you say?

Mrs. DUCKSTEIN. Yes.

Senator WHEELER. When you were down there in Mr. Burns's office, what have you to say as to whether Mr. Means frequently came in there?

Mrs. DUCKSTEIN. He was in there several times every day.

Senator WHEELER. He was in there all the time, was he not?

Mrs. DUCKSTEIN. A good bit of the time.

Senator WHEELER. He and Mr. Burns were very close friends, were they not?

Mrs. DUCKSTEIN. They seemed to be very close friends.

Senator WHEELER. And Mr. Means had access to the files down there, did he not, in the department?

Mrs. DUCKSTEIN. Yes; he did have.

Senator WHEELER. And Mr. Smith had access to the files, the confidential files and other files?

Mrs. DUCKSTEIN. I do not know about the files in Mr. Burns's safe. I do not know whether Mr. Smith had access to them; I do not know that he even knew they were there or not.

Senator WHEELER. He did not have the combination to the safe, but all other files around the department, outside of those in the safe, he had access to?

Mrs. DUCKSTEIN. I think he did.

Senator WHEELER. Would not he come down at times and get files from the investigating department?

Mrs. DUCKSTEIN. Well, I think he did. I do not remember any specific instance of it.

NOTE 11(a)

New York Times, January 23, 1926.

"It was learned yesterday that Mal Daugherty testified before the Grand Jury last Monday but that the fact of his appearance was kept from the public at that time. He said that he had turned over certain ledger sheets covering the period from January 1, 1921 to December 31, 1924 to Harry M. Daugherty and that he understood that his brother burned them.

Some of the ledger sheets in question contained the accounts of the late Jesse W. Smith who occupied a desk at the Attorney General's office at Washington and committed suicide. Harry M. Daugherty, Mal S. Daugherty, and other records were wanted, and any account in the name of Brady and any account with the Alien Property Custodian . . .

NOTE 11(b)

New York Times, February 9, 1927. (Re: American Metals Case.)

. . . Buckner (Federal Attorney in New York) shows that by their numbers and letters certain Liberty bonds sold through Otis & Company, bankers in Cleveland, Ohio, had been traced to the Midland National Bank which had ordered their sale, the proceeds of which are now in the form of certificates of deposit to the credit of Mr. Daugherty. Mr. Buckner said there were five such certificates for $10,000 each. Four of these he produced in evidence each bearing Mr. Daugherty's name."

NOTE 12

Investigation of Hon. Harry M. Daugherty. Page 2545.

Senator WHEELER. Do you remember when Jess Smith went to Florida in 1922 and when he returned?

Mrs. DUCKSTEIN. I think it was in February or March—a part of February and March. I do not know exactly when he returned, but it must have been in March or April.

Mr. CHAMBERLAIN. Was that in 1922?

Mrs. DUCKSTEIN. Yes. He went with President and Mrs. Harding.

Senator WHEELER. When he came back here, or when he was in Florida, do you remember something that Mr. Means was investigating at the time for President Harding?

Mrs. DUCKSTEIN. Yes; there were things I had sent a memorandum down to Mr. Means about. Mr. Means on two or three occasions asked me to write reports out for him to be mailed directly to Mr. Smith.

Senator WHEELER. Mr. Means had you write out reports which he himself mailed directly to Jess Smith.

Mrs. DUCKSTEIN. I put them in the mail box for him, and he has mailed them sometimes himself, I suppose. I handed them to him prepared for mailing.

Senator WHEELER. What were they?

Mrs. DUCKSTEIN. Various matters. Some of them were these same things about which I have spoken.

Senator WHEELER. About this Mrs. Cross or about this professor's book.

Mrs. DUCKSTEIN. About all these matters. I know all these matters were pending, but I do not remember just which ones I mailed out.

NOTE 13

Investigation of Hon. Harry M. Daugherty. P. 2533.

Senator WHEELER. A scurrilous book about the President?

Mrs. DUCKSTEIN. Yes, sir.

Senator WHEELER. Who, if anybody, worked on that case, if you know?

Mrs. DUCKSTEIN. Gaston Means worked on it.

Senator WHEELER. Gaston Means worked for whom?

Mrs. DUCKSTEIN. He worked for Mr. Smith about it?

Senator WHEELER. He worked for Mr. Jess Smith, do you mean?

Mrs. DUCKSTEIN. Yes, sir.

Senator WHEELER. For President Harding?

Mrs. DUCKSTEIN. Yes.

Senator WHEELER. Do you know what Mr. Means did in connection with that?

Mrs. DUCKSTEIN. I have not the faintest idea. I know that Mr. Smith sent for him and gave him some instructions, but I do not know what they were, or anything about it.

NOTE 14

This phase of President Harding's life is covered in detail in "The Answer," by Joseph de Barthe, a book on file at the Congressional Library in Washington, in which the author attempts to prove that President Harding was incapable of fatherhood, and therefore, not the father of Nan Britton's child.

NOTE 15

From "The President's Daughter."

"My independent thinking was of course inspired by my intimate knowledge of Mr. Harding's apparent unhappiness with his legal wife and his evident preference, in his relations with me, for subterfuge, which seemed to promote peace of mind, rather than open rebellion and consequent turmoil. 'She'd raise Hell!' had been Mr. Harding's frequent statements to me, and even though she seemed not to love him in the way a man has the right to expect to be loved by his wife, I knew without Mr. Harding's telling me, that she would not release him to another."

NOTE 16

Department of Justice,
Washington, D. C.
February 9, 1921

Mr. Gaston B. Means,
Department of Justice.
Sir:

You are hereby suspended without compensation from your position and employment of Special Agent until further notice.

Yours very truly,
Harry M. Daugherty,
Attorney General.

NOTE 17

New York Times, March 14, 1923.

Charles F. Cramer, General Counsel of the Veterans' Bureau committed suicide. Worried by critics Cramer takes life. He was found dead in his Washington home . . .

NOTE 18

New York City,
Hotel Pennsylvania,
Room 968.
December 2, 1921.

Mr. W. J. Burns,
Department of Justice,
Washington, D. C.
Dear Sir:

Attached is a detailed report covering the day's work on the Standard Aircraft Case, including conference with Attorney Lane and Auditor A. J. Pickering at Park Row, Federal Building, and with Mr. Meenan on this case.

Respectfully,
G. B. Means.

NOTE 19

Investigation of the Attorney General. Page 100.

Senator MOSES. Senator Ashurst wants to get the distribution of this money. You took from a Jap in a room in the Bellevue Hotel one hundred $1,000 bills?

Mr. MEANS. Yes, sir.

Senator MOSES. This was in February, 1922?

Mr. MEANS. Yes, sir.

Senator MOSES. What time of day was this?

Mr. MEANS. Night.

Senator MOSES. And from that room in the Bellevue Hotel you went where?

Mr. MEANS. I stayed there.

Senator MOSES. All night in that room?

Mr. MEANS. Yes, sir; Mr. Jess Smith came in and got it.

Senator MOSES. You were registered in your own name?

Mr. MEANS. Yes, sir; I guess I was registered there at that time.

Senator WHEELER. Under your own name?

Mr. MEANS. Yes; I was registered there at that time under my own name. My family was there, lived there; my wife and boy.

Senator MOSES. And you kept those bills under your possession in the hotel in your room?

Mr. MEANS. Yes, sir.

Senator MOSES. When did they go out of your possession?

Mr. MEANS. That same night.

Senator MOSES. In the hotel?

Mr. MEANS. Yes, sir.

Senator MOSES. They were passed on to whom?

Mr. MEANS. I gave them to Mr. Jess Smith.

Senator MOSES. Who came to your room?

Mr. MEANS. Yes, sir.

Senator MOSES. He came there for the purpose of receiving them?

Mr. MEANS. Yes, sir.

Senator MOSES. Did he tell you when he came: I came to get the hundred thousand dollars?

Mr. MEANS. Yes, sir. I did not know what they were given to me for at that time, but I was asked to receive—well, was told that this man would come.

Senator WHEELER. By whom were you told that?

Mr. MEANS. Mr. Jess Smith.

Senator WHEELER. He told you that a Jap would come to your room and give you 100 thousand-dollar bills?

Mr. MEANS. No; he did not say that.

Senator WHEELER. What did he say?

Mr. MEANS. He said he would come with $100,000, and for me to count; and I counted it. That was all.

Senator WHEELER. Now, you are looking over some records there, are you?

Mr. MEANS. Yes, sir. But you asked about this Standard Aircraft case, and when I had investigated it.

Senator WHEELER. One of the specifications that the Attorney General was charged with in his impeachment proceedings was the failure to prosecute the Standard Aircraft case, was it not?

Mr. MEANS. Yes; he was charged with that.

NOTE 20 (a)

Investigation of Hon. Harry M. Daugherty. P. 1026.

Senator WHEELER. Mr. Means became very active at Mrs. Willebrandt's investigation in prohibition enforcement?

Mr. BURNS. Yes; and at the request of the United States district attorney and his assistant in New York.

Senator WHEELER. He became very active in running down bootleggers in the city of New York?

Mr. BURNS. Yes.

Senator WHEELER. And he did uncover the whole whiskey ring?

Mr. BURNS. He certainly did.

Senator WHEELER. Yes; that is what he did.

Mr. BURNS. Oh, no; not all of it, of course, you understand.

Senator WHEELER. I understand. But he did uncover a great deal of the whisky ring in the city of New York.

Mr. BURNS. Yes; he did.

NOTE 20 (b)

Investigation of Hon. Harry M. Daugherty. P. 1555.

Senator WHEELER. Everybody knew that Mannington and Jess Smith were working directly with the Attorney General in the sale of the permits in New York City?

Mr. MEANS. Absolutely.

Senator JONES of Washington. When you use the word "everybody," who do you mean?

Mr. MEANS. John Gorini and Felder. When I refer to everybody, I refer to everybody inside the whisky ring there.

Senator JONES of Washington. Well, I do not know who they are.

Mr. MEANS. There is some of them.

Senator WHEELER. You have got a report that you did furnish to the Attorney General of the United States showing who the whisky ring was in New York City?

Mr. MEANS. Absolutely. When Mrs. Willebrandt sent me there I got the names of the officials that were in the ring. I went on Manny Kessler's boat and sailed with him and talked with him, and he offered me $80,000 or $100,000, in the Vanderbilt Hotel, to give to Holly Clarke, to take to him, he was the Assistant United States Attorney, to bribe him.

NOTE 21

Investigation of Hon. Harry M. Daugherty. P. 2377.

Mr. MILLER. No; he came from Mr. Crim with respect to some papers the department wanted in the Bosch magneto case. I had only heard of Mr. Means up to that time, and I said: "You will have to get some authority to get any papers out of my office." That was when I first knew him. There was some controversy between me and the people over at the Department of Justice about indiscriminately sending people over to get my files, because I am responsible for them, and I wanted to see where they were going. I understood Mr. Means to be on the staff of the Department of Justice, and I changed my earlier opinion of him, that I had heard, because he demonstrated to me that he was a very able investigator; he demonstrated that fact later on in one or two matters I asked him to look after for me.

Senator WHEELER. You had him investigate some matters for you?

Mr. MILLER. Yes.

Senator WHEELER. For your department?

Mr. MILLER. Yes; because he was an agent of the Department of Justice, a special agent, and as long as they had taken the liberty of sending him over to me I had no hesitancy in making use of a good find if it would be of some benefit to our office. I did not pay him anything, either officially or personally, because he was on their pay roll. But in the course of some of his conferences with me he brought out the fact that there were some things of interest to the Treasury Department and that the Treasury Department ought to know. I will not go into the details of what it was, because that probably you will develop.

NOTE 22

New York Times, February 20, 1924.

"Attorney General Daugherty was denounced by Senator Wheeler in the Senate this afternoon as a protector of criminals and an official whose friends had used his friendship to demand money for immunity from prosecution. The Montana Democrat also charged that appointments to office had been sold for money by men close to Mr. Daugherty and that there was evidence that the Attorney General was not actually ignorant of some phases of the naval oil lease transactions. 'If the Attorney General,' said Wheeler, 'has not actually got the money that has been collected in these various cases from one end of the country to the other he is a bigger fool than the people of the United States gave him credit for being.'"

NOTE 23

Congressional Record, March 18, 1924. Page 4422.

SENATOR CARAWAY:

The charge was made that a conspiracy had been entered into between the producers of these films and Mr. Muma—and who like all the other great men connected with this administration came from Washington Court House, Ohio—and the Attorney General and his agents—whereby they should be permitted to introduce this film into the various states upon a 50-50 division. That is, the man who made the film was to get one-half the profits and the man who violated the law, including the Attorney General were to get the other half.

NOTE 24

Investigation of the Attorney General. P. 545.

Senator WHEELER. Had Jess Smith ever used a gun, or ever owned a gun in his lifetime?

Miss STINSON. He wouldn't look at one, much less touch one.

Senator WHEELER. He was actually afraid of a gun, was he not?

Miss STINSON. He had a natural horror of a gun. I know it hadn't been later than last fall that we were going by a window where they had guns on display, and I stopped a moment, and he said, "Oh, come on, I wouldn't stop to look at the window." He might have been wanting to go on for something else, but I know his natural abhorrence of guns. After the war there was a lot of banditry going on in the neighborhod, and I wanted to get a gun, but he wouldn't permit me to have a gun.

Senator WHEELER. Now what, if anything, did Mal Daugherty tell you about any wounds upon his body?

Miss STINSON. Mal Daugherty said after he came to Washington, after he had taken out his necessary papers for administrator, that he came to Washington, and he was very much incensed because—he was named administrator in the will without bond by Jess, but when he came to Washington, and I told him where to find different accounts——

Senator WHEELER. Now just a moment. Mr. Mal Daugherty is made executor in the will without bond?

Miss STINSON. Yes, sir.

Senator WHEELER. And Mr. H. M. Daugherty is made executor in the will without bond also?

NOTE 25

Investigation of Hon. Harry M. Daugherty. P. 2532.

Senator WHEELER. When did you first become a stenographer in the Department of Justice?

Mrs. DUCKSTEIN. I believe the date was August 7, 1921.

Senator WHEELER. Did you say August 7, 1921?

Mrs. DUCKSTEIN. Yes.

Senator WHEELER. That was shortly after Mr. Daugherty became Attorney General?

Mrs. DUCKSTEIN. Yes.

Senator WHEELER. And had you known Mr. Daugherty previous to that time?

Mrs. DUCKSTEIN. No; I had not known him.

Senator WHEELER. Had you known Jess Smith previous to that time?

Mrs. DUCKSTEIN. No; I had not known either of them.

Senator WHEELER. When, if at all, did you first meet Jess Smith?

Mrs. DUCKSTEIN. I met him the day I went to the Department of Justice; the first day I went there.

Senator WHEELER. When did you first meet Mr. Daugherty?

Mrs. DUCKSTEIN. Oh, I do not remember.

Senator WHEELER. After that time?

Mrs. DUCKSTEIN. Some time along after that when I was working in his office.

Senator WHEELER. Did you say when you were working in his office?

Mrs. DUCKSTEIN. Yes, sir.

Senator WHEELER. During the time you were at the Department of Justice as a stenographer, did you have occasion to take dictation for Jess Smith?

Mrs. DUCKSTEIN. Yes; I did.

Senator WHEELER. Will you tell the committee under what circumstances you took the dictation and where you took it?

Mrs. DUCKSTEIN. Well, Mr. Smith wanted a very speedy stenographer, and he found out that I was, so he sent for me, and I took it in his private office on the sixth floor of the Department of Justice.

Senator WHEELER. In his private office on the sixth floor of the Department of Justice, you say?

Mrs. DUCKSTEIN. Yes, sir.

Senator WHEELER. What was the nature of the correspondence that you took for him?

Mrs. DUCKSTEIN. Oh, there were all kinds of letters. He wrote lots of personal letters to people all over the country, and he wrote business letters to his brokers about things, and he wrote about the conduct of his store in Washington Court House, and he wrote personal letters for the President and Mrs. Harding—well, not for the President, but for Mrs. Harding.

Senator WHEELER. He wrote personal letters for Mrs. Harding?

Mrs. DUCKSTEIN. Yes; and he attended to some things for President Harding. And he attended to matters for Mr. Daugherty.

Senator WHEELER. And what matters did he attend to for President Harding, if you know?

Mrs. DUCKSTEIN. Well the chief thing that is in my mind that he attended to for President Harding was about the investigation of a book, a scurrilous publication about the President.

NOTE 26

New York Times, May 31, 1923.

DAUGHERTY'S FRIEND SUICIDE IN HIS ROOM

Jesse W. Smith Shoots Himself in Attorney General's Washington Apartment. Brooded over ill health . . . There was always considerable mystery in Washington as to the exact relations Mr. Smith maintained toward the Administration, and particularly the Department of Justice. He was continually with Mr. Daugherty . . .

NOTE 27

Congressional Record, Page 4412. March 18, 1924.

Senator HEFLIN: "Mr. President, whenever crooks can lay their hands on the instrumentalities of justice in this country; and with the fruits of their crime buy immunity from prosecution, something is radically wrong and it's high time to cry out against such a dangerous and deadly condition.

Was the Attorney General prosecuting these people? No, he is a party to it so the testimony shows. One of the men connected with it, Jess Smith is dead, some say by his own hands and some do not know how he died, but he died in Mr. Daugherty's apartment, I understand.

Some people will a long time inquire why Jess Smith was brought here by Mr. Daugherty and put into the service of the Department of Justice—a plain dry goods clerk, I am told with no knowledge of law and no experience in the work to which he was assigned. I repeat why was this man brought here by Mr. Daugherty? And oh, how conspicuously he has figured in all the terrible things now being uncovered. He is dead. Some say he killed himself. Some think that he was murdered. He remembered some of his friends in the will. I understand, and of course, those who were remembered in his will profited by his death."

NOTE 28

From "Secrets of the White House," Mrs. Jeffray. P. 85.

"I remember one time particularly when Mr. Daugherty was a house guest. About half past seven in the morning, I heard him slam the door of his bedroom and hurry down the hall, go to the telephone, and in a loud voice demand of an usher the reason he had been unable to get a Mr. Smith on the telephone from Mr. Daugherty's rooms.

" 'Mr. Smith is dead,' the usher told him. 'He committed suicide early this morning.' This Mr. Smith was the famous Jess Smith, and it was understood that Mr. Daugherty had been with him the night before till almost midnight."

NOTE 29

Investigation of Hon. Harry M. Daugherty. P. 2850.

Mr. Means. Now, I made a report on Congressman Woodruff and said he absolutely had no motive. We were trying to find out if he had a motive behind what he was doing, what he was driving at. My report showed that he was absolutely sincere in what he was doing and that he believed measures obstructing the investigation of war-fraud cases had been brought to bear in the Department of Justice. Now, they wanted to ascertain whether Congressman Woodruff was sincere in what he was doing, and Congressman Johnson. I listened at their conversations. I was convinced they were absolutely sincere in what they were saying. When the Keller charges came up, though, Congressman Woodruff had little or nothing to do with that, and I so reported; neither he nor Captain Scaife. Captain Scaife came very near not joining in; in fact, he withdrew from it. The Keller charges came independent of the charges that Congressman Johnson and Captain Scaife had started in April, 1922.

Senator WHEELER. Means, what I want to get at is this: You did make reports from day to day during the investigation up there, during the impeachment proceedings?

Mr. MEANS. Not so much after the impeachment proceedings actually began, Senator. Not after they began, because they were public hearings, you see, and there was not much detective work to be done. Prior to that, though, I did.

Senator WHEELER. Prior to that time you did?

Mr. MEANS. Oh, yes. I reported on what the labor crowd was doing—that they were combining with Senator Keller——

Senator WHEELER (interposing). You mean Congressman Keller?

Mr. MEANS. Yes, sir; Congressman Keller. You see, the labor element joined in with Senator Keller——

Senator WHEELER (interposing). Congressman Keller.

Mr. MEANS. Yes; Congressman Keller, in drawing up these charges. That became an important matter to the Department of Justice, who Congressman Keller was being supported by. As a matter of fact, they undertook at that time to get, or were in hopes they would get, Mr. Samuel Untermyer down here to draw up the charges. I think he was in Europe. They started to wait until he got back. I would hear of information and——

Senator WHEELER (interposing). You reported back to the Department of Justice?

NOTE 30 (a)

Regarding the Death of President Harding. From the New York Times, August 3, 1923.

PRESIDENT HARDING DIES SUDDENLY

STROKE OF APOPLEXY AT 7.30 P. M.

Death Stroke came without warning. Mrs. Harding was reading to her husband when first signs appeared. She Ran For Doctor.

The President died at 7.30 P. M. Mrs. Harding and the two nurses, Miss Ruth Powderly and Miss Sue Drusser were in the room at the time. Mrs. Harding was reading to the President, when utterly without warning, a slight shudder passed through his frame; he collapsed; and all recognized that the end had come. A stroke of apoplexy was the cause of his death.

NOTE 30 (b)

From the New York Times, August 4, 1923.

REPORT OF WHAT HAPPENED IN THE SICK ROOM WHEN THE PRESIDENT'S SUDDEN STROKE CAME STILL SOMEWHAT CONFUSED

GENERAL SAWYER WAS EITHER IN THE ROOM OR JUST OUTSIDE

It was stated authoritatively tonight by Mr. Welliver who is taking Secretary Christian's place during the latter's absence that the official announcement of the President's death was in error in omitting that General Sawyer was in the room at the time, said Mr. Welliver.

NOTE 30 (c)

From the New York Times, August 4, 1923. Page 2, Column 2.

The exact time of the death of President Harding remains a mystery. Officially it is given at 7.30 o'clock but according to some of those with whom he talked General Sawyer, the President's chief physician said that after it was realized that the President had passed away he looked at his watch and it showed 7.20 o'clock.

General Sawyer was either in the room with the President or just outside the doorway when the fatal stroke came. He was the first physician to reach the stricken President.

NOTE 30 (d)

From the New York Times, August 5, 1923.

LAST MOMENTS OF MR. HARDING LATEST AND ACCEPTED VERSION

SAYS DR. SAWYER WAS HOLDING HIS FRIEND'S HAND WHILE WIFE WAS READING

There have been several versions of the incidents surrounding the death of President Harding. The shock and the resulting confusion prevented those immediately concerned in the final scene in Mr. Harding's bedroom in the Palace Hotel from taking note of the actual occurrence.

It was told by some of those in the vicinity that Mrs. Harding rushed to the door of the bedroom and called for help from her husband's physicians. It was said that General Sawyer, the late President Harding's chief physician, was not in the room when the President died. People with nerves on edge or stunned by the unexpected tragedy were unable to give any coherent account of what took place.

The *New York Times* correspondent believes that the following is as nearly correct a version as can be obtained. This account was the outcome of efforts of a member of the Presidential party to get all of the facts, etc., etc. The official bulletin was in error. Mrs. Harding and General Sawyer were alone with the late President at the time. Miss Ruth Powderly, the nurse, had left the sick room, etc., etc.

NOTE 31

New York World, August 4, 1923.

NO DEATH MASK MADE: MRS. HARDING OPPOSES

There will be no death mask made of President Harding. Cabinet officers with the Presidential party met last night and decided to ask Mrs. Harding to allow a mask of her husband to be made by J. Earl Cummings, a San Francisco sculptor.

Although, it is the usual custom, when a Chief Executive dies, to have a death mask made that his features may be preserved for posterity, Mrs. Harding demurred.

NOTE 32

From New York Times, August 5, 1923.

MRS. HARDING'S CONDUCT DURING THE ORDEAL

Mrs. Harding is calm. She said to friends of her party and relatives of the late President who gathered around her late this evening, that she did not fully realize the blow that had come to her. She had a duty to perform she said and must bear up . . .

(Describing the funeral New York Times). Mrs. Harding was dressed in deep mourning, etc., etc. Her eyes were dry at the finish of the prayers. . . . While Mrs. Harding a pathetic figure stood dry eyed, tears of sorrow streamed unchecked down the faces of many. . . . Mrs. Harding was very calm—she was remarkably self-contained. She showed the grit that was largely responsible for her recovery.

NOTE 33

Nan Britton revealed her affair with President Harding in a book which she wrote and published in 1927, entitled "The President's Daughter."

NOTE 34

Investigation of Hon. Harry M. Daugherty. P. 811.

Mr. CHAMBERLAIN. You will admit, Mr. Chairman, in fairness that the prosecution against Means was started before this investigation was started.

The CHAIRMAN. Yes; but there were several dockets started a year or two ago that were never tried.

Mr. CHAMBERLAIN. I am merely making the suggestion that Mr. Daugherty acted in all due speed in that matter.

Senator WHEELER. Let me say this, Senator Chamberlain: The Means case was never called, I understand, until it was charged that Means had first given me some information and after it came out in the newspapers of New York that Mr. Means had divulged some information to me, then there was a very speedy attempt made by the department to set those cases in New York.

NOTE 35

Investigation of Hon. Harry M. Daugherty. P. 2845.

Senator WHEELER. Let me ask you right there: During the impeachment proceedings in the House of Representatives of Mr. Daugherty, is it not a fact that you were working for Mr. Burns during that time?

Mr. MEANS. I was.

Senator WHEELER. And is it not a fact, Mr. Means that Mr. Burns and Mr. Daugherty asked you to go over to that committee and find out everything that you could that the committee was doing, and report it back to Mr. Daugherty and Mr. Burns?

Mr. MEANS. The night that the charges were drawn up against Attorney General Harry M. Daugherty, in the News office, I got a copy, and I am very sure they were the charges, for I had that crowd under surveillance. I carried it to the Department of Justice, walked into the room where Mr. Howland was sitting, and handed him those charges. He checked them up in connection with some other charges that he had. I told Mr. Burns, who was standing right there, that those were the official charges as they were going to be presented, and I had a carbon copy of them within eight minutes after they left the typewriter. I stood around waiting to get them.

I also drove to the Department of Justice with me that night five bootleggers that I was roping, finding out what they were doing. I had two or three duties to perform. I picked those bootleggers up over at the Hamilton Hotel, and Mr. Burns let me have his car to get those charges, and I roped them up as I went along. I picked the bootleggers up in the car, and as I drove along I talked to them, and learned a whole lot of information in regard to them. I came back with the charges and handed them to Mr. Howland, who was sitting there.

NOTE 36 (a)

Investigation of Hon. Harry M. Daugherty. P. 124.

Senator Ashurst. (After Means testified as to graft collected on the Dempsey-Carpentier fight pictures) Mr. Means you may be under indictment but you have today rendered the cause of truth and justice a valiant service. It is the first time I have ever seen the end justify the means.

NOTE 36 (b)

Page 657, Daugherty Investigation. (When Daugherty's counsel challenged reliability of Means' testimony.)

Senator Wheeler. Now I wish that those people who have stated that we are relying upon such unreliable evidence in this case would take the word of Mr. Goff and Mr. Burns, who are highly respectable citizens.

Senator Ashurst. And it might be well to take the word of the late President Harding, one of whose last official acts was to employ Mr. Means, as shown by abundant testimony.

NOTE 37

Harry Daugherty. From the New York Nation, October 1, 1924.

Harry Daugherty was afraid. After months of bluster and braggadocio he did not dare take the witness-stand publicly and face questions of his record. He cowered behind a technicality. He is not the kind of man who fights in the open. Twice he has exposed himself as the slimiest kind of fighter. . . .

Daugherty lapsed for a time into silence, appearing in the newspapers only in connection with his brother's fight to keep their bank accounts from being examined. Now he plays another card. One of the many witnesses who testified to the rottenness and corruption in his department was Gaston B. Means, a former department employee, an intimate of Daugherty. Mr. Means was under indictment in New York for violation of the liquor laws. No sooner had he appeared against Daugherty than the prosecution was pressed. Means was convicted and sentenced to two years imprisonment. He told Senator Wheeler that he had no money with which to appeal, and that a representative of Daugherty had approached him promising relief if he would repudiate his testimony.

NOTE 38

New York Times, May 14, 1926.

JOHN T. KING—NOTED POLITICIAN—DIES

. . . After the passing of his political career which ended in 1920 as far as any tangible connection was concerned, Mr. King became involved in difficulties connected with Harry Daugherty, former Attorney General of the United States and Col. T. W. Miller, former Alien Property Custodian, he was indicted early in 1926 on a charge of conspiracy to defraud the United States Government in the American Metals case. The indictment charged that the defendants brought about the transfer of $7,000,000 of the Company's funds from the custody of the Government, which had seized the money during the World War, to a Swiss Corporation. The defendants were charged with having accepted $441,000 in commission.

Col. Miller was the first of the three to be indicted. His indictment followed a long investigation by the Government. . . . It was said at the time that the Government expected to use Mr. King as a witness to prove the alleged payments of $391,000 in liberty bonds as part of a transaction, to Col. Miller, the late Jesse W. Smith, friend of Mr. Daugherty, and himself. Mr. King was subsequently indicted for alleged perjury in failing to include in his 1921 income tax returns his share of the Liberty bonds paid him in the American Metals transaction. . . .

NOTE 39

New York Times, September 24, 1924.

BRIGADIER GENERAL SAWYER DIES IN HIS SLEEP

General Sawyer's death was almost identical with the manner of death of the late Warren G. Harding when General Sawyer was with the President in San Francisco. Mrs. Harding was at White Oaks Farm (Sawyer's home) when General Sawyer was found dead.

Members of his family had no intimation of the seriousness of the General's condition up to the moment he expired.

NOTE 40

New York Times, November 22, 1924.

MRS. HARDING DIES AFTER LONG FIGHT

She succumbs to an old ailment in Sawyer home in Marion, Ohio.

APPENDIX B